Forgotten Founders and Other Neglected Social Theorists

Forgotten Founders and Other Neglected Social Theorists

Edited by
Christopher T. Conner
Nicholas M. Baxter
and David R. Dickens

LEXINGTON BOOKS
Lanham • Boulder • New York • London

Published by Lexington Books
An imprint of The Rowman & Littlefield Publishing Group, Inc.
4501 Forbes Boulevard, Suite 200, Lanham, Maryland 20706
www.rowman.com

6 Tinworth Street, London SE11 5AL

Copyright © 2019 by The Rowman & Littlefield Publishing Group, Inc.

All rights reserved. No part of this book may be reproduced in any form or by any electronic or mechanical means, including information storage and retrieval systems, without written permission from the publisher, except by a reviewer who may quote passages in a review.

British Library Cataloguing in Publication Information Available

Library of Congress Cataloging-in-Publication Data

Names: Conner, Christopher T., 1981- editor. | Baxter, Nicholas M., 1982- editor. | Dickens, David R. editor.
Title: Forgotten founders and other neglected social theorists / edited by Christopher T. Conner, Nicholas M. Baxter, and David R. Dickens.
Description: Lanham, Maryland : Lexington Books, [2019] | Includes bibliographical references and index.
Identifiers: LCCN 2019011841 (print) | LCCN 2019015685 (ebook) | ISBN 9781498573726 (Electronic) | ISBN 9781498573719 (cloth)
ISBN 9781498573733 (pbk)
Subjects: LCSH: Sociologists--Biography. | Sociology--History.
Classification: LCC HM478 (ebook) | LCC HM478 .F67 2019 (print) | DDC 301.09--dc23
LC record available at https://lccn.loc.gov/2019011841

Contents

Acknowledgments   vii

Introduction   1

Part I: Forgotten Founders

1   John Stuart-Glennie's Lost Legacy   11
    Eugene Halton

2   Annie Marion MacLean and Sociology at the University of Chicago and Hull House   27
    Mary Jo Deegan

3   Marianne Weber and the March for Our Lives Movement   45
    Stacy L. Smith

4   Luther Bernard   67
    Alan Sica and Christine Bucior

5   Radhakamal Mukerjee: A Regional, Social Ecological Outlook   95
    Diane M. Rodgers

Part II: Other Neglected Social Theorists

6   Pitirim A. Sorokin: Integral Science, Global Culture, and Love   117
    Lawrence T. Nichols

7   Gregory P. Stone's Contributions to Urban Sociology, Social Psychology, and the Sociology of Sport   143
    Harvey A. Farberman

8   Carl J. Couch   173
    Michael Katovich and Shing-Ling S. Chen

9 Jack Douglas: The Reinvention of Society and Sociology:
   Creative Deviance, the Construction of Meaning, and Social Order   191
   Thaddeus Müller
10 Ben Agger: Social Theory as Public Sociology   213
   Lukas Szrot

Index   227

About the Authors/Editors   239

Acknowledgments

This edited volume was suggested and inspired by the late Harold Orbach. This book would not have been possible without his persistence, in urging us to organize a conference session every year at the Midwest Sociological Society annual meetings that became the basis for this volume. It is in his honor that we dedicate this book.

We are also deeply grateful to all the contributors who believed in the project: Christine Bucior, Shing-Ling Chen, Mary Jo Deegan, Harvey Farberman, Eugene Halton, Michael Katovich, Thaddeus Muller, Lawrence Nichols, Diane Rodgers, Alan Sica, Stacy Smith, and Lukas Szrot. Not only did they agree to contribute to this volume, each of them has truly been a delight to work with on this project. The result of this collaboration is a work of which we are immensely proud. It was our aim to highlight theorists whose work, for one reason or another, has gone undeservedly unrecognized. Thanks to the hard work of those involved in this project, we feel this volume achieves our objective.

We would also like to thank Carrie Baxter, Connie Dye, Barbara J. Schulze, Stephanie Swanson and Pam Weiss. Each of these individuals encouraged, assisted, or helped coordinate the project in some way, across three different states and institutions, for which we are forever grateful. While each of the editors of this volume contributed an equal amount of time and effort toward completion of this project, Chris and Nick are extraordinarily thankful for David R. Dickens's continued mentorship. Finally, given the strains academia sometimes can place on us, we apologize for the fallout endured by our friends and family who have been caught in our struggle to make tough choices.

Introduction

Thomas Kuhn, in his classic work, *The Structure of Scientific Revolutions* (1962), points out that there is "an apparently arbitrary element, compounded of personal and historical accident" (4) embedded in science that plays a role in shaping the accepted views of a given scientific community. Thus, what is considered relevant scientific literature in any lasting scientific field is narrowed overtime to construct an academic canon (David and Zald 2009). While some may argue that such processes are beneficial (in helping provide disciplinary focus, development, and growth), this narrowing is also the product of internal disciplinary politics, sociocultural power dynamics, and historical shifts (see Kuhn 1962; Mills 1959). Given the politicized nature of sociology in America (see Frisby 1972; Fay and Moon 1977), the discipline has more than its share of forgotten or marginalized theorists whose work has potential significance for contemporary sociology. Still others, though not completely ignored, have fallen victim to a political or cultural climate not receptive to their work. This edited volume seeks to highlight the work of many of these forgotten and neglected social theorists in the hope of reinvigorating interest in their work and their potential contributions to the analysis of contemporary social issues.

Feminist, critical race, and queer theory scholars in particular have emphasized the significance of scholars marginalized from the sociological theory canon (Collins 1990; Harding 1991; Seidman 2017), primarily because of their social position and identity (Clough 1993; Weinstein 2006; Morris 2015; Chesney-Lind and Chagnon 2016). Similarly, others have criticized a Western bias in contemporary American Sociology, as few non-Western sociologists are recognized for their contributions to sociological theory (McLennan 2003).

Other significant scholars have been marginalized because of political and ideological infighting within the discipline, including arguments over research methodology, topic or group being researched, and/or theoretical perspective. For example, ethnographic research is largely dismissed by most mainstream sociologists, as is evidenced by the lack of qualitative articles published in the most prestigious sociology journals (Denzin and Lincoln 2008: vii; Compton et al. 2018). However, qualitative research has played a crucial role in the development of feminist (see Finch 2004), critical race (see Solorzano and Yosso 2002), and queer theories (see Gamson 2000).

Methodological biases may in turn become the basis for theoretical debates between perspectives within the discipline. These biased critiques are often disguised by rejecting certain types of work as being too micro, too ambitious, not scientific enough, having an overly political research agenda, or suffering from some other "methodological flaw" (Compton et al. 2018). Such critiques, while presented as arguments over the philosophy of social science, in fact hide the conservative bias of the dominant perspective in a discipline (see Kuhn 1962, Meltzer et al. 1975). One example of this is the limited journal publication of critical and interpretive sociological research in the United States prior to the 1960s, due to the dominance of structural functionalism and other positivist approaches. The heated intradisciplinary debates between symbolic interactionists and structural functionalists during this same time period provides further evidence for the systematic neglect of particular scholars (see Davis 1972). One such case involved that of Howard Becker and his contemporaries in the study of the sociology of deviance. Their attempts to qualitatively study deviant subcultures and provide insights into their perspectives were criticized for valorizing deviants (see Simon and Gagnon 1967; Davis 1972). While Becker, to a large extent, was able to successfully overcome these critiques and did not become a "forgotten theorist," others such as Jack Douglas (see chapter 9) faced similar opposition and were not as successful as Becker.

Additionally, as many critical and postmodern theorists are aware, a great deal of social theory is overlooked due to lack of translation, or misrepresented based on a single review (see Sprague 1997; Thomas and Kukulan 2004). Adding to these problems is the tendency for much of sociology to be transmitted as an oral tradition from mentor to mentee, which can result in theorists being forgotten or overlooked by the larger discipline (Meltzer et al. 1975; Denzin 1992; Reynolds 1993; Conner 2017). In these situations, those in power either hide or are unaware of ideological commitment to their own theories, and fear that their own work might fall out of favor (Cohen et al. 1975). This can be observed in cases of structural functionalism and critical theory, but also within symbolic interactionism as certain founders are just simply not discussed (see chapters 7, 8, 9 this volume). As a result, sociology is riddled with significant gaps and in some cases inaccurate interpretations

(Cohen et al. 1975), representations, and attributions (see Becker [1963] 1973; Plummer 2011; Goode 2016). Analysis of these gaps are important not only for reasons of historical accuracy, but also to reveal underlying theoretical or philosophical issues about the social world.

To address the lack of diversity in the sociology canon many scholars have begun to mine historical sociological writings to identify forgotten voices. This work has resulted in the recovery of several lost voices in the history of sociological theory, most notably that of W. E. B. Du Bois, Charlotte Perkins Gilman, and Jane Addams. The work of these "lost" scholars now can be found in most recent social theory textbooks, is featured in many sociology course syllabi (see American Sociological Association [ASA] Trails), and is increasingly cited in publications in academic sociology journals.

Attempts to resurrect the work of other marginalized voices in sociology continues (see Deegan 1988, 1991; Lengermann and Niebrugge 2006; Reed 2006; Lemert 2017), aimed primarily at diversifying the social theory canon. However, we believe that this progress is only getting started and there is still much work to be made in addressing the historical and contemporary marginalization of specific social theorists. This edited volume is thus meant to serve as another step in the direction of recognizing the contributions of marginalized social theorists.

While other similar texts tend to focus primarily on intellectual biography, our emphasis here is on the scholar's theories and their application to contemporary social issues. We provide a contextualization of each scholar's work, using present-day social issues or problems. Many of these individuals played a significant role in the development of sociology. Our hope is to provide a resource that will help re-integrate these marginalized social theorists, rescuing them from obscurity and elevating their status.

ORGANIZATION OF THE BOOK

Following this introduction, the text delves into a chronologically ordered set of theorists, who for one reason or another have fallen out of the sociological theory canon. We have organized these theorists into two parts. *Part 1, Forgotten Founders* (chapters 1–5) consists of social theorists active during the late nineteenth and early twentieth centuries. These scholars contributed to the early development of sociology and would be grouped by most theory textbooks as classical social theorists. *Part 2, Other Neglected Social Theorists* (chapters 6–10) focuses on more contemporary theorists whose contributions are nonetheless largely unrecognized. Each chapter includes a brief biographical sketch, an overview of the selected theorist's work and significance, and the relevance of their work to one or more contemporary social issues.

Collectively these ten chapters present forgotten and other neglected social theorists not only from classical and contemporary social theory, but also from a broad variety of theoretical perspectives (pragmatism, symbolic interaction, and critical theory), and a range of biographical backgrounds. In so doing, we seek to provide a more inclusive overview of neglected social theorists with an emphasis on their theoretical contributions and practical application to the analysis of contemporary social life.

In chapter 1, Eugene Halton examines the "lost legacy" of John Stuart-Glennie, a nineteenth century Scottish folklorist, historian, philosopher, and sociologist. Halton points out that, although he wrote several books and was well-known among leading scholars of his time, when he died in 1910 his work was quickly forgotten. Halton makes a convincing case that Stuart-Glennie's most original ideas were both ahead of their time and poorly understood. This is especially true of his concept of *the moral revolution*, which he used to describe a series of revolutionary changes across several different civilizations approximately 2,500 years ago, more popularly known as "the axial age." Halton further argues that Stuart-Glennie's conceptualization may be at least partially superior to the better known axial age model because of his focus on the significance of how human insights into nature in the deep past have shaped human nature in ways that may serve as resources for living today.

While Sandra Harding, Dorothy Smith, and Patricia Hill Collins are widely recognized as the progenitors of standpoint theory, in chapter 2, Mary Jo Deegan discusses the work of Annie Marion MacLean, as an important precursor to this influential contemporary approach. Deegan's chapter describes MacLean's role in the development of the Chicago School, providing new insights into its historical roots. MacLean's biography vividly demonstrates the hardships for women in academia. It is often said that women and other minorities must work twice as hard to get half as much recognition, and nowhere else is this clearer than in the case of Annie Marion MacLean.

In chapter 3, Stacy Smith shows that Marianne Weber was a renowned sociologist in her own right whose influence extended well beyond that of simply editing her husband's (Max Weber) writings. Marianne Weber's sociology was noticeably feminist in its theoretical orientation. She criticized marital relationships as subordinating women as a means to an end. Despite sharing many sociological views with her husband, Marianne Weber was critical of the "value-neutral" perspective, which she felt was an expression of male privilege. Smith attributes much of Marianne Weber's erasure from sociology to her rejection of the notion of objective or value free sociology in favor of a more activist oriented approach. As Smith argues, sociology has always struggled between the twin pillars of science on the one hand and more activist oriented approaches on the other. Marianne Weber's contributions to the sociology of culture and the significant role that women play in shaping culture, albeit in a subordinated role, provides a theory of culture that explores how culture can be resisted and in which social change can occur. She then applies her analysis to the March For Our Lives Movement.

In chapter 4, Alan Sica and Christine Bucior examine the sociological life and work of Luther Bernard. As they point out, between 1920 and the 1940s Bernard was one of the most well-known sociologists in America. He was founding editor of *The American Sociologist*, early editor of *Social Forces*, and a major figure behind the founding of the *American Sociological Review* in 1936. Today, however, Bernard is largely forgotten, recognized, if at all, as the spouse of Jessie Bernard. Yet he produced a remarkable number and variety of articles and books—on instincts, social control, social psychology, and the origins of social science, all of which raise important questions still being debated today. Equally impressive, Bernard tenaciously defended the standards of genuine scholarship against the facile careerism of his time. As Sica and Bucior so aptly put it (borrowing a line from Alvin Gouldner), Bernard lived "for sociology" rather than "off it."

In chapter 5, Diane Rodgers extends postcolonial critiques of the sociological canon, by drawing upon the work of Indian sociologist Radhakamal Mukerjee. A prolific scholar, Mukerjee was responsible for the founding of *The Indian Sociological Review* in 1934, and helped organize the All India Sociological Conference (AISC), which would later merge with the Indian Sociological Society (ISS). Rodgers also points out that Mukerjee developed a version of human ecology theory that was not in line with the then dominant model proposed by the Chicago School. Mukerjee's approach stressed the need for local indigenous diversity, based on a philosophical orientation that stressed humans living in closer balance with the natural environment, and "rurbanization." Finally, whereas many urban sociologists stress urban planning, Mukerjee was an advocate for prioritizing rural areas over urban ones.

In chapter 6, Lawrence Nichols provides a detailed overview of the life and work of Pitirim Sorokin, an émigré from the Russian Revolution who in 1929 became the first tenured full professor at Harvard. While he is perhaps most well-known for his monumental three volume work, *Social and Cultural Dynamics*, first published in 1937, Nichols points out that Sorokin addressed a variety of topics in his work, including altruism, prosocial behavior such as love, and spirituality, that were in his time far outside the sociological mainstream but which have become increasingly of interest among scholars today. Nichols also highlights the significance of Sorokin's integral model of sociology as a constructive antidote to the pervasive fragmentation and polarization in contemporary American sociology. As he describes it, Sorokin's approach provides a way to do science without abandoning ethical values such as creativity, love, and nonviolence.

Some sociologists become overlooked because their work did not center around one obvious central theme. Gregory Stone's work, for example, touched on a variety of areas including industrialization, urbanization, population growth, identity, social psychology, and the sociology of sport. As Harvey Farberman shows in chapter 7, however, a central thread can be found in Stone's work; how individuals maintain a sense of community in an increasingly depersonalized world. Farberman demonstrates the contemporary relevance of Stone's theoretical approach by means of an analysis of the role of professional athletes in contemporary American society—as both collective representations of the social consciousness and as a byproduct of an impersonal capitalistic society.

In chapter 8, Michael Katovich and Shing-Ling Chen provide a highly personal biography of Carl J. Couch as a man who sought to refine symbolic interactionism, making it more systematic and data driven, utilizing experiments, survey data, and a variety of different methodological approaches. As Katovich and Chen point out, Couch envisioned a symbolic interactionism that could produce generalizable insights into human social behavior—yet, it was also one flexible enough to be modified based on the particular study involved. His laboratory studies were not based on deception, but rather provided a setting in which participants and researchers could interact with one another. Beyond his methodological contributions, Couch also was instrumental in arguing for the practical utility of symbolic interactionism leading him, along with Gregory Stone, to co-found the Society for the Study of Symbolic Interaction (SSSI) in the mid-1970s. They also helped establish *Symbolic Interaction*, which serves as the flagship journal for the organization. Both men's legacies live on at the yearly Couch-Stone symposium—even if most contemporary interactionists are unaware of their specific contributions.

In chapter 9, Thaddeus Muller focuses on Jack Douglas's work. While not always given credit, many of Douglas's major claims can be found in much contemporary theoretical work. He also has been overlooked as a major theorist in the sociology of deviance. His concept of "creative deviance," in particular, was influential in cultural criminology long before it was recognized by many sociologists. Douglas also reminds us that statistics mean nothing without interpretation and he, who was once a quantitative sociologist himself, convincingly argued that other methods, be they archival, ethnographic, interview based, or even auto-ethnographic, must sometimes be employed in order to achieve the level of understanding necessary for sociology. Moreover, Douglas's version of ethnography was a blend of consideration for both micro-level interactions and macro-based social structure—providing a constrictive constructive alternative to a debate that many contemporary interactionists seem unable to resolve.

Lukas Szrot, in chapter 10, describes Ben Agger's arguments for public sociology and explores his critique of mainstream sociology. As Szrot demonstrates, Agger's sociology was activist driven and rooted in his own personal experiences. Moreover, Szrot unpacks some of Agger's criticisms of mainstream sociology including grand theorizing, abstracted empiricism, ideological debates on method and theory, and many others. In sum, Agger was not only a critical sociologist, he was critical of sociology in general.

Christopher T. Conner, Nicholas M. Baxter,
and David R. Dickens

WORKS CITED

Becker. [1963] 1973. *Outsiders: Studies in the Sociology of Deviance*. New York: The Free Press.
Chesney-Lind, Meda and Nicholas Chagnon. 2016. "Criminology, Gender, and Race: A Case Study of Privilege in the Academy." *Feminist Criminology* 11(4): 311–33.
Clough, Patricia T. 1993. "On the Brink of Deconstructing Sociology: A Critical Reading of Dorothy Smith's Standpoint Epistemology." *The Sociological Quarterly* 34(1): 169–82.
Cohen, Jere, Lawrence E. Hazelrigg, and Whitney Pope. 1975. "De-Parsonizing Weber: A Critique of Parsons Interpretation of Weber's Sociology." *American Sociological Review* 40(2): 229–41.
Collins, Patricia Hill. 1990. *Black Feminist Thought*. New York, NY: Routledge.
Compton, D'Lane, Tey Meadow, Kristen Schilt, eds. 2018. *Other, Please Specify: Queer Methods in Sociology*. Oakland, CA: University of California Press.
Conner, Christopher T. 2017. "The Astructural Bias and 'Sociological Amnesia' in Contemporary Interactionism: An Invitation to a Debate." *Symbolic Interaction* 40(2): 1533–8665.
David, Gerald F. and Mayer N. Zald. 2009. "Sociological Classics and the Canon in the Study of Organizations." In *The Oxford Handbook of Sociology and Organization Studies: Classical Foundations*, edited by Paul Adler. Oxford: Oxford University Press.
Davis, Nanette J. 1972. "Labeling Theory in Deviance Research: A Critique and Reconsideration." *The Sociological Quarterly* 13(4): 447–474.
Deegan, Mary Jo. 1988. *Jane Addams and the Men and the Chicago, 1892–1918*. New Brunswick, NJ: Transaction.
———. ed. 1991. *Women in Sociology: A Bio-Bibliographical Sourcebook*. New York, NY: Greenwood Press.
Denzin, Norman K. 1992. *Symbolic Interactionism and Cultural Studies*. Cambridge, MA: Blackwell.
Denzin, Norman K., and Yvonna Licoln. 2008. *Strategies of Qualitative Inquiry* 3rd edition. Thousand Oaks, CA: Sage.
Fay, Brian, and J. Donald Moon. 1977. "What Would An Adequate Philosophy of Social Science Look Like?" *Philosophy of the Social Sciences* 7(3): 209–27.
Finch, Janet. 2004. "Feminism and Qualitative Research." *International Journal of Social Research Methodology* 7(1): 61–64.
Frisby, David. 1972. "The Popper-Adorno Controversy: The Methodological Dispute in German Sociology." *Philosophy of Social Science* 2(1): 105–19.
Gamson, Joshua. 2000. "Sexualities, Queer Theory, and Qualitative Research." Pp. 347–365 in *Handbook of Qualitative Research*, edited by Norman Denzin and Yvonne Lincoln. Thousand Oaks, CA: Sage Publications.
Goode, Thomas. 2016. "The Paradox of Howard Becker's Intellectual Identity." *Deviant Behavior* 37(12): 1443–48.

Harding, Sandra. 1991. *Whose Science? Whose Knowledge?: Thinking From Women's Lives*. Ithaca, NY: Cornell University Press.

Kuhn, Thomas. 1962. *The Structure of Scientific Revolutions*. Chicago, IL: University of Chicago Press.

Lemert, Charles. 2017. *Social Theory: The Multicultural, Global, and Classical Readings, Sixth Edition*. Boulder, CO: Westview Press.

Lengermann, Patricia Madoo and Gillian Niebrugge. 2006. *The Women Founders: Sociology and Social Theory, 1830–1930*. Long Grove, IL: Waveland Press, Inc.

McLennan, Gregor. 2003. "Sociology, Eurocentrism and Postcolonial Theory." *European Journal of Social Theory* 6(1): 69–86.

Meltzer, B., J. Petras, and L. Reynolds. 1975. *Symbolic Interactionism: Genesis, Varieties, and Criticism*. New York, NY: Routledge.

Mills, C. Wright. 1959. *The Sociological Imagination*. New York, NY: Oxford University Press.

Morris, Aldon. 2015. *The Scholar Denied. Los Angeles*. Oakland, CA: University of California Press.

Plummer, Ken. 2011. "Labeling Theory Revisited: Forty Years On." Pp. 83–103 in *Langweiliges Verbrechen (Boring Crimes)*, edited by Helge Peters and Michael Dellwing.

Reed, Kate. 2006. *New Directions in Social Theory: Race, Gender and the Canon*. Thousand Oaks, CA: SAGE Publications Inc.

Reynolds, Larry T. 1993. *Interactionism: Exposition and Critique*. New York: Rowman & Littlefield.

Seidman, Steven. 2017. *Contested Knowledge: Social Theory Today*, Sixth Edition. Sussex, UK: John Wiley & Sons.

Simon, W. and J. H. Gagnon. 1967. "Feminity in the Lesbian Community." *Social Problems* 15 (Fall): 212–221.

Solorzano, Daniel G. and Tara J. Yosso. 2002. "Critical Race Methodology: Counter-Storytelling as Analytical Framework for Educational Research." *Qualitative Inquiry* 8(1): 23–44.

Sprague, Joey. 1997. "Holy Men and Big Guns: The Can[n]on in Social Theory." *Gender & Society* 11: 88–107.

Thomas, Jan E. and Annis Kukulan. 2004. "'Why Don't I Know about these Women?': The Integration of Early Women Sociologists in Classical Theory Courses." *Teaching Sociology* 32 (July): 252–263.

Weinstein, Jay. 2006. "The Marginalization of Application in U.S. Sociology." *Journal of Applied Sociology* 23(2): 20–30.

Part I

Forgotten Founders

Chapter One

John Stuart-Glennie's Lost Legacy

Eugene Halton

THE CASE OF THE MISSING JOHN STUART-GLENNIE

John Stuart-Glennie (1841–1910) was a Scottish folklorist, historian, philosopher, and sociologist. He was educated at the University of Aberdeen and the University of Bonn. After having become a barrister, he left law to pursue folklore research, including a series of travels throughout Greece and Turkey. He wrote numerous books and articles throughout his life, and interacted with many of the most well-known scholars and intellectuals of his time. Yet when he died in 1910, he not only became quickly forgotten, but his most original ideas, many well in advance of their time, were never understood. He died at a time when sociology was still in formation, and many of his most important writings from the 1870s on were published before the discipline of sociology was established.

Stuart-Glennie's most significant idea in hindsight was his theory of what he termed in 1873 *the moral revolution*, delineating the revolutionary changes across different civilizations in the period 2,500 years ago, roughly centered around 500–600 BCE. This is the era currently known as "the axial age," after Karl Jaspers coined that term in 1949 and published his book translated in 1953 as *The Origin and Goal of History*. Stuart-Glennie's theory of the moral revolution is framed within a three-stage view of history, the first of which involved an outlook he characterized as *panzoonism*, and sometimes as *naturianism*. This theory of aboriginal and early civilizational outlooks is also notable and worthy of consideration in contemporary context, as I will describe later.

Jaspers is widely known as the originator of the theory that there were shared affinities in new ideas erupting across different civilizations of this period, notably ancient Greece, China, Israel, and India. The accepted history of the axial age, as spelled out by Jaspers, is that whereas the earliest civilizations showed "islands of light" of some spiritual significance, it was only the outbreak of the axial age that marked a radical transformation to a new kind of consciousness, a pivotal revolution and achievement of the human spirit. Some of the chief characteristics, as Jaspers put it, were that, "Rationality and rationally clarified experience launched a struggle against the myth (logos against mythos)" (Jaspers 1953: 5), philosophers appeared, religion was "rendered ethical."

There were a few other scholars cited by Jaspers who noted the phenomena before him, including Ernst von Lasaulx in 1856 and Viktor von Strauss in 1870. But Jaspers claimed their comments were "marginal," and that he was the first to give it full theoretical articulation. Jaspers was unaware of Stuart-Glennie. Interest in Jaspers's work gradually grew over decades and seeped into sociology through the work of Shmuel Eisenstadt and others, and more recently Robert Bellah. And there is increasing interest in the idea of the axial age across a variety of disciplines today.

Bellah's 2011 book, *Religion in Human Evolution: From the Paleolithic to the Axial Age*, is directly influenced by Jaspers, and Bellah did not know of Stuart-Glennie when I first informed him in 2013. Bellah also edited a book in 2012 with Hans Joas, *The Axial Age and Its Consequences*, which has contributors from a range of disciplines. There is also no discussion of Stuart-Glennie, though a quotation from his work appears in a bibliographical footnote. In 2009 I had informed Hans Joas about Stuart-Glennie after a lecture he gave at my university on "The Axial Age Debate as Religious Discourse" and the note he wrote down at that time then made it into the quotation in the bibliography footnote. But still there was no discussion there.

I rediscovered Stuart-Glennie through the books of one of the most well-known public intellectuals in America in mid-twentieth century, but today also strangely eclipsed, Lewis Mumford. Mumford had even served as editor of *The Sociological Review* in 1920, so could be considered a sociologist, among other professions. I was a student of Mumford's works, and corresponded and met with him a few times.

As of this writing, my efforts have begun to be vindicated. Egyptologist Jan Assmann published a new book at the end of 2018, *Achsenzeit* (Axial Age), which includes a chapter on John Stuart-Glennie, based on my book, and he notes: "Had he not found his rediscoverer in the American sociologist Eugene Halton, he would undoubtedly have remained in oblivion, in which he disappeared soon after his death" (Assmann 2018, my translation).

To give further biographical evidence of how Stuart-Glennie was actively involved in the intellectual life of his times, here are a few examples of Stuart-Glennie's social contacts in his lifetime. In 1885 he met and became a friend of Irish playwright, critic, and political activist George Bernard Shaw, with whom he shared an interest in socialism. Twenty years later in his preface to his play *Major Barbara*, Shaw compared Stuart-Glennie favorably to Friedrich Nietzsche:

> Now it is true that Captain Wilson's moral criticism of Christianity was not a historical theory of it, like Nietzsche's; but this objection cannot be made to Mr. Stuart-Glennie, the successor of Buckle as a philosophic historian, who has devoted his life to the elaboration and propagation of his theory that Christianity is part of an epoch (or rather an aberration, since it began as recently as 6000 BC and is already collapsing) produced by the necessity in which the numerically inferior white races found themselves to impose their domination on the colored races by priestcraft, making a virtue and a popular religion of drudgery and submissiveness in this world not only as a means of achieving saintliness of character but of securing a reward in heaven. Here you have the slave-morality view formulated by a Scotch philosopher long before English writers began chattering about Nietzsche. (Shaw 1907)

Shaw was lamenting how British theater critics ignored British thinkers. He was describing Stuart-Glennie's writing on how religious legitimation could be used for social dominance, instilling fear and subordination in the underclass, and false hope in a just afterlife: the rise of the "Hell religions."

Shaw also noted how Stuart-Glennie's problematic race-based theory of the origins of civilization clashed with Marx's class-conflict theory: "As Mr. Stuart-Glennie traced the evolution of society to the conflict of races, his theory made some sensation among Socialists—that is, among the only people who were seriously thinking about historical evolution at all—by its collision with the class-conflict theory of Karl Marx" (Shaw 1907). Under the thrall of then reputable scientific racism, Stuart-Glennie mistakenly attempted to describe the origins of civilization as rooted in conflicts between dominant lighter races and darker races, as I have addressed elsewhere (Halton 2017). He failed to see how Marx's class conflict theory could better explain the phenomena. Stuart-Glennie also corresponded with Karl Marx's daughter Eleanor, and was well aware of Marx's work, though I have not discovered any contacts or correspondence between them.

Earlier Stuart-Glennie traveled and corresponded with philosopher John Stuart Mill, whose middle name was given to Mill by his father James Mill in honor of Stuart-Glennie's grandfather, Sir John Stuart. Shortly after meeting the young twenty-one-year-old Stuart-Glennie, John Stuart Mill wrote to Henry Fawcett, on July 21, 1862: "(Henry) Buckle's untimely end grieved me deeply. I knew of it early, having met at Athens with his travelling companion Mr. Glennie, a young man of, I think, considerable promise, who occupies himself very earnestly with the higher philosophical problems on the basis of positive science" (Mill 1972). This is high praise from one of the most prominent philosophers of the time.

Stuart-Glennie was also a friend of early sociologist and fellow Scotsman Patrick Geddes and also Victor Branford. Geddes published an obituary for Stuart-Glennie in the new sociological journal *The Sociological Review* in 1910. Geddes' review begins: "Of the many historical, sociological, and philosophical writings of the late Mr. J. S. Stuart-Glennie three characteristic examples are to be found in *Sociological Papers*, Vol. II" (Geddes 1910: 317). *Sociological Papers* was an annual volume published between 1905 and 1907, which then turned into *The Sociological Review*. Stuart-Glennie's three papers appeared under the heading "Sociological Studies." In the first volume, Stuart-Glennie had commented on a chapter by Emile Durkheim. These are some serious sociological credentials.

From these brief examples from Stuart-Glennie's biography, one might expect that he came to be regarded as also one of the early contributors to the emergence of sociology. But history did not happen that way. Despite publishing a number of books and articles throughout his life, including important contributions in the late nineteenth century to the Folklore Society, an organization that preceded organized sociology and anthropology, Stuart-Glennie's works seemed to drop from the face of the earth after he died in 1910. And, whether through the complexity, or possibly the obscurity of his writing style (he invented a number of new terms and neologisms, including alternatives to the "barbaric mongrelism" of Comte's term "sociology"), or the obtuseness of readers to the originality of some of his key ideas, or the possibility that those ideas were simply ahead of their time, his most significant original ideas never were given the understanding they deserved in his lifetime.

THE LOST LEGACY OF THE MORAL REVOLUTION

As mentioned, John Stuart-Glennie formulated the first systematic theory of "the moral revolution" in 1873 (later independently theorized by Karl Jaspers as "the axial age") to characterize the historical shift around roughly 600 BCE in a variety of civilizations, most notably ancient China, India, Judaism, and Greece (Stuart-Glennie 1873). He returned to the theme many times over the succeeding decades, and explicitly in a sociological context later in his life. Here is his statement from his contribution to the Sociological Society meeting in London, published in 1906 in *Sociological Papers, Volume 2*:

> [O]ne great epoch can be signalised—that which I was, I believe, the first, thirty-two years ago ([*In the Morningland*:] "New Philosophy of History," 1873), to point out as having occurred in the sixth (or fifth-sixth) century B.C. in all the countries of civilisation from the Hoangho to the Tiber. There arose then, as revolts against the old religions of outward observance or custom, new religions of inward purification or conscience—in China, Confucianism; in

India, Buddhism; in Persia, Zoroastrianism; in Syria, Yahvehism (as a religion of the people rather than merely of the prophets), and changes of a similar character in the religions also of Egypt, of Greece, and of Italy. (Stuart-Glennie 1906: 262)

And as he put it in his original 1873 publication: "Anterior to the Sixth Century, and to the New Religions of the Second Age of Humanity, Religion had no specially moral character" (Stuart-Glennie 1873). Acknowledging that religion had no special moral character before this time may seem odd to us today who live in a time of those world religions which emerged from the legacy of the moral revolution, including Christianity and Islam.

Stuart-Glennie's theory of the moral revolution was part of a broader critical philosophy of history, which included gradations unexplored by Jaspers. Where Jaspers had viewed prehistory and non-civilizational aboriginal peoples as insignificant in the history of spirit, and even early polytheistic civilizations as but "islands of light" at most, Stuart-Glennie's comparative theory of history gave more weight to pre-axial folk cultures and civilizations, which Jaspers undervalued or ignored. A key term introduced by Stuart-Glennie for aboriginal and early folk cultures is *panzoonism*, a worldview of revering "all life" as a religious basis for conceiving nature. I will return to this later, after providing examples of Stuart-Glennie's theory of the moral revolution.

Speaking of the likely origins of civilizations about 8000 BCE in his 1901 paper, "The Law of Intellectual Development," Stuart-Glennie noted a period of gradual development until the time of the moral revolution:

[S]uch religions as those against which, in the sixth century B. C, broke out that great revolution which substituted, or attempted to substitute, for these religions of custom, Religions of Conscience. I was, I believe, the first, thirty years ago, to generalize the very remarkable synchronous facts of this great epoch as a moral revolution embracing all the countries of civilization from the Hoang-ho to the Tiber. (Stuart-Glennie 1901: 457)

Some of the characteristics that Stuart-Glennie drew attention to were religion transforming from custom to conscience, new ascetic outlooks marked also by the rise of prophets (which he termed "prophetianism"), and a greater level of self-reflection.

Five years earlier, in his 1896 paper, "The Survival of Paganism," Stuart-Glennie also restated his theory, claiming that the accepted history of the time which held that the origins of European philosophy and science were uniquely Greek was both superficial and myopic. As Stuart-Glennie saw it, the paganism of pre-civilizational "folk culture" as well as early civilizational polytheism, however falsely conceived, retained "intuitions" of the "Solidarity of Nature" he termed *panzoonism*, which provided a basis out of which reflective science could emerge as a manifestation of the moral revolution. Another aspect of the revolution of the sixth century BCE was the rise of Judaism, a new expression of divinity as transcendent rather than immanent, a new outlook of "anthropomorphic supernaturalism." The rise of the "New Moral Religions" in the Western lineage from Judaism through Christianity and Islam, the "religions of the book," set up an antagonism between science and religion, a dialectic that would mark the history of the West. It is:

> A very superficial view . . . which represents the origin of European Philosophy and Science . . . as due merely to the splendor of Greek genius. It was but part of the general Revolution of the Sixth Century B.C., and a publication and development of ideas far from unknown in Priestly Colleges, notwithstanding the mythological forms of their exoteric Cosmologies. But synchronously with this New Philosophy developed by nameable individual thinkers, and recorded, not in mythic, but in scientific language, and not in hieroglyphic, but in alphabetic writing, there arose those New Moral Religions which made of this great Revolution the true Epoch from which date the Modern as distinguished from the Ancient Civilisations. Among these New Religions of the Sixth Century B.C. was one in which the general revolt against Mythologic Polytheism took the form of a specially absolute and anthropomorphic Supernaturalism—the Yahvehism of the Jews after the Babylonian Captivity. And the Semitic conception of a Creator-God outside and independent of Nature, becoming 500 years later the intellectual core of Aryan Christianism, such an antagonism was set up between the fundamental conceptions of Religion and Science as to this day endures. (Stuart-Glennie 1896: 517–18)

Stuart-Glennie notes the revolt against "Mythologic Polytheism," not only through "scientific language," but also through the "New Moral Religions," a more general revolution whose legacy begat the origin of what he called elsewhere "the modern revolution." His observations on the rise of new critical outlooks in science and religion, a new reflectiveness, resonate with those of Jaspers. Yet Jaspers did not credit the earliest pre-civilizational outlooks with any spiritual significance, and only grudgingly admitted that pre-axial civilizations held some "islands of light," in contrast to Stuart-Glennie. Though their theories of history are markedly different, there are also strong parallels between Stuart-Glennie and Jaspers in their understandings of the ideas, cultures, and representative figures marking the transformation effected by the moral revolution/axial age.

One of the aspects of my book to make Stuart-Glennie's original ideas known that stood out for me was how closely many of Stuart-Glennie and Jaspers's characterizations of the phenomena were. The fact that many of their observations closely overlap was interesting in itself for me, despite their differences. Jaspers's outlook involves a view of spirit as transcendence, poised between the poles of religion and secularism, neither of which by themselves are adequate to do justice to the openness of transcendence.

By contrast, Stuart-Glennie was a socialist and philosopher, an empirical folklorist and philologist, who pursued a naturalistic account of history and mind.

Of course they also had significant differences, perhaps most notably in Jaspers's insistence that the axial age remains the standard by which to understand all of human history: "the spiritual foundations of humanity were laid simultaneously and independently. . . . And these are the foundations upon which humanity still subsists today" (Jaspers 1953: 98). And as he put it elsewhere:

> The conception of the Axial Period furnishes the questions and standards with which to approach all preceding and subsequent developments. The outlines of the preceding civilisations dissolve. The peoples that bore them vanish from sight as they join in the movement of the Axial Period. The prehistoric peoples remain prehistoric until they merge into the historical movement that proceeds from the Axial Period, or die out. The Axial Period assimilates everything that remains. From it world history receives the only structure and unity that has endured—at least until our own time. (Jaspers 1953: 8)

Jaspers sought to get at how the axial divide has distanced that which was outside of its mindset, so that the legacies of the religions of the book, for example, still dominate world religious outlooks, whereas ancient Egyptian and Babylonian polytheisms have dissolved. Still, the yet living "prehistoric peoples," or what is better termed indigenous peoples, would strongly differ with Jaspers's civilizational-centric depiction, despite the ways civilizations have brutally sought to eliminate them. The pre-axial civilized peoples might also beg to differ, given that the Neolithic diet they bequeathed us remains the staple of the world food system.

Stuart-Glennie, in contrast with Jaspers, saw the moral revolution/axial age as a transitional phase between the first and third stages of history. He described the first stage, the panzoonist outlook of aboriginal and early civilizational mind, as true intuitions of nature, but as clothed in false conceptions. By true intuitions of nature Stuart-Glennie meant to draw attention to the ways in which natural phenomena are central to many non-civilizational peoples, from the close attention to wildlife to, for example, skilled practices of wayfinding and tracking. Stuart-Glennie's definition of religion showed perhaps the influence of socialism on him, given how he connected it to "Environments of Existence." In his 1891 essay on "The Origins of Mythology" he stated: "Religion is, subjectively, the Social Emotion excited by the Environments of Existence, conceived in the progressive forms determined by Economic and Intellectual Conditions; and is, objectively, the Ritual Observances in which that Emotion is expressed" (Stuart-Glennie 1891: 225). Stuart-Glennie's definition allows that life experience can enter into religious sensibility and human consciousness. It does not deny ideological or alienating elements, but also does not reduce religion to them. It allows that the social construction of religion may be informed by physical and social conditions of relations to environs. This gets particularly interesting when considering the two-sided practical and reverential attuning to the wild habitat as teacher and role model one sees in a wide variety of hunter-gatherer societies.

Early civilizational polytheisms also give significant attention to patterns of nature, which are vital for agriculturally based societies, through fertility and weather deities. Such practices and beliefs, "naturianism," expressed true subjective intuitions about nature, but, as Stuart-Glennie saw it, lacked objective conceptualization. He saw in the developments of modern science of his time the rise of a potential "third age of humanity," which would involve true intuitions of nature, but now clothed in true scientific conceptions.

The second stage of humanity, the period and legacy of the moral revolution, is regarded by Stuart-Glennie as a transitional time whose main task was to develop subject-object differentiation. It is the age of "transcendence" and of a greater reflective outlook, as Jaspers characterized it, but rather than seeing that as the pivot of all history, Stuart-Glennie holds it as a 2500 year phase of development of subjective and objective dimensions of consciousness, much as a child develops a differentiation of self and other:

> [A] Revolution should be discoverable in the general history of Mankind . . . the great historical period of Transition, or Middle Stage of Mental Development which it initiated . . . that of a Differentiation of Subjective and Objective. . . . If one conceives the distinction of Subjective and Objective as, generally, but a short way of indicating the distinction between consciousness of Oneself and consciousness of what is not Oneself; between the Internal World of our own thought and emotions, and the External World of those persons and Things that excite thought and emotion; between reflection on Ourselves—the sequences of inward want and satisfaction, of pain and pleasure that constitute our own solitary selves—and reflection on the coexisting phenomena of Outward Objects,—I think that no difficulty should be found in attaching a perfectly clear and definite meaning to the distinction of "Subjective and Objective." (Stuart-Glennie 1878: 208)

Whereas the earlier felt intuitions of the laws of nature characterizing pan-zoonism lacked objective conceptualization in Stuart-Glennie's view, the result of the legacy of the moral revolution, the 2500 year, as he put it, Modern Revolution, would be a stage that could, through science, *objectively conceptualize* the subjective *intuitions* of nature. That 2500 year period was marked by a dialectic of 500 year cycles in the West between the supernaturalism of the Judeo-Christian tradition and the naturalism of science, culminating in the triumph of science, a religion of humanism, and a polity of socialism by the year 2000. The actual history turned out to be far messier than Stuart-Glennie surmised: Global capitalism stretching new levels of inequality enabled by advanced science and technology, and a rise of religious fundamentalism.

I have dealt with Stuart-Glennie's idea of 500 year cycles in history and this historical dialectic in the West in my book, and cannot address it further in the space here. What is of interest, however, is that Stuart-Glennie was able to include nature as a key element in the development of human consciousness and religious sensibility, whereas Jaspers largely excluded it from "the history of the spirit." Despite abundant evidence for the attunement to wild nature in the whole range of aboriginal religions, Jaspers denied that nature can be a source of profound spiritual significance and even transcendence: "We see the vast territories of Northern Asia, Africa, and America, which were inhabited by men but saw the birth of nothing of importance to the history of spirit" (Jaspers 1953: 22). Stuart-Glennie's position is markedly opposed to that of Jaspers on this point.

In an 1876 work of Stuart-Glennie, *The Modern Revolution. Proemia 1: Pilgrim Memories*, there is a wonderfully succinct sentence that goes to the heart of the differences between Stuart-Glennie and Jaspers's accounts: "the Civilisations prior to the Sixth Century B.C. were chiefly determined by the Powers and Aspects of Nature, and those posterior thereto by the Activities and Myths of Mind" (Stuart-Glennie 1876: 479). Whether one accepts the powers of nature as elements of the history of spirit which continue as such, as Stuart-Glennie does, or whether one denies them spiritual significance, as Jaspers does, marks a major fissure in understanding the role of the moral revolution/axial age in history (see also Halton, forthcoming). To give an example, both Stuart-Glennie and Jaspers noted parallels between the eastern Asian movements in ancient China and India and those of the West in ancient Greece and Israel, and the legacies of Christianity and Islam. But Stuart-Glennie noted how the Eastern outlooks retained a connection to the *panzoonism*, or "the conception of immanence of power in nature itself," whereas the Western religious outlooks developed as supernatural and independent of nature:

> Common as an exoteric Polytheism and esoteric Pantheism were to all the earlier religions, we find the new religions of, and subsequent to, the sixth century BC, distinguishable into two antagonistically different classes. The new religions of Farther Asia, though, so far, like the new religions of Hither Asia and Europe, that they were religions of conscience rather than, like those of which they took the place, religions of custom, were yet clearly distinguishable from the western religions in retaining the fundamental conception of panzoism, the conception of immanence of power in nature itself, and were, therefore, still esoterically pantheistic and atheistic. But the new religions of Western Asia and of Europe,—Judaism, half a millennium later, Christianism, and, after another half millennium, Islamism,—were, on the contrary, for the

> first time supernatural religions, not in their popular forms only, but in their essential principle, the conception, not of a power immanent in, but of a creator independent of, nature. (Stuart-Glennie 1901: 457–58)

Another forgotten facet of Stuart-Glennie's outlook worth recalling is this idea of *panzoonism*, meaning "all life," the livingness of things, the intuition of a "Solidarity of Nature" as characterizing the first stage of humanity. He published his book articulating his theory of the moral revolution, *In the Morningland*, in 1873, two years after Edward B. Tylor published *Primitive Culture* and introduced the term and theory of *animism*. There Stuart-Glennie gave a devastating critique of animism that scholars never picked up on, a critique that remains interesting.

Tylor claimed that animism involves an attitude toward an object imbued with a spirit from without. Stuart-Glennie claimed Tylor's theory would be more correctly titled "spiritism," not animism, because it was not about the life of the object per se. Stuart-Glennie's alternative, panzoonism, concerns the power inherent in the object and the relation to that power. I view it as involving a relational consciousness, a participation attitude, thoroughly involved in its living and signifying habitat. In this relational outlook things are not inanimate substances, but rather animate signs through which one finds clues and cues for living. In this sense Stuart-Glennie's panzoonism finds resonance in contemporary theorizing on "the new animism," among writers such as David Abram, Tim Ingold, Nurit Bird-David, Robin Wall Kimmerer, and myself.

IS THE MORAL REVOLUTION/ AXIAL AGE UNSUSTAINABLE?

Almost 4.5 billion people today are Christian or Muslim, more than half the people on earth. Their religious beliefs stem from the moral revolution of post-exile Judaism and its "religions of the book" legacy in the development of Christianity and Islam. Contemporary global civilization is also heavily influenced by the legacies of developments from the moral revolution/axial age of Greek science and Athenian democracy, of political empire building from Cyrus on, of the reflective spirit that broke out back then to reshape things in ways still present. Though it is true that many leading figures of the philosophic and religious movements, the "renouncers," ultimately "failed" in having their ideas co-opted by the power systems they rose up against, many of their ideas lived on through those power structures, for example, in the Christian Roman Empire and in Islam. These are some of the reasons Jaspers could say "Man, as we know him today, came into being. For short we may style this the 'Axial Period'" (Jaspers 1953: 2).

Stuart-Glennie was incorrect in thinking that a new stage of humanity would come into being by the year 2000 in which religion would be purified through science. He also was naïve in seeing that the developments of science and technology would be solely benign. Jaspers, living through the Second World War and its atomic bomb finale, saw and wrote about how science and technology had become deeply problematic, even while he held to axial ideals. Stuart-Glennie did make some prescient predictions, such as that a "United States of Europe" would come into being around the year 2000, which it did, though it now shows signs of dissembling. But instead of arriving at a new age of humanism, humanity has proliferated a world "human-all-too-human," as Nietzsche put it, replete with dehumanization side by side with human rights and institutions.

Stuart-Glennie's philosophy of history and account of the moral revolution has its deficits, such as his racist ideas on the origins of civilization and his overly optimistic belief in a necessary historical progress. But there remain elements of his thinking related to the moral revolution relevant to contemporary issues.

The moral revolution/axial age introduced ideas of transcendence, such as in religions of the Abrahamic tradition, where, as Robert Bellah said of ancient Judaism in his recent book on the axial age, "A God who is finally outside of society and the world provides the point of reference from which all existing presuppositions can be questioned, a basic criterion for the axial transition" (Bellah 2011: 322). This new transcendent "point of reference," the greater reflectiveness, was celebrated by Jaspers and Bellah. Bellah saw it as the rise of "theoretic culture," and that it "certainly proclaimed the sacredness of the person" (Bellah 2013).

Both Bellah and Jaspers were critical of the ways science and technology had become dominant and potentially out-of-control forces in modern life. As Jaspers put it, it was "possible for technology, released from human meaning, to become a frenzy in the hands of monsters" (Jaspers 1953: 125). Both saw the ideals of the axial age as having continuing contemporary relevance in restoring humane values. Stuart-Glennie, by contrast, lived in the hopes of the Victorian era that science and technology were benign forces, and lacked the critical perspective that Jaspers and Bellah shared.

Yet Stuart-Glennie's philosophy of history offers an unexpected corrective to the axial-centrism of Jaspers and Bellah. Remember that the era of the moral revolution, his second stage of humanity, was a transitional phase, a developmental working out of subjective and objective perspectives, and that he saw a forthcoming third stage as completing the partial intuitions of the first panzooinist stage of true insights into nature. Science and humanism would return to true intuitions of nature and add true conceptualizations of nature. Despite the many lacunae in Stuart-Glennie's schematic account, I see an unappreciated insight in it, one that I have been working out from another perspective in my own work: how human insight into nature in the long-term deep past have informed, shaped, and tempered human nature in ways that may serve as resources for living today (Halton 2019).

What would some of the allegedly true insights into nature from panzoonism be? What could their possible relevance be for today? The most significant insight might be what I have called "sustainable wisdom," an outlook of accord with the earth and its limits instead of one set apart from it. As I put it in 2013:

> Though we may think ourselves modern, we retain Pleistocene bodies, as ecological philosopher Paul Shepard put it, and Pleistocene needs, bodied into being over our longer two million year evolution. What Shepard termed "the sacred game," the dramatic interplay of predator and prey, reminds us of that older evolutionary story, wherein [humans emerge] into being wide-eyed in wonder at circumambient life, a child of the earth foraging for edible, sensible, thinkable, and sustainable wisdom. (Halton 2013: 279–92)

The two million year trajectory into anatomically modern humans, embodied in our psyches and genomes, reveal practiced modes of wisdom available for use in contemporary society, including diet and parenting, and even potentials for economic life. The Paleolithic diet, for example, in its many varieties, represents an optimum diet, a far healthier alternative to the industrial diet, and one that can be selected for today. The Neolithic diet, basis for the global food system today, brought its eaters reduced nutrition over most of its history from the earlier Paleolithic model, actually causing people to become 4–6 inches shorter wherever it was introduced. It is only in the past 150 or so years in advanced industrial countries that heights began to return to their pre-neolithic normalcy (Mummert et al. 2011). The Paleolithic model is less meat dependent and grain dependent than the industrial diet, suggesting more sustainable practices for the earth.

Human nature involves a complex, nuanced innate sociality, bodying forth in the "communicative musicality" of banter between infants and their mothers, as neuroscientists Colwyn Trevarthen and Stephen Malloch have demonstrated (Malloch and Trevarthen 2009). This inborn social, musical capacity is dialogical and expressive, and is coming from the subcortical brain of the infant. The synaptic connections of our vaunted prefrontal cortex have not yet been made, but this expressive banter will help body them into being in the course of development. This is a truly social *and* biological interaction, one that, when adequately undergone, will result in a couple of years in a child capable of symbolic interaction. Human plasticity in early childhood operates within developmental patterns that can be optimized or pathologized.

As Jean Liedloff, who spent years studying Venezuelan Amazonian hunter-gatherers and their parenting argued:

> The assumption of innate sociality is at direct odds with the fairly universal civilized belief that a child's impulses need to be curbed in order to make him social. There are those who believe that reasoning and pleading for "cooperativeness" with the child will accomplish this curbing better than threat, insult, or hickory sticks, but the assumption that every child has an antisocial nature, in need of manipulation to become socially acceptable, is germane to both these points of view as well as to all the more common ones between the two extremes. If there is anything fundamentally foreign to us in continuum societies like the Yequana, it is this assumption of innate sociality. It is by starting from this assumption and its implications that the seemingly unbridgeable gap between their strange behavior, with resultant high well-being, and our careful calculations, with an enormously lower degree of well-being, becomes intelligible. (Liedloff 1977: 84)

Liedloff calls this general outlook "the continuum concept," the two million years of evolution embodied in the genome. From this perspective it is our human birthright that a child is born with the expectation of being worthy and welcomed.

Consider by contrast the Christian idea of "innate depravity" so celebrated by the Puritans, that a baby is born evil, a viper, a child of the devil as Jonathan Edwards put it, an amped up version of St. Augustine's idea of original sin. Augustine: "A baby's limbs are feeble as it kicks and strikes out, but its mind is sinful." This is an alienated outlook which has falsely separated from human nature, then declared that separation to be human nature. One might call this outlook, which vilifies the newborn, the real "original sin."

Would a mother ever come up with such a depraved view of newborns? I don't believe so. Only a chauvinist patriarchal mindset, the same one which redefined the first appearance of woman as "born" from a man's rib, could fabricate such an absurdity to invert the innate goodness and sociality of the newborn into depravity. Here is an outright cost of the legacy of the moral revolution/axial age, with its idea of transcendence, that gulf between earth and the divine, and which was supposed to produce a "universal compassion" and a new valuation of "the sacredness of the person" as Bellah put it and Hans Joas has also written about. It is the loss of the touch of the earth and the forgetting of its lessons and limits as central.

This example illustrates the potential dangers represented in Bellah's idealization of axial cognitive mind and Bellah and Jaspers's undervaluing of passional mind, of the sustainable wisdom in parenting practices it can carry. This idealizing of reflective mind also prevented Bellah and Jaspers, in my opinion, from fully appreciating the place of perceptive relations to wild habitat in the evolutionary origins of religion. Stuart-Glennie's definition of religion cited earlier as involving "subjectively, the Social Emotion excited by the Environments of Existence" (Stuart-Glennie 1873: 220) provides an interesting contrast.

Here is an opening for the panzooinist outlook to inform contemporary life, the attunement to wild nature and modeling of its informing properties for human ways, in this case parenting. One sees repeated examples of such outlooks in extant hunter-gatherers, over a range of parenting practices. To be sure, one can also find examples of infanticide, practiced of necessity in extreme cases when times are hard. Now infanticide is clearly morally objectionable to us, and is clearly not necessary in settled society today. But there remains much to learn of optimal parenting practices based on the long-term continuum that threads through a diversity of still extant hunter-gatherers. A colleague, psychologist Darcia Narvaez, has been exploring these possibilities through a series of conferences and publications on child well-being (Narvaez 2014; Narvaez et al. 2014). In short, there is room for the original intuitions into nature, to paraphrase Stuart-Glennie, to inform contemporary life, not in a regressive sense, but in a progressive and selective re-incorporation.

More generally, the anthropological and archaeological record reveals that humans evolved as foragers, out of increasing modes of prosocial behavior, relatively equitable clan based societies, and sustainable relations to habitat through an outlook of few wants that could be easily met (Sahlins 1973; Suzman 2017). This not only was, but remains, our human nature. Neolithic civilization reversed that, creating "the economic problem" of unlimited desires and limited means to meet them, a development that the moral revolution attempted, in part, to offset, but overall failed to achieve. The idea of "economic man" as having unlimited wants, of a Hobbesian "state of nature," is a civilizational construct, not human nature.

Agriculturally based civilization spawned wealth and poverty, great inequality, and unlimited wants as part of its mistaken idea that it could transcend nature. More recently, between 1970 and 2018 human population doubled. In that same time period there was a global average decline of 60 percent of vertebrate species populations, and regionally an 89 percent decline in Central and South America (WWF 2018). The various scenarios of unsustainability puncture the happy never-ending ascent of the myth of progress, as well as question the role of science and technology as manifestations of the myth of progress.

More than half the world are believers in the religions of the book and, one must assume, active contributors to the increasingly unsustainable world we live in. One would hope that the wisdom of the moral revolution/axial age could be turned to address and overcome these problems, as indeed, many of the writers, including Stuart-Glennie, Jaspers, Lewis Mumford, Robert Bellah, and others, including another writer I discovered had written on the theme 20 years before Jaspers, D. H. Lawrence, have attempted to do. They share a hope that understanding the revolutionary past of the moral revolution/axial age, as Jaspers put it, might "assist in heightening our awareness of the present." And in this milieu Stuart-Glennie's idea of panzoonism, admittedly abstract, does suggest that a reimagining of our relations to nature in our scientific, economic, and religious beliefs might be necessary, not in the context of his optimistic progressivism, but rather in something like holism: a recovery of a more primal way of consciousness, already embedded but forgotten within us.

WORKS CITED

Assmann, Jan. *Achsenzeit: Eine Archäologie Der Moderne.* Frankfurt, GER: C. H. Beck, 2018: 141.
Bellah, Robert. 2011. *Religion in Human Evolution: From the Paleolithic to the Axial Age.* Cambridge: Belknap Press of Harvard University Press.
———. 2013. "The Modern Project in Light of Human Evolution." Lecture Presented at University of Notre Dame, Notre Dame, IN, March 19, 2013. http://csrs.nd.edu/events/special-event----robert-bellah-to-lecture-at-notre-dame/.
Bellah, Robert, and Hans Joas. 2012. *The Axial Age and Its Consequences.* Cambridge, MA: The Belknap Press of Harvard University Press.
Geddes, Patrick. 1910. "The Late Mr. JS Stuart-Glennie." *The Sociological Review* 3(4): 317–23.
Halton, Eugene. 2013. "Planet of the Degenerate Monkeys." In *Planet of the Apes and Philosophy.* Edited by John Huss, Chicago: Open Court Press: 279–92.
———. 2014. *From the Axial Age to the Moral Revolution: John Stuart-Glennie, Karl Jaspers, and a New Understanding of the Idea.* New York: Palgrave Macmillan.
———. 2017. "Sociology's Missed Opportunity: John Stuart-Glennie's Lost Theory of the Moral Revolution, also Known as the Axial Age." *Journal of Classical Sociology* 17(3): 191–212.
———. 2019. "Indigenous Bodies, Civilized Selves, and the Escape from the Earth." In *Indigenous Sustainable Wisdom: First-Nation Know-how for Global Flourishing.* Edited by Darcia Narvaez, Four Arrows, Eugene Halton, Brian Collier, and Georges Enderle. New York: Peter Lang Publishing: 47–73.
———. Forthcoming. "The Forgotten Earth: Nature, World Religions, and Worldlessness in the Legacy of the Axial Age/Moral Revolution." In *From World Religions to Axial Civilizations.* Edited by Said Arjomand and Stephen Kalberg. Albany, NY: SUNY Press. Submitted for publication.
Jaspers, Karl. 1953. *The Origin and Goal of History.* New Haven: Yale University Press.
Liedloff, Jean. 1977. *The Continuum Concept.* New York: De Capo Press.
Malloch, Stephen, and Colwyn Trevarthen. 2009. *Communicative Musicality: Exploring the Basis of Human Companionship.* Oxford: Oxford University Press.
Mill, John Stuart. 1972. "Letter to Henry Fawcett, Vienna, July 21, 1862." In *The Collected Works of John Stuart Mill, Volume XV—The Later Letters of John Stuart Mill 1849–1873 Part II* [1856]. Edited by Francis E. Mineka and Dwight N. Lindley. Toronto: University of Toronto Press. Accessed January 22, 2018, http://oll.libertyfund.org/titles/mill-the-collected-works-of-john-stuart-mill-volume-xv-the-later-letters-1849-1873-part-ii.
Mummert, Amanda, Emily Esche, and Joshua Robinson. 2011. "Stature and Robusticity During the Agricultural Transition: Evidence From the Bioarchaeological Record." *Economics and Human Biology* 9(3): 284–301.
Narvaez, Darcia. 2014. *Neurobiology and the Development of Human Morality: Evolution, Culture, and Wisdom.* New York: Norton.
Narvaez, Darcia, Kristin Valentino, and Agustin Fuentes, eds. 2014. *Ancestral Landscapes in Human Evolution: Culture, Childrearing and Social Wellbeing.* Oxford: Oxford University Press.
Sahlins, Marshall. 1973. *Stone-Age Economics.* Chicago, IL: Aldine.

Shaw, George Bernard. 1907. "Preface." In *Major Barbara*. London: George Bernard Shaw.
Stuart-Glennie, John. 1873. *In the Morningland: Or, the Law of the Origin and Transformation of Christianity—Volume 1: The New Philosophy of History*. London: Longmans, Green, and Co.
———. 1876. *The Modern Revolution. Proemia 1: Pilgrim Memories*. London: Longmans, Green, and Co.
———. 1878. *The Modern Revolution. Proemia 1: Isis and Osiris*. London: Longmans, Green, and Co.
———. 1891. "Origins of Mythology." Pp. 215–29 in *The International Folk-Lore Congress, 1891: Papers and Transactions*. Edited by J. Jacobs and Alfred Nutt. London: David Nutt.
———. 1896. "The Survival of Paganism." Pp. 519–20 in *Greek Folk Poesy: Volume 2, Folk Prose*. Edited by Lucy MJ Garnett. London: David Nutt.
———. 1901. "The Law of Historical Intellectual Development." *The International Quarterly* 1901(3): 444–63.
———. 1906. "Sociological Studies." Pp. 243–78 in *Sociological Papers*, Volume 2. Edited by F. Galton, P. Geddes, M. E. Sadler, et al. London: Macmillan & Co. Ltd.
Suzman, James 2017. "The Bushmen Who Had the Whole Work-Life Thing Figured Out." *New York Times*, July 24, 2017.
Tylor, Edward B. 1871. *Primitive Culture*. New York, NY: G.P. Putnam's Sons.
WWF. 2018. *Living Planet Report—2018: Aiming Higher*. Edited by M. Grooten and R. E. A. Almond. Gland, Switzerland: WWF. Accessed November 3, 2018. https://www.wwf.org.uk/updates/living-planet-report-2018.

Chapter Two

Annie Marion MacLean and Sociology at the University of Chicago and Hull House

Mary Jo Deegan

Annie Marion MacLean is a forgotten founder of American sociology. She accomplished many vital tasks as a 1900 graduate of the then-most important school of sociology, the Chicago school, at the University of Chicago. She did this in several ways: (1) as a faculty member in the Extension Division there from 1902 until 1934; (2) as the author of nine articles in the leading professional outlet, *The American Journal of Sociology (AJS)*, more than any other woman in the history of the discipline; (3) as a precedent setting leader of several areas of study, such as the Chicago school of occupations or the Chicago school of race relations; (4) as a part of the Hull-House school of sociology, the leading institution in women's work in the profession; (5) as an innovator in critical quantitative and qualitative methods; (6) as the author of over 200 publications; and (7) as an early feminist theorist and activist. Any one of these accomplishments would have made her an important early sociologist; the combination of them makes her a stellar professional leader.

In this chapter I introduce MacLean's intellectual biography and examine her professional role in light of the Chicago schools of sociology at the University of Chicago and at the world famous social settlement, Hull-House. I then examine her contributions to the study of women and their paid labor. I use these studies to analyze her work in quantitative and qualitative data collection techniques. I finish by connecting her corpus with some contemporary social issues.

ANNIE MARION MACLEAN'S BIOGRAPHY

MacLean was part of the first generation of "new women," educated women who wanted to bring women into public life and social equality with men, who became sociologists (Deegan 1991, 1996; Smith-Rosenberg 1985). She received her undergraduate and graduate training at Acadia University in Wolfville, Nova Scotia (N.S.). She earned her bachelor's degree there in 1893 and her master's degree in 1894. MacLean then turned to new challenges hundreds of miles away, and in another country she found what she wanted at the University of Chicago in the department of sociology. She completed her second master's degree in 1897 and her doctorate in 1900 and became part of the early Chicago school of sociology (ECSS).

She studied sociology with Charles R. Henderson, George H. Mead, Albion W. Small, who chaired her master's and doctoral committees, and Charles Zueblin. These men of the ECSS were associated with the social settlement Hull-House. This was a center of sociological theory and practices, led by the founder Jane Addams (Deegan 1988). Several settlement residents also taught sociology at the university including Edith Abbott, Addams, Sophonisba Breckinridge, Florence Kelley, and Mary E. McDowell. Another female sociologist and Hull-House ally, Marion Talbot, was a member of the department and the Dean of Women at the university. All these women and MacLean formed a female Chicago school of sociology (FCSS; Deegan 1978).

Her mentors, friends, and colleagues encompassed other full-time faculty at the University of Chicago, including John Dewey, James Tufts, and Graham Taylor. Prior to World War I, these faculty, friends, and colleagues created an extraordinary American theory of human action and meaning. The full-time faculty's ideas, especially for Mead and Dewey, is called "Chicago pragmatism" (Feffer 1993; James 1904; Rucker 1969), and the women's approach is called "feminist pragmatism" (Deegan 1988, 1991, 1996, 1999, 2001a, 2001b, 2006; Seigfried 1991, 1993, 1996, 2002). Thus MacLean sprang from two sociology schools in Chicago and merged their interests and methods in her work. These blended topics are part of her intellectual apparatus; her career as a teacher, mentor, and researcher; and identify her place in intellectual history.

MacLean articulated radical changes in American life and politics, altering the possibilities for human growth and action for the poor, the working class, immigrants, people of color, youth, the aged, and women. MacLean was a central figure in the study of women and in applied sociology between 1897 and 1911. In the latter year she contracted infectious rheumatism. Her failing physical strength increasingly restricted her activities for the rest of her life. She continued, nevertheless, to teach correspondence courses and write dozens of books, essays, and articles after this date.

MacLean worked with a large and powerful cohort of women who influenced her and whom she influenced in return (Lengermann and Niebrugge 2007; MacDonald 1994a, 1994b). She reflected on her physically and emotionally painful journey from the heights of intellectual activity and accomplishments (MacLean 1910) to the nearly total incapacitation of a body racked by pain, inflammation, and restrictions (MacLean 1914, 1918). She turned away from the temptations of self-pity and despair and took notes on the world of hospitals, care-taking, and medicine. She triumphed over her losses and sought happiness in daily living. She, who could have taught the most outstanding and advanced students, reveled in her correspondence students and their struggles to be educated (MacLean 1923a, 1930).

MACLEAN'S INTERESTS FROM TWO CHICAGO SCHOOLS OF SOCIOLOGY

A significant number of MacLean's colleagues, ideas, and practices merged the Hull-House social settlement (HHSS) and the Chicago school of sociology (CSS) into one process. This large Chicago circle included Henderson, Mead, Small, and Zueblin as men of the CSS with whom she studied *and* were associated with Hull-House. It also included the women of the FCSS who held various faculty positions at the university *and*, except for Talbot, were residents of Hull-House. MacLean also made friends with other CSS alumni, especially Amy Hewes (1903, 1911), Frances A. Kellor (1904, 1905), Monroe Work (1903), and Richard Wright, Jr. (1903; Deegan 2014). MacLean served as an intellectual liaison between the HHSS and the CSS and powerfully illustrates their collaborative approach. Both groups were engaged in liberation sociology (Feagin and Vera 2008), and fought for social justice, education, and democracy.

The use of qualitative and quantitative methodology was common to both the HHSS and the CSS, although the women tended to be more empirically oriented than the men. Both groups were interested in using sociology to inform the public and empower them in a democracy, often engaging in critical ethnography, participant observation, experiential analysis, feminist ethnography, and critical quantitative studies (Deegan under review). For MacLean, women's right to fair wages was high on her list of political goals. Both schools of thought believed in education as part of shaping human authority and citizenship. Both groups supported social settlements, with the residents of the settlements, who were usually female sociologists, more committed to these institutions than the male sociologists who visited them. Similarly, the male sociologists worked full-time and primarily at the University of Chicago while the women held more marginal faculty positions there, although both groups supported the academy and higher education (Deegan 1978, 2014).

Her mentors, friends, and colleagues encompassed other full-time faculty at the University of Chicago, including John Dewey, and the president of the university, William R. Harper. At Hull-House, her allies included Abbott, Addams, Breckinridge, and Kelley. All these women also taught at the University of Chicago in the FCSS, but they did not specifically teach MacLean there. Talbot was an important liaison between the university and the social settlement who also influenced MacLean.

MacLean held a series of positions at colleges between 1899, before she finished her doctorate, and 1911 when she was stricken with a quick-acting form of rheumatism. These institutions included Royal Victoria College, the women's branch of McGill University in Montreal, Canada, John B. Stetson University in Deland, Florida, and Adelphi College (now University) in NYC.

MACLEAN'S THEORETICAL INTERESTS

The men of the early CSS trained MacLean and strongly influenced her work. MacLean's (1897a, 1897b) master's degree, again, showed an overlapping interest between the CSS and the HHSS with an emphasis on women's factory legislation, inspection, and childhood rights, and her degree was among the earliest granted in the CSS. MacLean (1900) was the first woman to earn a doctorate in the CSS with her focus on *The Acadian Element in the Population of Nova Scotia* and the immigrant experience.

Even today, MacLean (1897b, 1899a, 1899b, 1903a, 1905a, 1908, 1909, 1915, 1926) holds the record for publishing more articles in *AJS* than any other female sociologist since the journal was founded in 1895. Her mentors in the CSS, moreover, respected her ideas and practices more than their successors in the 1920s and the 1930s (Faris 1967), who never promoted her from her assistant professorship in the Extension Division, did not cite her work, and apparently did not mourn her passing.

MacLean developed not only "Chicago ethnographies" and "Chicago case studies" which, in turn, profoundly influenced the career of Edwin Sutherland (1937), but also "Chicago community studies," the "Chicago school of work and occupations," "Chicago urban sociology, the "Chicago school of social movements," the "Chicago school of race relations," and "Chicago quantitative studies" (Faris 1967; Fine 1995; Kurtz 1984).

MacLean also was a pioneer in experiential studies and participant observation of physical disability, gender, medical institutions, and occupations. She drew on similar interests in the HHSS. She honed her "female standpoint" (e.g., Smith 1987); her "feminist ethnographic skills" (Reinharz 1992) and her ability to cross class and ethnic boundaries. The sociology of physical disability remains understudied and under researched today (e.g., Deegan and Brooks 1985), but her books and writings set a high standard for analysis, courage, and documentation. The thorny complexities of problematic care for people with chronic disabilities continues (Deegan 2011; Deegan and Brooks 1985), and MacLean helps us understand that process.

MacLean's scholarship on women's organizations, including women's housing, occupations, the Young Women's Christian Association (YWCA), the American Association of University Women (AAUW), consumerism, and suffrage remains a historical baseline for our understanding of contemporary feminism and voluntary associations, topics also examined by scholars in the HHSS and the FCSS. These social movement organizations mobilized resources for the common good. MacLean helped develop many social movements and their activist networks, and her skills as a feminist pragmatist still have much to teach us today. Women, labor, people of color, people with physical disabilities, and other disenfranchised groups continue to struggle to attain the ideals that MacLean supported and advanced. The feminist pragmatist welfare state accomplished many of their goals but it has also suffered from many attacks and setbacks in the intervening decades (Goodwin 1997). The linkages between race, class, and gender are a major area of inquiry today and scholars studying this intersection of statuses suffer from historical amnesia about MacLean.

Finally, MacLean and other Canadian sociologists have an important history that needs further research and interpretation. MacLean was part of a group of Canadian women and another group of Scottish Canadians who were trained in the CSS for more than a century. They are pioneers in Canadian studies, too, and their complex analyses call for more adequate documentation. Their work and legacies will be strengthened by understanding MacLean's formerly forgotten ties to her homeland (MacLean 1914).

We know more about primary and secondary labor markets, gender and trade unions, women and religion, the modern civil rights movement and its supporting organizations, and the historical complexity surrounding the CSS both before and after 1920 than MacLean could know about her own era. The work of women from the FCSS, the HHSS, and that of her colleagues, friends, and mentors, moreover, is only being rediscovered today. But as that story is revealed in greater detail, MacLean will have a central position in it. MacLean (1923b: 28–29) herself gives us the tools to help us better understand her legacy:

> Work is one of the permanent satisfactions of life. Something to do that links us to the rest of mankind. . . . It is cowardly to hide behind physical ills or sorrows. I am part of a reasoned social process, and I shall not shirk respon-

sibility even though disease has me by the throat.... Suffering is not futile if it can teach us that beside even the still waters lies happiness.

MacLean left us a vibrant legacy of thought and action that provides a foundation for contemporary sociology.

MACLEAN, WOMEN, AND THE SOCIOLOGY OF WORK AND OCCUPATIONS

MacLean was one of the first people to study a series of famous Chicago schools: urban (MacLean 1910, 1916a), race relations (1903b), social movements, women (1899a, 1899b), and work and occupations. MacLean also combined specialties with both schools of sociology: for example, in her analyses of women's organizations and the sociology of social movements or the sociology of immigration and race relations. Each of these topics is discussed in Deegan (1914), but due to space constraints I focus here on women and paid labor to demonstrate her type of analyses and practices. In addition to creating these empirical studies, MacLean employed multiple methodologies to document them, and these techniques are analyzed, too.

Women's status in the marketplace was a central question to MacLean. Thus, she studied department stores (1899a), "The Sweat-Shop in the Summer" (1903a); and "The Diary of a Domestic Drudge" (1905b). Her analyses of "Women in the Industrial World" (1905c) and vignettes in "Silhouettes from Life" (1905d; the latter study directly influenced the subsequent work of Sutherland [1937], whom she introduced to sociology in 1906) also demonstrate her focus on women in the marketplace.

MacLean's greatest intellectual achievement, *Wage-Earning Women* (1910), drew on her participatory background and the work of an impressive team of investigators. MacLean used the women's sociology network to hire a research staff that included twenty-nine women. This massive study surveyed 13,500 women laborers employed in 400 institutions in more than 20 cities. Amy Tanner, a Chicago-trained sociologist, played a major role in collecting the data to study "Life in the Pennsylvania Coal Fields, with Particular Reference to Women" (MacLean 1908, 1910: 130–59). MacLean's sister Mildred helped document "The Chicago Worker" (1910: 55–73), especially in the garment industry. The women in Chicago and New York were compared and exhibited many similar patterns of age, wages, marital status, and religion. The women workers in New York, however, displayed higher statistics for pursuing "some study" and using libraries (72).

Variations in state legislation made some occupations safer or easier (MacLean 1910, Table 1, p. 165), but wages were generally low. Working hours were long. Having sufficient money for housing, clothing, health, and recreation was a constant challenge. Living in physically safe buildings and neighborhoods was also difficult and many working young women lived with their families and helped support not only themselves but others, too. Questions of sexuality and reputations were important for women workers who were often suspected of having "loose morals." Regional statistics were offered for New England, New Jersey, the Midwest, and the West Coast. Industries in food processing, clothing, printing, and sales showed gendered and national patterns as well as localized ones. Wage-earning women were increasingly common throughout the country, and the number of married women was increasing, too. MacLean and her team documented sweeping changes in the expectations of women's paid labor.

One of MacLean's more acclaimed ethnographies, and a subsequent chapter in *Wage-Earning Women* (1910), was her work "With Oregon Hop Pickers" (1909), published in the leading professional journal, *AJS*. The section on "Chicago Garment Workers" is a brief report of a central thrust of both the HHSS and CSS' work on labor unions in Chicago's booming industry.

The YWCA was the sponsoring and funding resource behind *Wage-Earning Women*. It documented the range of women's paid labor, their wages, their distribution in different industries in various regions, and their work with labor unions. MacLean employed her students at Adelphi College to help amass and calculate the study, training them in research techniques and analysis. This massive team research was the beginning of a pattern that is common practice today. MacLean, however, worked before computers and research centers were available. After publishing *Wage-Earning Women* in 1910, she created a more popular version in *Women Workers and Society* in 1916(a) with recommendations to improve the lives of working women.

MacLean's Critical Quantitative Methods Used in the Study of Women's Paid Labor

Quantitative methods were fundamental to MacLean's work on wage-earning women and her cross-national studies of legislation, two topics of major interest to other Chicago sociologists. "Critical quantitative methods" are strikingly different from the mainstream, contemporary practices of numerical research. In the past, this mathematical work was dominated by women, while today it is dominated by men (Deegan 1988; Reinharz 1992). The early liberation sociologists (see, for example, Residents of Hull-House 1895) shared this mathematical work with the public because it made complex arguments clearer, whereas mathematical work today is oriented toward experts and viewed as too complex for the public to understand. The public of the past could use this evidence to argue for more democracy and social justice, while experts and policy-makers today use this evidence to maintain elite control and understand what the public is doing and thinking. Sociologists in both eras saw science as aligned with numbers, but scientific goals did not hold a higher priority than community values for the early sociologists, while many contemporary sociologists define science as having a separate and superior set of "objective" values. Many of the patriarchal stances of Park were augmented and ultimately supplemented in the U.S. by the ideas of the French sociologist Emile Durkheim ([1913] 1964), who made sharp divisions between the expert and the public and the importance of "objective reality." Scientific rules for Durkheim were more important than any other principles when conducting research.

The HHSS created knowledge and practices with unique characteristics. Thus female sociologists, like MacLean (1910), engaged in massive statistical studies that were subsequently translated into everyday language and application (MacLean 1916a). The residents of Hull-House (1895), as noted above, clearly demonstrated this in their monumental work, *Hull-House Maps and Papers*. Hull-House was a sociological "home" that was radically different from male-dominated academic sociology, and these distinctions grew over time. In MacLean's (e.g., 1903a) era, qualitative and quantitative methods worked hand in hand, not as opposing ideas and evidence (see Deegan, Hill, and Wortman 2009). Whatever proof or evidence that could make an argument or plan of action clearer was used for the common good. A sample of these critical methods are discussed here but MacLean's work is replete with such examples.

The Distribution of Canadian Migration by States and Nations

Canadians migrated to all the states in the Union, but especially to Massachusetts. MacLean (1905a: 816) provided a table listing the number of Canadians in the U.S. for each state. This massive relocation of Canadians to the U.S. was for economic reasons and easily accomplished. Canadians also disproportionately migrated to the U.S. in comparison to immigration from the old country. MacLean (1905a: 817) dramatically presented this data by the use of bar graphs comparing Canadian migration to that of eleven other countries.

The Distribution of Correspondence Students by Geography and Occupation

MacLean often provided simple statistics showing the range of types included in her analysis. Thus in her review of her twenty years of teaching in correspondence courses, where she was

> leading seekers after knowledge along the inky way, I have had 799 students in 47 states in the Union and in 10 foreign countries, including in this group

Hawaii and the Philippines. The geographical distribution of students may be seen from Tables I and II. The following list of fifty-three occupations represented shows some duplications. This is due to the fact that the student's designation of his vocation was accepted. (MacLean 1923a: 462)

The tables provided information on this distribution and documented how she usually did not teach undergraduate students of sociology, let alone advanced graduate ones. She was not promoting a prestigious career but enjoying the process of teaching and learning.

Calculating a Living Wage

MacLean repeatedly compared the cost of living to the typical wages in various occupations. She did this for hop-pickers (1908, 1910), saleswomen (1899a), and maids (1905c). These early mathematical calculations repeatedly showed that women could not live independently on the wages from their paid labor. These economic formulations of "a living wage" were innovative and in the forefront of critical quantitative work. If women could not survive, let alone thrive, on their salaries, these wages were unjust. The public, as consumers, voters, friends, and families needed to raise a democratic voice to protest and change this situation. Capitalist greed was insatiable, and the conscience of the people needed to be aroused.

DOCUMENTING THE STRUCTURE OF WOMEN'S PAID LABOR IN THE U.S.

MacLean traced the emergence of the factory system and the movement of labor out of the home, especially in the garment industry, to the eighteenth century. She demonstrated the increasing proportion of women workers and their presence in different occupations (1897b, 1899a, 1903a, 1905b, 1905c, 1905d). Women's low wages became accepted practice as employers assumed that women could receive more money through their families. Oppression resulted, and the employment of mothers of young children produced particularly disturbing situations. MacLean summarized protective legislation for women and supported their unionization. Chicago was one of the centers for this movement (MacLean 1910) and the YWCA was another source of hope (1916b). Clearly MacLean created a structural, statistical analysis calling for fairer wages and working conditions for women in a number of articles. Those set the background for her massive, national investigation for the YWCA in 1910.

These articles and *Wage-Earning Women* established several precedents that were part of Florence Kelley's public sociology to educate consumers, provide safe working conditions for labor, and bring women into the public sphere of state governance. Kelley's (1896, 1898a, 1904) work on behalf of working children, what she called "The Working Boy" who needed "The Illinois Child-Labor Law," was also supported by Addams (1896), Abbott (1908), and Abbott and Breckinridge (1910, 1911a, 1911b) of the HHSS and FCSS. These articles, and others on the eight-hour day (Kelley 1898b), the consumers' league (Kelley 1898a, 1905b, 1914), women's clubwork (Kelley 1901), and minimum wages (Kelley 1911), were published in *AJS* along with MacLean's extensive work on these same topics that appeared in that journal. This sociological cooperation and platform was augmented by numerous book reviews of collegial, team efforts (e.g., Kelley 1905a, 1905b, 1912a, 1912b, 1912c, 1915, 1916). This gendered division of labor created a major voice for female sociologists especially both within and outside of the discipline. This statistical work was supported by Henderson, Mead, and Zueblin, who comprised a sizable proportion of the men of the ECSS.

MACLEAN'S CRITICAL QUALITATIVE METHODS

MacLean used a range of qualitative methods. Her participant observation of department store clerks was the first Chicago ethnography (MacLean 1899a). Her engagement with the political rights of consumers also makes this a very early example of "participant action research," a characteristic method for liberation sociology. MacLean (e.g., 1920) wrote sociological poetry revealing the emotions underlying women's low wage employment. She used an informant for her analysis of the everyday life of domestic laborers (MacLean 1905b). She was employed in a sweat-shop working under dreadful working conditions, conducting her work in conjunction with consumer activists (MacLean 1903a). She studied three small Black churches in the South and provided information on their limited funds (MacLean 1903b). I examine two of her politically involved "critical qualitative methods" below, her ethnographic studies and feminist standpoint.

Shortly after MacLean moved to Florida, she began an important and innovative study of a nearby Black community, continuing her pioneering work in ethnography two decades before the now famous Chicago studies that are credited with beginning this technique (Deegan 2001b). Her political commitments to the people she observed and interviewed anticipated the later social movements in liberation sociology (Feagin and Vera 2008) and critical ethnography (Thomas 1993). Her ethnographic community study of African Americans resulted in her working with the eminent Black sociologists, W. E. B. Du Bois, Monroe Work, and Richard Wright at Du Bois's Atlanta Conferences in 1903. Her work demonstrated the negative effects of Jim Crow society and the positive spirit of Black church-goers.

MacLean often revealed her own everyday life by adopting a woman's standpoint (Smith 1987) in a variety of writings. She analyzed immigration (1925a), the problems of being wealthy in a democracy (1915), loving her dogs (1925b), friendship and teaching (1923a, 1930), but most powerfully, her lived experience of physical disability (1914, 1918). Her sociology of disability, especially for women, is pioneering and a strong voice in the literatures of both the HHSS and the CSS (Deegan and Brooks 1985). Her experiential method employing her standpoint theory was at the forefront of connecting her experiences with sociological perspectives while she lived in the midst of pain and conflicting diagnoses and treatments.

MACLEAN AND CONTEMPORARY STUDIES OF LIBERATION SOCIOLOGY

Liberation sociology is a tradition of social activism and social justice within the discipline:

> Liberation sociology is concerned with alleviating or eliminating various social oppressions and with creating societies that are more just and egalitarian societies. Liberation *from what* is linked to liberation *for what.* An emancipatory sociology not only seeks sound scientific knowledge but also takes sides with, and takes the outlook of, the oppressed and envisions an end to that oppression. (Feagin and Vera 2008: 1)

MacLean was a pioneering liberation sociologist who fought *against* discrimination and capitalist exploitation and *for* social justice and equality for people of color, the poor, women, and the disabled.

Feagin and Vera embed liberation sociology in more than a century of struggle, rightly placing Hull-House and some Chicago sociologists in a central, founding position, and MacLean is an integral part of this history. Hull-House and Chicago sociologists founded a sociology that recognized the public as central to the discipline and, the Chicago pragmatists especially, trusted the public in a democratic society (Neeley and Deegan 2005; Seigfried 1993). These early American sociologists encouraged education for citizenship, led and articulated reasons for social movements, and transformed the United States, especially the American welfare state and our understanding of race, class, gender, and nonviolence (Deegan 2008).

The HHSS and the CSS also encouraged the study of social class and labor relations, analyzing the processes of work, unionization, and worker exploitation. They adapted Fabian socialism to help create an American welfare state. During the 1890s, the HHSS successfully worked to enact legislation to end child labor. They were integral to the development of a Federal Children's Bureau, which provided information and collected data to help achieve children's optimal development. The bureau also established many public policies, such as initiating the birth and death registry of children; supporting well-baby clinics; and investigating infant, children's, and maternal mortality, juvenile delinquency, child labor, mothers' pensions, and nutrition (Skocpol 1992). They widely distributed this information and advice to thousands of young mothers (Addams 1910; 1930).

The HHSS and the ECSS, including MacLean, also emphasized urban sociology and the benefits of city life and urban planning, as well as working to solve the problems of poor housing and sanitation. They studied criminology, focusing especially on juvenile delinquency, the court system, and notions of justice (Addams et al. 1927; Neeley and Deegan 2005). The HHSS, in conjunction with Chicago clubwomen, faculty wives, and female faculty and students in the CSS (Deegan 1996), was instrumental in establishing a series of world-class institutions associated with juvenile delinquency and justice. They founded the world's first juvenile court in 1899, developed probation and parole procedures to reconnect juvenile offenders with the community, and helped to found the family court system, the Juvenile Psychopathic Institute, and the Institute for Juvenile Research (Addams et al. 1927). Mead and Henderson were involved in some of these groups, as well (Deegan 2003a, 2003b; Neeley and Deegan 2005).

Women were the focus of study for the HHSS and part of the CSS, especially as mothers, wage-earners, homemakers, and forces for social change (Abbott 1905, 1908, 1910; MacLean 1910). The feminist pragmatists built on traditional and modern ideas of women, which they developed in their writings. The feminist pragmatist welfare state applied this epistemology as praxis to the state apparatus, creating a system of social welfare with strong support for women and children (Goodwin 1997; Skocpol 1992).

All of the women and most of the men in these two groups supported suffrage between 1900 and 1920. Many of them also supported women's work in sociology as an ideal profession, breaking through traditional barriers to women in the workplace (Deegan 1991). But the women were usually far more radical in their view of women's role in the discipline and in public life than the men. This reflected a gendered political division between the groups. The work on gender in the HHSS was directly linked to their commitment to world peace (Addams, Balch, and Hamilton [1915] 2003), but MacLean identified with a pro-World War I stance that she shared with the men of the CSS (Deegan 2014). This was one of the few times that MacLean split with the HHSS and sided with the politics of the ECSS. In general, MacLean united now polarized positions in theory and methods, showing a way to combine a range of interests and political perspectives.

Finally, MacLean produced "Life in the Pennsylvania Coal Fields, with Particular Reference to Women" in 1910, where she documented the harsh living and working conditions there and the need for labor unions to fight for higher wages. Women's support of these struggles was vital to keep families and communities together. In the spring of 2018 we see the school teachers, many of them the daughters and granddaughters of the coal miners in this region, draw on this historical legacy as they successfully fought together to raise their collective wages. In her groundbreaking work MacLean documented this regional and gendered heritage.

CONCLUSION

Recovering the work of Annie Marion MacLean is crucial to understanding women's founding role in the profession. This is more than a historical exercise: She provides a needed historical foundation for many contemporary studies, in gender, race, and class; in disability, and so on. She is, moreover, a liberation sociologist who fought for social justice and the application of sociology to achieve the common good.

The use of qualitative and quantitative methodology was common to both the HHSS and the ECSS, although the women tended to be more empirically oriented than the men. Both groups were interested in using sociology to inform the public and empower them in a democracy, often engaging in critical ethnography, participant observation, experiential analysis, feminist ethnography, and critical quantitative studies. For MacLean, women's right to fair wages was high on her list of political goals. Both schools of thought believed in the crucial role of education in shaping human authority and citizenship. Both groups supported social settlements, with the residents of the settlements, who were usually female sociologists, more committed to these institutions than the male sociologists who visited them. Similarly, the male sociologists worked full-time and primarily at the University of Chicago while the women, including MacLean, held more marginal faculty positions there, although both groups supported the academy and higher education. The men, however, are widely recognized founders of sociology, while the women, including MacLean, are not. Restoring her, as well as her fellow female scholars, to the sociological canon is an urgent and necessary goal.

WORKS CITED

Abbott, Edith. 1905. "A Statistical Study of the Wages of Unskilled Labor in the United States, 1830–1900." PhD dissertation, University of Chicago.
———. 1908. "A Study of the Early History of Child Labor Legislation in America." *American Journal of Sociology* 14 (July): 15–37.
———. 1910. *Women in Industry*, intro. by Sophonisba P. Breckinridge. New York: D. Appleton.
Abbott, Edith, and Sophonisba P. Breckinridge. 1910. "Chicago's Housing Problems." *American Journal of Sociology* 16 (November): 289–308.

———. 1911a. "Housing Conditions in Chicago: III." *American Journal of Sociology* 16 (January): 433–68.

———. 1911b. "Chicago Housing Conditions: IV." *American Journal of Sociology* 17 (July): 1–34.

Addams, Jane. 1896. "A Belated Industry." *American Journal of Sociology* 1 (March): 536–50.

———. 1910. *Twenty Years at Hull-House*, illustrated by Norah Hamilton. New York: Macmillan.

———. 1930. *The Second Twenty Years at Hull-House*. New York: Macmillan.

Addams, Jane, Emily Greene Balch, and Alice Hamilton. [1915] 2003. *Women at the Hague*, ed. and intro. by Mary Jo Deegan. Amherst, NY: Humanity Books.

Addams, Jane, et al. 1927. *The Child, the Clinic and the Court*, intro. by Jane Addams. New York: New Republic.

Deegan, Mary Jo. 1978. "Women in Sociology, 1890–1930." *Journal of the History of Sociology* 1 (Fall): 11–34.

———. 1988. *Jane Addams and the Men of the Chicago School, 1892–1920*. New Brunswick, NJ: Transaction Books.

———, ed. 1991. *Women in Sociology*, intro. by Mary Jo Deegan. New York: Greenwood Press.

———. 1996. "'Dear Love, Dear Love': Feminist Pragmatism and the Chicago Female World of Love and Ritual." *Gender & Society* 10 (October): 590–607.

———, ed. 1999. *George Herbert Mead Play, School and Society*. New York: Peter Lang.

———. 2001a. "Introduction: George Herbert Mead's First Book." Pp. xi-xliv in *Essays in Social Psychology*, edited and introduction by Mary Jo Deegan. New Brunswick, NJ: Transaction Publishers.

———. 2001b. "The Chicago School of Ethnography." Pp. 11–25 in *Handbook of Ethnography*, edited by Paul Atkinson, Amanda Coffey, Sara Delamont, John Lofland, and Lyn Lofland. London (United Kingdom): Sage.

———. 2003a. "Introduction." Pp. 11–34 in *Women at the Hague: The International Congress of Women and Its Results*, by Jane Addams, Emily Greene Balch; and Alice Hamilton, edited and introduction by Mary Jo Deegan. Amherst, NY: Humanity Books.

———. 2003b. "Katharine Bement Davis: Her Theory and Praxis of Feminist Pragmatism." *Women & Criminal Justice* 14 (2/3): 15–40.

———. 2006. "The Human Drama Behind the Study of People as Potato Bugs: The Curious Marriage of Robert E. Park and Clara Cahill Park." *Journal of Classical Sociology* 6 (January): 101–22.

———. 2008. *Self, War, and Society: The Macrosociology of George Herbert Mead*. New Brunswick, NJ: Transaction Publishers.

———. 2011. "Democratic Ethnography." Paper presented at the Couch/Stone Symposium, Las Vegas, NV. 1 April.

———. 2014. *Annie Marion MacLean and the Chicago Schools of Sociology, 1894–1934*. New Brunswick, NJ: Transaction Publishers.

———. Under review. "Annie Marion MacLean." *Encyclopedia of Social Research Methods*, edited by Sara Delamont. UK: Sage.

Deegan, Mary Jo, and Nancy A. Brooks, eds. 1985. *Women and Disability: The Double Handicap*. New Brunswick, NJ: Transaction.

Deegan, Mary Jo, Michael R. Hill, and Susan Wortmann. 2009. "Annie Marion MacLean, Feminist Pragmatist and Methodologist." *Journal of Contemporary Ethnography* 38 (December): 655–64.

Durkheim, Emile. [1913] 1964. *The Rules of Sociological Method*, 8th ed., tr. by Sarah A. Solovay and John H. Mueller, edited by George E. G. Catlin, and intro. by Steven Lukes. New York: Free Press.

Faris, Robert E.L. 1967. *Chicago Sociology: 1920–1932*. Chicago: University of Chicago Press.

Feagin, Joe R., and Hernan Vera. 2008. *Liberation Sociology*. Boulder, CO: Paradigm.

Feffer, Andrew. 1993. *The Chicago Pragmatists and American Progressivism*. Chicago: University of Chicago Press.

Fine, Gary A., ed. 1995. *The Second Chicago School?* Chicago: University of Chicago Press.
Gaylord, Mark S., and John F. Galliher. 1988. *The Criminology of Edwin Sutherland*. New Brunswick, NJ: Transaction Books.
Goodwin, Joanne L. 1997. *Gender and the Politics of Welfare Reform*. Chicago, IL: University of Chicago Press.
Hewes, Amy. 1903. "The Part of Invention in the Social Process." PhD dissertation, Department of Sociology, University of Chicago.
———. 1911. "Marital and Occupational Statistics of Graduates of Mount Holyoke." *American Statistical Association Publications* 12 (December): 771–97.
James, William. 1904. "The Chicago School." *Psychological Bulletin* 1 (15 January): 1–5.
Kelley, Florence. 1896. "The Working Boy." *American Journal of Sociology* 2 (November 1896): 358–68.
———. 1898a. "The Illinois Child-Labor Law." *American Journal of Sociology* 3 (January): 490–501.
———. 1898b. "United States Supreme Court and the Utah Eight Hours' Law." *American Journal of Sociology* 3 (July): 21–34.
———. 1901. "The Committee of the General Federation of Women's Clubs on the Industrial Problem as It Affects Women and Children." *American Journal of Nursing* 1 (August): 813–15.
———. 1904. "Has Illinois the Best Laws for Protection of Children in Illinois?" *American Journal of Sociology* 10 (November): 299–314.
———. 1905a. Review of *Poverty*. *American Journal of Sociology* 10 (January): 555–56.
———. 1905b. *Ethical Gains in Legislation*. New York: Macmillan.
———. 1911. "Minimum-Wage Boards." *American Journal of Sociology* 17 (November): 303–14.
———. 1912a. Review of *The Report on the Condition of Women and Child Wage-Earners in the United States* (Vols. 7 and 8). *American Journal of Sociology* 17 (January): 550–52.
———. 1912b. Review of *Beyond War: A Chapter in the Natural History of Man*. *American Journal of Sociology* 18 (July): 270–72.
———. 1912c. Review of *A New Conscience and an Ancient Evil*. *American Journal of Sociology* 18 (September): 271–72.
———. 1914. *Modern Industry in Relation to the Family, Health, Education, Morality*. New York: Longmans, Green, and Co.
———. 1915. Review of The Modern Factory." *American Journal of Sociology* 20 (March): 711–12.
———. 1916. Review of *Wage-Earning Pittsburgh*. *American Journal of Sociology* 21 (January): 557–59.
Kellor, Frances A. 1904. *Out of Work*. New York: G.P. Putnam's Sons.
———. 1905. "A New Phase of Welfare Work: Domestics Now Share the Attention of Social Well Wishers." *Woman's Welfare* 3 (November): 84–88.
Kurtz, Lester R. 1984. *Evaluating Chicago Sociology: A Guide to the Literature, with An Annotated Bibliography*. Chicago: University of Chicago Press.
Lengermann, Patricia Madoo, and Jill Niebrugge, eds. 2007. *The Women Founders: Sociology and Social Theory, 1830–1930*. Long Grove, IL: Waveland.
MacLean, Annie Marion. 1897a. *Factory Legislation for Women in the United States*. Master's Thesis, Department of Sociology, University of Chicago, Chicago, Illinois.
———. 1897b. "Factory Legislation for Women in the United States." *American Journal of Sociology* 3 (September): 183–205.
———. 1899a. "Two Weeks in Department Stores." *American Journal of Sociology* 4 (May): 721–41.
———. 1899b. "Factory Legislation for Women in Canada." *American Journal of Sociology* 5 (September): 172–81.
———. 1900. *The Acadian Element in the Population of Nova Scotia*. PhDdissertation, Department of Sociology, University of Chicago. Chicago, Illinois. (No complete extant copy.)
———. 1903a. "The Sweat-Shop in the Summer." *American Journal of Sociology* 9 (November): 289–309.

———. 1903b. "A Town in Florida." Pp. 64–9 in *Negro Church: Report of a Social Study made under the Direction of Atlanta University; together with the Proceedings of the Eighth Conference for the Study of the Negro Problems*, held at Atlanta University, May 26, 1903, edited by W. E. Burghardt Du Bois. Atlanta, Ga: The Atlanta University Press.

———. 1905a. "Significance of the Canadian Migration." *American Journal of Sociology* 10 (May): 814–23.

———. 1905b. "The Diary of a Domestic Drudge." *World To-day* 8 (June): 601–05.

———. 1905c. "Women in the Industrial World." *The Evangel* n.v. (October): 23–28.

———. 1905d. "Silhouettes from Life." *World To-day* 9 (November): 1195–96.

———. 1908. "Life in the Pennsylvania Coal Fields, with Particular Reference to Women." *American Journal of Sociology* 14 (November): 329–51.

———. 1909. "With Oregon Hop Pickers." *American Journal of Sociology* 15 (July): 83–95.

———. 1910. *Wage-Earning Women*. New York: Macmillan.

———. 1914. *Mary Ann's Malady: Fragmentary Papers Dealing with a Woman and Rheumatism*. New York: Broadway Publishing Co.

———. 1915. "The Plight of the Rich Man in a Democracy." *American Journal of Sociology* 21 (November): 339–44.

———. 1916a. *Women Workers and Society*. Chicago: A.C. McClurg.

———. 1916b. "Fifty Years of the Y.W.C.A." *Survey* 35 (22 January): 481–84.

———. 1918. *Cheero!* New York: Woman's Press.

———. 1920. "Among Ourselves." *The Association Monthly* 14 (May): 237.

———. 1923a. "Twenty Years of Sociology by Correspondence." *American Journal of Sociology* 28 (January): 461–72.

———. 1923b. "This Way Lies Happiness." *Open Court* 37 (January): 23–29.

———. 1925a. *Modern Immigration*. Philadelphia, PA. J.B. Lippincott.

———. 1925b. "Love My Dog!" *Forum* 74 (July): 143–45.

———. 1926. "Albion Woodbury Small: An Appreciation." *American Journal of Sociology* 32 (July): 45–48.

———. 1930. "Conveying Personality at Long Range." Pp. 130–32 in *Proceedings of the University Extension Association*, vol. 15. Bloomington, IN: University of Indiana Press.

McDonald, Lynn. 1994a. *The Early Origins of the Social Sciences*. Montreal: McGill-Queen's University.

———. 1994b. *The Women Founders of the Social Sciences*. Ottawa, Canada: Carleton University Press.

Neeley, Elizabeth, and Mary Jo Deegan. 2005. "George Herbert Mead on Punitive Justice: A Critical Analysis of Contemporary Practices." *Humanity & Society* 29 (February): 71–83.

Reinharz, Shulamit. 1992. *Feminist Methods in Social Science Research*. New York: Oxford University Press.

Residents of Hull-House. 1895. *Hull-House Maps and Papers*, ed. by Jane Addams. New York: Crowell.

Rucker, Darnell. 1969. *The Chicago Pragmatists*. Minneapolis: Minnesota Press.

Seigfried, Charlene Haddock. 1991. "Where are All the Feminist Pragmatists?" *Hypatia* 6 (Summer): 1–19.

———, ed. 1993. Special issue on "Feminism and Pragmatism." *Hypatia* 8 (Spring 1993).

———. 1996. *Pragmatism and Feminism*. Chicago: University of Chicago Press.

———, ed. 2002. *Feminist Interpretations of John Dewey*. University Park, PA: Pennsylvania State University Press.

Skocpol, Theda. 1992. *Protecting Soldiers and Mothers*. Cambridge, MA: Belknap Press of Harvard University Press.

Smith, Dorothy E. 1987. *The Everyday World As Problematic: A Feminist Sociology*. Boston: Northeastern University Press.

Smith-Rosenberg, Carroll. 1985. "The New Woman as Androgyne." Pp. 245–96 in *Visions of Gender in Victorian America*, edited by Carroll Smith-Rosenberg. New York: Oxford University Press.

Sutherland, Edwin. 1937. *The Professional Thief*. Chicago: University of Chicago Press.

Thomas, Jim. 1993. *Doing Critical Ethnography*. Thousand Oaks, CA: Sage.

Work, Monroe. 1903. "The Middle West, Illinois." Pp. 88–92 in *Negro Church: Report of a Social Study Made Under the Direction of Atlanta University; Together with the Proceedings of the Eighth Conference for the Study of the Negro Problems, Held at Atlanta University, May 26, 1903*, edited by W. E. Burghardt Du Bois. Atlanta, GA: The Atlanta University Press.

Wright, R. Richard, Jr. 1903. "The Middle West, Ohio." Pp. 92–108 in *Negro Church: Report of a Social Study Made Under the Direction of Atlanta University; Together with the Proceedings of the Eighth Conference for the Study of the Negro Problems, Held at Atlanta University, May 26, 1903*, edited by W. E. Burghardt Du Bois. Atlanta, GA: The Atlanta University Press.

Chapter Three

Marianne Weber and the March for Our Lives Movement

Stacy L. Smith

Marianne Schnitger Weber (August 2, 1870–March 21, 1954) was a classical sociologist, feminist, and popular speaker and activist. She wrote books, scholarly and popular articles, was active in organizations largely occupied by and organized for men, and was a leader in the German feminist movement. Her academic social circle included Georg Simmel and his wife Gertrud, husband Max Weber, and a host of other prominent activists and scholars. Weber maintained an active lecture and publication schedule and was renowned for her own effort and intellect. When her husband Max died, Weber collected and edited his writings for publication. For her activism and scholarship, which promoted the legal status of German women, as well as for her curation of Max's work, the University of Heidelberg granted Weber an honorary law doctorate in 1924. Yet for all of these accomplishments, Weber is, today, best known only as the wife of and biographer of Max Weber (Britton 1979; Lengermann and Niebrugge-Brantley 1998; Lengermann and Niebrugge-Brantley 2003; Zohn 1988).

MARIANNE WEBER: BIOGRAPHY

Weber's childhood and young adulthood were characterized by personal upheaval and a striving for a place where she could develop her intellectual abilities. Weber's wealthy grandfather, Karl Weber, did not approve of his daughter's choice of husband, and cut off the young couple's access to the family money. Her mother died when she was two, and Weber was sent to live in genteel poverty with a grandmother and maiden aunt in the small town of Lemgo, Germany (Britton 1979). At the age of 16, her grandfather agreed to send her to finishing school, and from there she became a live-in nanny for a maternal aunt in Oerlinghausen, caring for her six cousins. Weber disliked the work and prevailed upon her grandfather to send her to Berlin for a year when she was 19, to the home of her great-uncle, Max Weber, senior, where she was to develop her artistic talent. There, she met second cousin Max Weber, only a few years her senior. Her introduction to Helene Weber, Max's mother, was perhaps as important. Helene was an activist, and it was in meeting her that Weber realized that she had an opportunity to be married *and* have a career. She saw Helene as having rescued her from "a life without hope of achievement or intellectual scope" (Britton 1979: 11). After a brief return to Oerlinghausen and misery, Weber returned to her great-uncle's house in Berlin permanently (Britton 1979).

When Weber first came to Berlin, Max was engaged to another cousin, Emmy. In the fall of 1892, Max broke off that engagement and soon thereafter asked Marianne to marry him. The family refused to acknowledge the engagement until the following year, out of concern that Marianne would not make a good wife, as she was not interested in the "domestic arts." Max, however, was more interested in her ability to maintain "her individuality, her freedoms, and her independence" than her housekeeping skills, and she solved the issue by retaining loyal housekeepers for the rest of her life. Max and Marianne Weber married in Berlin in 1893 (Britton 1979).

Building a Household and a Career

Throughout their lives together, Weber's freedom and independence would be great, but bounded by her husband's professional and personal needs. In 1894, at the age of 30, Max became a professor of economics at the University of Freiburg (Britton 1979). At Freiburg, Marianne caused a sensation by becoming the first woman to attend classes at the university. Because the finishing school had not provided the type of education she needed to sit for university entrance exams, Weber audited these classes with permission of the instructor (Hanke 2011; Whimster 2005). At Freiburg, she began work on her first book, a study of Marx and Fichte, which was published in 1900 as part of a series edited by her husband. It was also in Freiburg that she began a life as a social activist (Britton 1979; Hanke 2011, Lengermann and Niebrugge-Brantley 1992). It was in Heidelberg, however, where Weber would ultimately establish herself and become a prominent citizen in her own right. In 1897, Max accepted a position as Professor of Philosophy at the University of Heidelberg. At Heidelberg, women were beginning to enter a university as students for the first time, and Max insisted that Weber have the same kind of "full intellectual life" and study alongside these women (Weber [1926] 1988: 229). Weber continued her study of philosophy and attended Max's lectures on political economy. She also continued her activism, becoming the leader of the Heidelberg Association for Women's Education and Study, an organization that focused on getting women admitted to higher education (Hanke 2011).

This happiness and productivity would be short-lived, however. A visit from Max's parents ended with an explosive argument between Max and his father. When his father became ill and died in the summer of 1897 with the argument unresolved, Max became, according to Weber, "ill in spirit" (Britton 1979: 19). Five years after the beginning of his illness, and after alternating between travel, visits to sanitoriums, and a failed attempt to return to work at the university, Max resigned his professorship. In Weber's eyes, at the age of 37, Max had "lost his entire career" (Britton 1979: 23). Shortly afterward, Weber began lecturing to "keep [Max's] name before the public" (Britton 1979: 23).

By 1904, Max was recovering, had been offered co-editorship of a journal, and had finished writing *The Protestant Ethic and the Spirit of Capitalism*. Three years later, the couple used a small inheritance from Weber's grandfather to move back to Heidelberg and, after several years of research and writing begun when Max was ill, Weber published *Ehefrau und Mutter in der Rechtsentwicklung* ("Marriage, Motherhood, and the Law"). *Ehefrau* was the first work to trace the influence of culture and religion on women's rights, law, custom, and family structure in Germany. It was reviewed favorably by Emile Durkheim in *L'Année Sociologique*, and cited by Max in his *General Economic History* (Adams and Sydie 2001; Britton 1979, Lengermann and Niebrugge-Brantley 1998, Lengermann and Niebrugge-Brantley 2001, McDonald 1994, Whimster 2005). *Ehefrau* established Weber as the authority on gender inequality and family law, a position that allowed her greater reach as a writer and lecturer and established her as "a leading intellectual of the liberal feminist movement" in Germany (Britton 1979; Lengermann and Niebrugge-Brantley 1998: 201). Between 1907–1924, Weber was an invited speaker and member or leader of several activist organizations. Along with friend and fellow activist Gertrud Simmel, she helped to found a branch of the *Bund Deutscher Frauenverein* (Federated Women's Association; BDF) in Heidelberg. Weber wrote that the organization was influential in supporting a feeling of independence in working class married women (Britton 1979). Beginning in 1919, Weber occupied the prestigious position of president of the BDF network, which situated her as a highly visible member of the liberal middle class women's movement in Germany and required that she travel extensively and maintain an active lecturing schedule (Hanke 2011; Roth 1990).

In 1920, Weber was 50 years old and well respected as a lecturer and political advocate. Max had recovered his career and accepted a position as Professor of Economics at the University of Munich (Britton 1979). In May of that year, Weber returned to Munich after completing a lecture series: a few weeks later Max became ill with influenza. The illness progressed over the next several weeks into pneumonia, and on June, 14, 1920, Max Weber died in his home. Marianne was devastated. "He had moved to some distant, inaccessible place," she wrote. "The earth had changed" (Weber [1926] 1988: 698).

Weber soon returned to Heidelberg, where she would spend the rest of her life. She resigned her leadership positions and withdrew from public life, and until 1926 dedicated herself to editing her husband's writings and to writing his biography (Britton 1979; Hanke 2009; Roth 1990). Weber's friends saw her dedication to Max's legacy as an "unjustifiable loss to the women's movement" (Whimster 2005: 137), but her work would become, according to many scholars, critically important to the preservation and promotion of Max's legacy. In 1926 Weber re-emerged into public life and her successful lecturing career, speaking to crowds of up to 5,000 (Britton 1979). Throughout her career, Weber spoke and wrote about issues of sexual morality, marriage, and the position of women in society (Roth 1990), issues that were important to her and to her audiences. In her popular lecture, "Personal Problems for the Individual," for example, she situated the expectations laid on women for housework and caregiving as a societal issue, stating that society expected women to sacrifice their lives for their children and the elderly while men were allowed to focus entirely on their careers. Women attempting to do both were left to feel guilty (Britton 1979). Her lecture is still relevant today.

Influence on German Intellectual Culture

In addition to women's rights, Weber was also concerned with the state of Germany as a nation. World War I had been disastrous for the German economy and society, and had, Weber felt, stripped away much of German culture. She was convinced that it was important to foster a mentoring culture between the old and the young in Germany in order to restore lost cultural values. In 1924, she began inviting university students into her home for "educational evenings" or *Geistertees*: an hour of mingling on a Sunday afternoon, then an hour-long formal presentation, followed by a question-and-answer session. Speakers included leading male academics and prominent women, and the audience was often as much as two-thirds female. Weber was one of the first to encourage intellectual exchange between women and men (Britton 1979; Roth 1990).

As Weber once again became involved in public life, she also organized and participated in local organizations that focused on social and cultural change. She was at her most popular as a public speaker when the Nazi party began its rise to power (Roth 1990). In 1933, Hitler dissolved the BDF, effectively exiling women from public life (Britton 1979). Despite the risk, she continued to speak publicly and in 1939 was the principal speaker at the annual meeting of *Die Kommende Gemeinde* (The Coming Community) (Britton 1979). As World War II loomed, Weber watched as Heidelberg was drained of intellectual talent. Friends emigrated to the United States rather than abandon Jewish spouses. Roughly forty members of the University of Heidelberg faculty were dismissed for refusing to alter their teaching to suit the Nazi regime. As a long-time activist, Weber was shocked that the university community did not resist these dismissals (Britton 1979). She continued to hold her Geistertees, but in smaller numbers and with attendees who were careful not to overtly criticize the Nazi regime. When some members felt compelled to join the Nazi party, Weber broke off contact with them (Becker 1951). Despite the growing danger, she continued to invite Jewish colleagues to the Geistertees and continued to associate and travel with Jewish friends. Roth (1990: 68) wrote that Weber's "mode of opposing the Nazi regime was more a matter of persistence than resistance." Weber herself, in spite of her activities, was not persecuted: she speculated that she was left alone because of her age (Becker 1951).

The United States bombed and then occupied Heidelberg on March 23, 1945. The end of the war brought U.S. Army investigators from the Office of Strategic Services to her door (one of whom was sociologist Howard P. Becker). The investigators were charged with, she wrote, "root[ing] out [and] purify[ing] our culture from Nazism," turning the German people's attention away from conquest and toward freedom and law (Becker 1951; Britton 1979: 153). Weber felt guilt and shame for the inaction of the Heidelberg intellectual community (although she told Becker that she was involved with those who attempted to assassinate Hitler), but she also asserted that the combination of propaganda and fear of death was sufficiently powerful to motivate most of the populace to stay silent (Becker 1951, Britton 1979). Becker also brought Weber good news: *Max Weber: A Biography*, along with several of her edited volumes of Max's work, had been translated into English and were very popular in the United States (Britton 1979).

Following the war, Weber continued to be intellectually and socially active for the next seven years. She continued to host the Geistertees until 1952, and died in Heidelberg in 1954 (Zohn 1988). Her circle continued to meet until at least the late 1950s, "[h]onoring her memory with a picture [of her] surrounded by flowers" (Roth 1990: 68). Marianne Weber, scholar and activist, lived through four distinct periods of German history, many of them rife with hardship and violence: the rule of Willhelm Kaiser, the Weimar Republic, Nazism, and post WWII-reconstruction. She survived two world wars and many years of hunger and hardship (Britton 1979; Hanke 2011). "The foundations of her life," wrote Hanke (2011: 141), "were always precarious, both personally and materially." And yet, she persisted.

MARIANNE WEBER'S SCHOLARLY CONTRIBUTION

In her lifetime, Marianne Weber was as well known as her husband, Max. She was well respected as a scholar and an academic, remarkable in a time where society was almost completely dominated by men (Roth 1990; Lengermann and Niebrugge-Brantley 1998). She made a distinct contribution to the political milieu of her time as a feminist activist and lecturer, speaking and writing on women's equality, marriage, ethics, and education (Hanke 2011). She wrote eight books, edited and secured the publication of nine of Max's works, and, in addition to academic articles, published essays in women's journals and organizational newsletters. In total Weber left behind approximately 100 pieces of written work (Hanke 2011; Lengermann and Niebrugge-Brantley 1992). Her contribution to sociology can be divided into two parts: her editing of Max's unpublished manuscripts and her scholarly works.

Contribution to Max's Legacy

Begun, perhaps, as a coping strategy for her overwhelming grief at his sudden death, Weber spent six years immersed in editing for or writing about her husband and is credited with preserving his intellectual legacy. Max had left behind a wealth of unfinished manuscripts; Weber began by collecting and publishing Max's correspondence. In the fall of 1920 she began work on the unpublished manuscripts. Between 1920 and 1922, with an undisclosed amount of help from Max's former students, she edited *Economy and Society*, *Religion and Capitalism*, *Politics as a Vocation*, and *Science as a Vocation*, among others (Britton 1979; Hanke 2009; Lengermann and Niebrugge-Brantley 1998).

The work of editing complete, Weber then spent the next four years writing what many consider to be the definitive biography of her husband's life and work. The book is not, and was not intended to be, an academically rigorous piece (Britton 1979), and contemporary responses to the biography were mixed. Current scholars acknowledge that the purpose and tone of the book are not consistent with the academic style we expect today; however, it remains "the" biography of Max today (Hanke 2009; Kaesler 2007). The nature of the book aside, Weber is widely credited for preserving and promoting Max Weber's legacy as a sociologist (Lengermann and Niebrugge-Brantley 1998). It is "fair to say," according to Roth (1990: 63), "that without Marianne Weber, her husband's work might not have gained its later importance for the course of social science."

Contributions to Sociology and Feminism

Weber's unique scholarly work stands in contrast to the "male" approach to sociology; therefore, it is necessary to begin this section with an overview of how male sociologists (including Max, Georg Simmel, and others) conceived of the science of sociology. The couple toured the United States in 1904 and in her biography, Weber ([1926] 1988) wrote that Max entered a "new phase" of thought following the tour that he would maintain throughout the rest of his career, positing that logic and method are the only acceptable tools for understanding concrete problems. Max argued that every individual is socialized within a particular culture and thus experiences the world from a particular cultural standpoint. There is, therefore, no universal truth; only a culturally relative one. The researcher must maintain a mental and emotional distance from the subject to avoid contaminating the study with his/her/zir viewpoint (Lengermann and Niebrugge-Brantley 1998; Weber [1926] 1988). The ideal researcher, then, is capable of being *value-neutral*: separating the self from the subject and keeping a distance that allows one to look for significance from various angles. The researcher's purpose is to observe human activity and determine what it means to the people involved, what Max called *verstehen* (understanding) (Adams and Sydie 2001; Lengermann and Niebrugge-Brantley 1998).

According to Weber ([1926] 1988), Max made a distinction between *theoretical value relationships* and *practical value judgments*. The ideal researcher defines theoretical value relationships as verifiable explanations of human behavior based on the rational employment of reason and assessment of cultural values affecting behavior. In contrast, practical value judgments are not value-neutral, but emotional: ethical judgments about what is "good" and "bad" that are unverifiable because thought and emotion cannot be observed (see table 3.1).

A scientist who fails to maintain this focus on theoretical value relationships is at risk of not only producing faulty research, but also of unwittingly reinforcing the cultural values of the ruling class, since most researchers, Max argued, were themselves members of that class (Weber [1926] 1988).

Table 3.1. Theoretical Value Relationships and Practical Value Judgments.

Theoretical Value Relationships	Practical Value Judgment
Verifiable	Unverifiable
Cognition	Volition
Reason	Emotion
Cultural Values	Ethics

(Adapted from Weber [1926] 1988)

Even as a teacher, Max believed that, while it was acceptable for a professor to show students the consequences of a choice, value judgments should be avoided so that the professor does not exert undue influence on the students. This is not to say that Max was not concerned with social issues. Weber ([1926] 1988: 321) noted that he was very much active in social issues—but movement to action, according to Max, unlike science, is "made with means other than the intellect."

In her work, Weber employed the same methodologies as Max and other male sociologists, and she agreed that one's socialization profoundly affected one's viewpoint. But she did not agree that sociology should be value-neutral; in fact, she criticized the "value-neutral" perspective as an expression of male perspective and privilege (Lengermann and Niebrugge-Brantley 1998; McDonald 1994). In this new phase, Max had turned, Weber wrote, toward a "thinking orientation toward scientific truth—a task without any direct relationship to reality" (Weber [1926] 1988: 308). As a woman, she was aware of very real social issues that were devalued or simply overlooked by male sociologists, and she centered her social analysis on those issues, grounding her sociology in her own experience of living in a world dominated by men (Lengermann and Niebrugge-Brantley 1998; Roth 1990). Weber's sociology was thus feminist in both theory and method (Adams and Sydie 2001; Lengermann and Niebrugge-Brantley 1998; Lengermann and Niebrugge-Brantley 2001; Lengermann and Niebrugge-Brantley 2003; Roth 1990; Roth 2005).

In addition to her contribution to feminist epistemology, Weber broadened concepts proposed by male sociologists by adapting them to the lived experience of women (Lengermann and Niebrugge-Brantley 1998; Roth 1990). First, in *The Protestant Ethic*, Max had argued that because all individuals are capable of reason, are able to self-actualize, and are ultimately only responsible to their creator for their choices, then it follows that it is unethical for an individual to subordinate another human being to their needs. Weber criticized marital relationships within patriarchal societies as doing just that: suborning women such that they served as a means to an end for men. Furthermore, in "The Types of Legitimate Domination," Max argued that a key characteristic of forms of legitimate power is the consent of those not in power (Weber [1925] 2016). In "Authority and Autonomy in Marriage," Weber argued that, legitimate or not, the subordinated experience that power as a loss of personal autonomy (Weber [1919] 1998). Her reaction to *The Protestant Ethic*, therefore, challenges Max's conception of legitimate authority as inadvertently making an argument for "moral, legal, and political equality" for women (Lengermann and Niebrugge-Brantley 1998: 218). Second, unlike male sociologists, Weber acknowledged that differences in class affect how individuals experience the world, that there is, therefore, no one value-neutral truth but instead multiple perspectives. In "On the Valuation of

Housework," she identified flexible solutions for households that would work across various economic circumstances, an approach that Lengermann and Niebrugge-Brantley (1998) call *practical verstehen*. Finally, in "Women's Special Cultural Tasks," Weber redefined and broadened the sociological concept of culture and applied Simmel's cultural categories to gender (Whimster 2005).

Erasure from the Canon

It is Weber's distinctiveness that likely resulted in her erasure, until recently, from the classical sociological canon. Sociology is a relatively young science, and in its early years was inhabited by female researchers as well as males. Sociologists disagreed, as did Marianne and Max Weber, over whether sociology should serve activism and reform, or if it should be objective and value-neutral. As sociology developed into a formal discipline, however, it was absorbed into academic institutions, where women and men could be students but only men could be professors. Working within the university system, during this time period (between 1890–1947) male sociologists came to a general consensus in favor of a focus on objectivity and scientific rigor, which delegitimized and marginalized female sociological work (Lengermann and Niebrugge-Brantley 2001). Contemporary academia is more inclusive overall, but subtle biases remain. Reading "between the lines" of modern scholarship on Weber, it is clear that she is viewed through a gendered lens, in a society that insists on seeing women as wives and mothers rather than as scholars. The Webers were childless until they adopted the children of Max's sister, Lili, who died in the spring of 1920 (Britton 1979). Several scholars (see for example Roth 1990; Whimster 2005) speculated, based on the couple's childlessness and other clues in Weber's writings, that their marriage was unconsummated or that one or the other was either infertile or unfaithful. Some of them considered her remarkable productivity in writing, lectures, and other activism, to have been a replacement for the children she wanted but did not have. These assumptions reflect a patriarchal belief that a woman's "true" fulfillment comes in the form of procreation, with intellectual work being a poor substitute. This derogatory view of Weber and her life's work was not always the case. Meurer (2012: 249) noted that Weber originally was seen as a "figure in her own right," with no speculation about the significance of her marriage. In the 1970s, a major German newspaper (*Frankfurter Allgemeine Zeitung*) published a similar tribute to Weber, but one author described this view of her and her work as existing "in the shadow of" Max Meurer (2012: 249) dismissed this claim, stating that "Marianne Weber never stood in the shadow of her husband. She was an independent, highly regarded and prominent personality in public life."

As mentioned earlier, Weber's biography of Max was not universally well received. In addition to the charge of not being sufficiently scholarly, Weber's biography has also been criticized as emotional and erroneous (see for example Hanke 2009; Kaesler 2007). Scholars have also argued that Weber deliberately de-emphasized herself in the biography and thus chose to be seen as "less than" her husband. The most common assertion is that her choice to write in the third person was an attempt to diminish herself in favor of her husband (see, for example, Adair-Toteff 2013; Hanke 2009). Hanke (2009: 356) goes so far as to state that "it would probably not have offended Marianne Weber in the slightest to know that she has gone down in history as Max Weber's *wife* because of her biography" (emphasis in original). This argument, however, is flawed. Writing conventions, such as use of first or third person, vary over time and between writing genres; the choice of narrative voice may have been one of convention rather than emotional expression. Furthermore, Zohn, who translated *Max Weber: A Biography* into English, found Weber's personality to be very present in her writing. He described her language choices as "flavorful" and "colorful" and her examples as often dramatic and emotional. In translating the text, he chose to stay as close as possible to the original language, because, he wrote, "Weber's stylistic peculiarities must be allowed to shine through . . . for certainly this author's style reflects her personality and her special way of looking at the world" (Zohn 1988: vii). Far from writing herself out of the biography, Weber instead bursts off of the page; one cannot read the biography without a sense of coming to know her.

Although *Max Weber: A Biography* has been translated and widely read, Weber's other scholarly work has been largely neglected; very little of it was translated into English. Also, most of the information about the woman herself available in English comes from secondary sources: her memoir has not been translated, and records of her lectures and activist publications are sparse. After more than fifty years, it is unlikely that new material (such as her published essays) will be translated (Britton 1979; Meurer 2012). However, in 1998, Lengermann and Niebrugge-Brantley published excerpts from an unpublished translation of three of Weber's most important articles: "Authority and Autonomy in Marriage," "On the Valuation of Housework," and "Women's Special Cultural Tasks."

Excerpt from "Authority and Autonomy in Marriage"

Weber's "Authority and Autonomy in Marriage" built on and challenged *The Protestant Ethic*. The two works are similar in method and in their argument that individual autonomy and personal responsibility were brought about by cultural, political, and religious shifts over time, but Weber broadened Max's argument to include the autonomy of women (Lengermann and Niebrugge-

Brantley 1998). The Protestant Reformation, for example, altered the relationship between god, society, and the individual, with the result that humans became responsible to god over earthly authority. For women, this established a certain amount of inherent ethical separation from their husbands. In the secular world, abstract principles laid out by Enlightenment writers insisted that each individual's unique personality is a sign of humanity, and that therefore the individual must not be used "as a means to another's ends; but must be treated as an end in themself" (Thomas 1985: 413). Male Enlightenment writers tried to find a rational argument for the subordination of women, but the ethical system they proposed was general and structured society in a way that eventually favored increasing female autonomy (Thomas 1985). Weber argued that because individuals have this autonomy, they have a responsibility to themselves and to god to use it. Subordinating one's self to another person against one's own ethical and personal conscience is thus tantamount to the individual failing themselves, the human race, and god (Weber [1919] 1998).

Beginning from the premise that each individual has inalienable rights that must be recognized by others and by social institutions, it follows, according to Weber, that individuals (1) have a capacity to think for themselves and understand the consequences of their actions, (2) recognize themselves as autonomous human beings, and (3) have an understanding of moral and social laws that preserve the social order by inhibiting impulsive, self-serving behavior. Thus, it becomes immoral to use other human beings for one's gain, a concept Weber extended to marriage as well. She saw it as immoral for a wife to give up her will to her husband and follow his demands when those demands required acting against her conscience. The wife, Weber asserted, is not to be used for her husband's benefit without consideration of her own wants and needs. Yet within the patriarchal systems that Weber studied, the authority of the husband and individual autonomy of both partners existed in tension (Weber [1919] 1998).

For Weber, this tension between authority and autonomy created an ethical problem, because of its effect on the wife and the marriage. Weber wrote that because of the patriarchal authority structure, a wife had two potential methods of coping with challenges to her autonomy. First, she could suppress her autonomous self in favor of her husband's wishes. Eventually, however, Weber wrote that the wife would lose the ability to repress herself. To the husband, this "new" person would seem like a stranger. The alternative involved a wife who so thoroughly suppressed her sense of self that she became submissive, mindless, and childlike. In addition to the damage to the wife's persona, the husband, Weber wrote, would become bored with the relationship and seek intellectual stimulation elsewhere (Weber [1919] 1998). A healthy marriage, for Weber, involved mutual struggle and growth where, if the woman suborned herself willingly, it was a "gift of love" that had "beauty and worth," and where the husband recognized that occasionally ceding authority to his wife was not an affront to his masculinity. Women are willing, Weber wrote, to make sacrifices in marriage, but as respected companions, not as submissive children (Weber [1919] 1998). A woman who suppressed her own self to follow her husband's directives, Weber argued, committed "an offense against her own human worth; she then downgrades herself to a second-class being" (Weber [1919] 1998: 219).

Excerpt from "On the Valuation of Housework"

Weber wrote "On the Valuation of Housework" in response to Charlotte Perkins Gilman's ([1898] 1998) publication, *Women and Economics*. Gilman argued that women's utter reliance on men for food, clothing, and shelter for both themselves and their children was unique to humankind and detrimental to women, their offspring and, ultimately, the species. Gilman interrogated each of the arguments commonly used to support women's subordination and dismantled each in turn. She argued that the solution to the detrimental effects of inequality was for women to become economically independent: that is, to work for a wage (Gilman [1898] 1998). Weber agreed with Gilman on several points: women were expected to do all housework and child-rearing duties by social custom, not biological determinism; women and men are equally capable of work of all kinds; class differences result in different financial circumstances for women (women of lower classes already worked outside of the home out of necessity); and female dependence is detrimental to individuals and social institutions alike. They differed in method and conclusion, however. Although both considered the role of culture in preserving the status quo, where Gilman's piece is theoretical, Weber's response is practical. Weber used census data to expose the flaws in Gilman's argument that gender inequality can be rectified through the economic independence of women.

Weber saw marriage as, in part, a legal and social means to ensure that men were responsible to their progeny. She therefore disagreed with Gilman, asserting that full economic independence for women, and especially for mothers, would likely result in greater independence for *men*, who would be freed from the duty of providing economically for their children. Furthermore, Weber determined that the vast majority of women were already working for a wage, but at low-paying jobs (agriculture, housekeeping staff, laundresses, etc.) that would not allow them to support themselves or a family. She determined that only two percent of the female population were part of wealthy households, with access to education and professional work. A different solution was necessary: one that would consider class and economic differences to find a solution that would benefit all households (Weber [1919] 1998).

To arrive at this solution, Weber examined how culture and interaction at the micro-level prevented women, even working women or those with an inheritance, from asserting their economic independence. She argued that male domination of the family's finances was detrimental to the marriage and to the woman's emotional and psychological well-being, and that those problems existed irrespective of the wealth of the family. By custom, Weber wrote, husbands managed the financial affairs of the family, and doled out money for household and personal expenses in small amounts. Because they did not run the household, they likely did not understand and could not predict upcoming expenses. As a result, the wife was forced to routinely ask her husband for money. These repeated small requests ran the risk of upsetting the family's emotional harmony. Even the most generous of husbands, Weber predicted, would become angry and make derogatory comments about his wife's abilities, even within an otherwise happy marriage. To avoid these outbursts, the wife resorted to "pleading and coaxing": manipulation that was emotionally and mentally draining, demeaning, and that created a sense of dependence, damaging the wife's sense of self. The wife was thus forced to "reach her goals by all sorts of roundabout ways and trickery" that Weber labeled "disfiguring" (Weber [1919] 1998: 221). Lack of access to household funds threatened the wife's autonomy and damaged the marital relationship.

This gendered economic practice was held in place by two distinct forms of cultural norms, according to Weber: law and custom. Weber argued that custom was easier to change than the law, and so focused on methods that could be implemented, household by household, eventually affecting the law through mounting public pressure. Weber noted that some upper-class families had established budgets that accounted for all household needs and curtailed male recreational spending, thus ensuring that the wife had a steady source of funds for which she was not required to beg her husband. She advocated developing a family budget in every household according to its income, with disputes mediated through family court. Her solution is practical, acknowledges her own privilege, works across social classes, and expresses a confidence in the ability of people to effect powerful changes that will alter the law, rather than the law changing society (Weber [1919] 1998).

Excerpt from "Women's Special Cultural Tasks"

Georg Simmel and his wife Gertrud, a feminist and political activist, were colleagues and friends of Marianne. Weber wrote "Women's Special Cultural Tasks" as a public response to Simmel's 1890 essay, "The Psychology of Women" (Wobbe 2004). In his article, Simmel wrote about how modernization and the increasingly gendered divisions of labor had resulted in "fragmented" and highly differentiated male lives while women remained "unified."

Unlike his contemporary colleagues, Simmel considered gender to be a social rather than a biological construct. Ultimately, however, he remained an essentialist, believing that men and women are "naturally" different and thus suited for different tasks: men in the world, and women at home (Wobbe 2004). Simmel explored the nature of gender roles in relation to his famous theory of culture, where he distinguished between *objective culture*, as what we think of as "cultural forms and their artifacts" that are external to human beings, and *subjective culture*, which is shaped by the individual, personal self (Tijssen 1991: 204). We become human, Simmel argued, when we use objective culture to transform ourselves into a cultural being. Objective culture is created by and supported by men, according to Simmel: therefore, there is no subjective culture without men. Men are especially suited to the creation and support of objective culture because they have the ability to disassociate themselves from their personal values and work within a highly specialized, goal-oriented, and rational division of labor, focusing on "grand ideas." The unfortunate consequence is that men become fragmented; split between the objective and the personal. Women, on the other hand, are "whole," having escaped the tension between objective and subjective culture. They are less fit for objective culture, according to Simmel, because, due to their sex, they are less rational, logical, objective, and "not naturally inclined to specialization or to the pursuit of objective ideas," having "no need for the pursuit of grand ideas" (Tijssen 1991: 212). Thus they cannot become, for example, artistic geniuses. This is not to say that Simmel believed that women should not work outside the home, but rather he saw only a narrow range of employment as appropriate for women. Women are more emotional, intuitive, and naturally moral, he wrote, which makes them better suited for careers that make use of their intuitive skills, such as the performing arts or medicine (Tijssen 1991).

Simmel regarded women as existing in a desired condition: their lack of masculine disassociation means that they have a closer connection to the universe as "more authentic human being[s]." For this reason, he argued, society should reconsider how women are valued (Tijssen 1991: 207). His view of women, however, was overly romanticized and limited, an observation Gertrud and Marianne shared with each other in private letters (Wobbe 2004; Lengermann and Niebrugge-Brantley 1998). Although Weber agreed that men and women are different, she argued that women are as capable as men and therefore should be granted the same opportunities as men to develop their talents and intellect. In fact, because women's experiences included both the world of paid labor and home-life work, women had the added advantage of being able to bridge the two worlds (Wobbe 2004).

Weber's purpose in "Cultural Tasks" was primarily to examine the difference between subjective and objective culture and, considering women as producers of culture, identify cultural tasks that were important for women. She accepted Simmel's definition of objective and subjective culture, but argued that the tension they caused was not between fragmentation and unity but rather between the individual and what she called "timeless values." She redefined culture as "any intellectually determined, purposeful working on and shaping of material given by nature," and argued that we only get the full meaning of culture when objective and subjective culture are brought together in the individual, through self-actualization. Therefore, Weber argued, "culture in its deepest sense signifies the *perfecting of the soul through the development of all its inherent shoots and possibilities in the objective intellectual and spiritual works of humanity*," including disciplines like art and law that "stand in contrast to the individual as timeless values" and against which "the individual is challenged and formed" (Weber [1919] 1998: 224, emphasis in original). By arguing that culture is comprised of any intentional shaping of "natural" materials and that personal, inner development occurs through thoughtful contact with higher levels of reasoning (fields that concern "timeless values"), Weber situated women as producers and shapers of objective culture and defined participation in the public realm as a necessity for *all* human life. Women with the natural ability and the economic means to become educated, therefore, should do so, she urged, especially if they wished to shape culture (Weber [1919] 1998).

Weber rejected Simmel's claim that only men produce and maintain objective culture. She did believe that differences in men and women gave them advantages concerning certain tasks, but not because a gender was biologically coded for specific types of work. In her article, then, she identified the "special cultural tasks" that fall to women due to gendered social expectations. Far from being unimportant, the tasks that women perform in the home were irreplaceable and ultimately responsible for making social order possible (Weber [1919] 1998). Morality originates in the home, Weber noted, beginning with mothers and other caregivers (generally women), who were often the first to teach children the unwritten norms and values that make social interaction, and ultimately society, possible. Children also learn high forms of morality, that require the suppression of individual desires, in the home. Through observation of others, children develop their inner character, learning respect for others, kindness, empathy, humility, and developing the ability to take another person's perspective. Weber called this the "entire How of our being" and identified it as the "daily, painstaking task of the mother," modeled through caretaking and the intentional creation of a harmonious home (Weber [1919] 1998: 226).

Through the choices that they make for their households, women consciously shaped the social order of cultural objects and practices for the entire household, which in turn shaped the nature of objective culture that men produced for female consumption. Women created an environment that supported personal relationships, within the family, among friends, and so on that were essential for developing close networks of individuals within modern societies. Finally, the home, Weber argued, should offer a restful respite for family members. The integration of objective culture and subjective culture requires self-reflection that can only happen within the stress-free environment that a well-run household provides. Far from being simple individuals and consumers of culture they had no part in creating, Weber saw women as having a deep influence on culture, occupying a "unique middle ground" between subjective and objective culture where the individual personality was shaped in daily life and where the ability to build community was developed. Therefore, "the *plain, uneventful everyday [life], too*," Weber wrote, "*is worthy in itself of being lived*, [and] is a formative task that falls, first of all, to the woman" (Weber [1919] 1998: 225; emphasis in original). Without women, then, there is no objective culture.

Autonomy and Production of Culture in the March For Our Lives Movement

Although in the United States today women are formally recognized as autonomous individuals and producers of culture (by law, if not always by custom), the struggle for equality is far from over for women, as well as for other subordinate or marginalized groups. The March For Our Lives movement emerged from one such subordinate group: schoolchildren. Although the two groups are in many ways quite distinct, primary and secondary school students, like the women of Weber's era, are generally considered to be "naturally" subordinate and therefore insignificant in the maintenance or creation of culture. Yet, the March For Our Lives movement sparked national attention in a way that other anti-gun violence activist groups, whether youth- or adult-led, have not. Using Weber's work, this section suggests an explanation for emergence of the movement and the groundswell of support that it enjoys.

The Genesis of March for Our Lives

Fifteen minutes before the dismissal bell would have rung on Wednesday, February 14, 2018, a gunman entered Marjory Stoneman Douglas High School in Parkland, Florida and opened fire, killing seventeen and injuring fourteen. The shooting was one of the ten deadliest mass school shootings in American history. At 3:41 p.m., the gunman dropped his AR-15, discarded his ammunition vest, and mingled with the students fleeing the school. Parents waited for their children for hours, while police officers cleared the building. News helicopters filmed what has become a familiar scene: groups of children walking away from the building in single file, with their hands in the air, under the direction of police officers. The gunman was arrested later, walking along a road two miles from the school, after having stopped for a soda (Mettler et al. 2018).

During the attack, students used their cell phones to call loved ones, and to post comments, photos, and video on social media as the shooter was moving through the school. Before the gunman was even caught, some social media users began criticizing students for posting to social media from inside the classroom as classmates were shot. Other commentators criticized students as being so attached to social media that they could not stop, even under dire circumstances. In some respects, this response can be attributed to a cultural discomfort with real images of terror, death, and suffering, especially involving children, and social media provides an immediacy that demands attention in a way that conventional news reporting does not. Once conventional media sources began interviewing students about their experiences, however, they were once again vilified by some, mislabeling them as "crisis actors" and photoshopping their photographs into offensive images. These tactics are by no means isolated; other shooting victims and their families have also been labeled as crisis actors and as hoax perpetrators. The practice is particularly jarring when applied to youth. Parkland survivors and high school seniors David Hogg and Emma Gonzalez, for example, two of the more vocal students, have drawn significant negative attention. A photoshopped image of Gonzalez tearing up the Constitution of the United States, for example, went viral on the internet. The message is clear: an undetermined, but apparently significant portion of the population would like for these children to be silent about their experiences.

But they have not been silent. Grief over the shooting and anger over the social media attacks quickly morphed into social action (Darrough 2018) as a group of students took to Twitter with the hashtag #NeverAgain, and across the nation, school walkouts were quickly organized, in support of the Parkland students and on the anniversary of the Columbine shooting. #NeverAgain became March For Our Lives, the name given to the protest march and rally held on March 24, 2018. The mission of March For Our Lives is to end gun violence in schools and elsewhere, with its stated goals ranging from restoring funding for research on gun violence and intervention programs, to better control of weapons sales, including improved background checks (March For Our Lives 2018).

The Connection between Home and School

Weber defended women's work in the home as a primary site for the development of individuals who were capable of forming social networks, and for the integration of objective culture into subjective culture. By extension, she argued, the home creates society. After the home, primary and secondary schools serve as important locations for cultural transmission in the United States. Adults in these classrooms perform tasks similar to those identified by Weber as women's cultural tasks. At school, children learn to follow rules so that the society of the classroom functions smoothly. They learn higher morals, like sharing, respect for others, and role-taking. They are methodically presented with objective culture like math, science, and art in an environment that is intended to be conducive to learning (bringing objective culture into the subjective). Ideally, this education is expected to produce graduates who, at minimum, both understand social rules and act from an internal moral compass, as an educated and involved citizenry is central to the preservation of democracy in the United States (Stitzlein 2017). The omnipresent threat of mass shootings in our schools, however, disrupts the learning process. Across the nation, schools have installed security cameras, locks, and metal detectors, invited school resource officers (police officers) into daily operations, and added active shooter/lockdown drills to disaster drills. Children as young as age five learn, and are reminded on a regular basis, that they can become the targets of extreme violence. This situation creates high levels of anxiety: in a study conducted two months after the Parkland shooting, more than half (57 percent) of teens aged 13–17 reported being worried about a shooting at their school (Graf 2018). When a majority of students are forced to cope with constant anxiety in a space that should be safe, it is reasonable to assume that the socialization and learning process Weber described is disrupted. If the school, like the home, is instrumental in creating society, then the disruption caused by the omnipresent threat of school gun violence represents not only a mortal danger to students, but a danger to society as well.

Rejecting Subordination, Claiming Autonomy

The safety of children in the United States is a cultural value guaranteed by law and is the responsibility of adults. Laws constrain the age at which children are allowed to work, marry, control financial accounts, join the military, and even drop out of school. For those children who attend a brick-and-mortar school, their routines are highly regimented, not only for the sake of education, but for safety as well. A failure in this regard is seen as a failure of the dominant (adults and institutions) to protect the subordinate (schoolchildren). Rectifying the problem has been the responsibility of adults and institutions as well. Yet the safety measures and lockdown drills have not stopped school shootings, and legal solutions have been immobilized by divisive political narratives that frame the problem as a choice between the lives of children and constitutionally guaranteed gun rights.

Weber argued for equality and autonomy for women as a matter of ethics and women's psychological well-being. Similarly, Parkland students feel that they must reject subordination and attain autonomy as a matter of survival for themselves and other schoolchildren. In her speech at the March 24, 2018 rally in Washington, DC, Gonzalez summed up this sentiment: "Maybe the adults have gotten used to saying 'it is what it is,' but . . . if you actively do nothing, people continuously end up dead, so it's time to start doing something" (Grinberg and Muaddi, 2018). Parkland survivor Jaclyn Corin pointed toward a lack of political action: "we have to be the adults in this situation," she explained, "because clearly people have failed us in government" (NBC Washington 2018). Responses to these sentiments have been mixed. Where Weber experienced a tension between women's abilities and what the patriarchal society believed they were capable of, Parkland students have experienced a similar disconnect based on age rather than on sex. Although they have received support from adult organizations, the organizers of March For Our Lives and its events are teens, and they have successfully built alliances with other youth-oriented groups across the country (Guarino 2018, March For Our Lives 2018). The youngest speaker at the Washington, DC, rally was 13 years old. Ironically, although these students are clearly demonstrating a grasp of history and civic engagement, they are often told that they should be silent. Lauren Hogg, 15-year-old Parkland survivor, told Bustle reporter Celia Darrough (2018):

> I've had so many people come up to me and say "You're too young to be talking about gun reform, [or] You're too young to be talking about mental health policy." When they tell me this, I simply respond . . . if I'm old enough to be shot in my school. . . . I'm old enough to talk about guns.

Youth, Shaping Culture

In the United States, children and especially teens are generally considered consumers of culture, rather than producers. From clothing, to filmmaking, marketing, and education, young people's needs and tastes are considered to be different from adults. This popular conception of culture as something to be consumed echoes Simmel's description of objective culture as external "cultural forms and their artifacts" (Tijssen 1991: 204). Weber's definition, the "purposeful working on and shaping of material given by nature" (Lengermann and Niebrugge-Brantley 1998: 224), instead highlights the importance of process, which is crucial for understanding the emergence of the March For Our Lives movement. The speed with which the school walkouts and the rally were organized and promoted relied heavily on the same social media networking skills for which the students were initially criticized. School walkout dates, for example, were shared from Twitter accounts to organization websites and from person to person on various social media platforms.

Parkland students surprised the nation by stepping forcefully outside of their everyday lives and into activism, and in so doing are modifying and creating culture. The movement has sparked a remarkable response in the U.S. public as a "mass movement" that has the potential to sway votes in favor of gun control (Lopez 2018). The first March For Our Lives rally attracted at least 1.2 million to Washington, DC, and other cities across the United States, and was "one of the biggest youth protests since the Vietnam War" (Lopez 2018). During the summer of 2018, March for Our Lives organizers conducted a twenty-state bus tour focused on encouraging firearms and voter registration among young people, traditionally a low voting demographic (March For Our Lives 2018). In Weber's terms, the youth of Parkland, Florida, and their allies, may effect a real change in American culture through a rejection of their subordinate status and an insistence on exercising the autonomy they have been trained, at home and at school, to wield.

WORKS CITED

Adair-Toteff. 2013. "The 'Real' Marianne?—Commentary on the Meurer-Hanke Dispute." *Max Weber Studies* 13(1): 81–85.
Adams, Bert N. and R. Sydie. 2001. *Classical Social Theory*. Thousand Oaks, CA: Pine Forge Press.
Becker, Howard P. 1951. "Max Weber, Assassination, and German Guilt: An Interview with Marianne Weber." *The American Journal of Economics & Sociology* 10(4): 401–05.
Britton, Anne Camden. 1979. *The Life and Thought of Marianne Weber*. Master's Thesis, Department of History, San Francisco State University.
Darrough, Celia. 2018. "I Was Old Enough to Watch My Friends Die, So Don't Say I'm Too Young to Talk About Guns." *Bustle*. https://www.bustle.com/p/i-was-old-enough-to-watch-my-friends-die-so-dont-say-im-too-young-to-talk-about-guns-9511328
Gilman, Charlotte Perkins. [1898] 1998. *Women and Economics*. Mineola, NY: Dover.
Graf, Nikki. 2018. "A Majority of U.S. Teens Fear a Shooting Could Happen at Their School, and Most Parents Share Their Concern," *Pew Research Center*. http://www.pewresearch.org/fact-tank/2018/04/18/a-majority-of-u-s-teens-fear-a-shooting-could-happen-at-their-school-and-most-parents-share-their-concern/
Grinberg, Emanuelia and Nadeem Muaddi. 2018. "How the Parkland Students Pulled Off a Massive National Protest in Only 5 Weeks," *CNN*. https://www.cnn.com/2018/03/26/us/march-for-our-lives/index.html
Guarino, Mark. 2018. "Students Being Tour to Address Gun Violence, Uniting Suburban and Urban Survivors in Chicago," *The Washington Post*. https://www.washingtonpost.com/national/students-begin-tour-to-address-gun-violence-uniting-suburban-and-urban-survivors-in-chicago/2018/06/17/799226b2-7219-11e8-b4b7-308400242c2e_story.html?noredirect=on&utm_term=.ae2d6c1a43a6
Hanke, Edith. 2009. "'Max Weber's Desk is now my Altar': Marianne Weber and the intellectual heritage of her husband." *History of European Ideas* 35: 349–59.
———. 2011. "Review Essay. In the Shadow of Max Weber: Bärbel Meurer's Portrait of Marianne Weber." Translated by Sam Whimster. *Max Weber Studies* 11(1): 141–46.
Kaesler, Dirk. 2007. "Still Waiting for an Intellectual Biography of Max Weber." *Max Weber Studies* 7(1): 97–118.

Lengermann, Patricia Madoo and Gillian Niebrugge-Brantley. 1998. *The Women Founders: Sociology and Social Theory 1830–1930*. New York: McGraw-Hill.

Lengermann, Patricia Madoo and Gillian Niebrugge-Brantley. 1992. "Early Women Sociologists and Classical Sociological Theory, 1830–1930." Pp. 288–330 in *Classical Sociological Theory*, edited by G. Ritzer. New York: McGraw-Hill.

———. 2001. "Classical Feminist Social Theory." Pp. 125–38 in *A Handbook of Social Theory*, edited by G. Ritzer and B. Smart. Thousand Oaks, CA: Sage Publications.

———. 2003. "Commentary on Craig R. Bermingham's 'Translation with Introduction and Commentary' of Marianne Weber's 'Authority and Autonomy in Marriage.'" *Sociological Theory* 21(4): 424–27.

Lopez, German. 2018. "It's Official: March For Our Lives Was One of the Biggest Youth Protests Since the Vietnam War," *Vox*. https://www.vox.com/policy-and politics/2018/3/26/17160646/march-for-our-lives-crowd-size-count

March For Our Lives. 2018. Home Page. https://marchforourlives.com/policy/.

McDonald, Lynn. 1994. *The Women Founders of the Social Sciences*. Ottawa, Canada: Carleton University Press.

Mettler, Katie, Clare Ramirez, Nick Kirkpatrick, Joanne Lee, Zhiyan Zhong, and Leslie Shapiro. 2018. "How the Florida School Shooting Unfolded: Visual Timeline." *The Washington Post*. https://www.washingtonpost.com/graphics/2018/national/amp-stories/florida-shooting-reconstruction/

Meurer, Bärbel. 2012. "Barbel Meurer Responds to Edith Hanke and Other Critics of her Marianne Weber Biography." Translated by Sam Whimster. *Max Weber Studies* 12(2): 247–58.

NBC Washington. 2018. "'We Have to Be the Adults': Thousands of Students Expected in DC for Saturday's 'March for Our Lives,'" *4Washington*. https://www.nbcwashington.com/news/local/Thousands-of-Students-Expected-in-DC-for-Saturdays-March-for-Our-Lives-477637213.html

Roth, Guenther. 1990. "Marianne Weber and Her Circle." *Society* 127: 63–70.

———. 2005. "Transatlantic Connections: A Cosmopolitan Context for Max and Marianne Weber's New York Visit 1904." *Max Weber Studies* 5(1): 81–112.

Stitzlein, Sarah M. 2017. "Public Schooling and Democracy in the United States." *Oxford Research Encyclopedia of Education*, 22 July. 10.1093/acrefore/9780190264093.013.25

Thomas, J. J. R. 1985. "Rationalization and the Status of Gender Divisions." *Sociology* 19(3): 409–20.

Tijssen, Lietake van Vucht. 1991. "Women and Objective Culture: Georg Simmel and Marianne Weber." *Theory, Culture & Society* 9: 203–18.

Weber, Marianne. [1926] 1988. *Max Weber: A Biography*. Translated and edited by Harry Zohn. New York: John Wiley & Sons.

———. [1919] 1998. "'Authority and Autonomy in Marriage,' 'On the Valuation of Housework,' 'Women and Objective Culture'—Selections from *Marianne Weber's Reflections on Women and Women's Issues (Frauenfrage and Frauengedanke)*." Pp. 215–28 in *The Women Founders: Sociology and Social Theory*, translated by E. Kirchen and edited by P. Lengermann and J. Niebrugge-Brantley. New York: McGraw-Hill.

Weber, Max. [1925] 2016. "The Types of Legitimate Domination." Pp. 183–91 in *Classical and Contemporary Sociological Theory: Text and Readings*, edited by Scott Appelrouth and Laura Desfor Edles. Thousand Oaks, CA: Sage Publications.

Whimster, Sam. 2005. Review of *Marianne Weber: Beiträge zu Werk und Person* by Bärbel Meurer. *Max Weber Studies* 5(1): 131–67.

Wobbe, Theresa. 2004. "Elective Affinities." Pp. 54–68 in *Engendering the Social: Feminist Encounters with Sociological Theory*, edited by B. L. Marshall and A. Witz. New York: Open University Press.

Zohn, Harry. 1988. "Translator's Preface." Pp. v–vii in *Max Weber: A Biography*, translated and edited by Harry Zohn. New York: John Wiley & Sons.

Chapter Four

Luther Bernard

Alan Sica and Christine Bucior

"They don't make 'em like they used to" is a retrogressive platitude usually applied to machinery or film stars or sports heroes. This wearied expression, however, perfectly captures in its most profound sense the professional life and achievements of Luther Lee Bernard (October 29, 1881–January 23, 1951). Between 1920 and the 1940s, he was among the best known U.S. sociologists in the country, partly through personal contacts with virtually every sociologist then at work. Following a pattern established when he was a graduate student at Chicago, between 1927 and 1932 he sent detailed questionnaires to every sociologist he could find, asking for their complete professional autobiographies. Many of them responded at great length, both regarding their careers as well as the history of sociology at their institutions. The results of this elaborate project, known then as "Luther's Onion Skins," still comprise the single best and broadest source of data about early American sociology (Luther Bernard Papers, Boxes 11–13). He was founding editor of *The American Sociologist*, early editor of *Social Forces*, as well as a motive force behind creation of the *American Sociological Review* in 1936.

Not surprisingly given his notoriety, he was elected in 1932 as the 23rd president of the American Sociological Society (renamed the American Sociological Association in 1959). While writing or editing a slew of books, he meantime taught all over the country at institutions which did not sufficiently value his unusual talents, nor appreciate his frank West Texas personality and phenomenal energy. But more important than, and the inspiration for, all his achievements as recorded in his vita was a belief he shared with other "founders" of American sociology: that no other field of study promised such fecund intellectual and political rewards, could prove so useful in banishing provincialism and ideologically driven nonsense from responsible thought, and was therefore entirely worthy of energetic, lifelong pursuit.

PRIVATE CONCERNS

In the years following his death in 1951 at the age of 69, Luther became known exclusively, if at all, as the hectoring husband of Jessie Bernard, a grandmother of sociological "first wave" feminism, who outlived him by 45 years. Whereas the American Sociological Association (ASA) since 1979 has bestowed an annual Jessie Bernard Award for scholarly excellence in the study of women, Luther Bernard is no longer mentioned by anyone. But his story, personal and professional, is uniquely valuable when attempting to gauge the history of the discipline, and thanks to the fact that Luther "had the abiding good sense to save stuff most of us throw away" (Bannister 1991: vii), it can be told, and probably should be, especially now as sociology undergoes yet another sea change (see Bucior and Sica 2018). Whereas one can easily learn the rudiments of Jessie's life from Wikipedia, no entry for Luther Lee Bernard has yet been written, nor is it likely to be.

The most thorough analysis so far published of Luther's professional and personal life (often within the context of Jessie's) occurs in Chapters 8 and 9 (111–143) of Robert Bannister's 1987 monograph, *Sociology and Scientism: The American Quest for Objectivity, 1880–1940*. Bannister begins Chapter 8, "An Objective Standard," by quoting a 1911 letter from Luther to his first sociology teacher and mentor, Charles Ellwood: "[My doctoral] thesis was a protest against instinctive control, pointing out its inadequacy and its essentially subjective and individualistic reference." Bannister then begins his short treatment of Luther's life with "A born maverick, Luther Bernard had a special talent for making trouble" (111), which is a polite understatement. But he did not create "trouble" for recreational purposes or due to neuroses. He always had in mind—as clearly explained, at length, in his enormous correspondence and diary entries—certain ways of going about social research and teaching and committee work which held everyone else to his own stratospheric standards, and that, along with a penchant for involving himself with complicated women, brought him fame of the sort that did not always serve him well. Nowadays his behavior would be considered "normal," but in the 1910s and 1920s, he (like W. I. Thomas at Chicago) was viewed as pushing the limits of propriety, both professionally and interpersonally.

The simplest "facts" regarding Luther's harried life and compendious work are outlined by the "finding aid" to his papers in the Paterno Library of Pennsylvania State University, and in the ASA's brief online commemoration of his 1932 presidency (which simply reprints Howard Odum's excellent summary in *American Sociology* [1951]). He was born on October 29, 1881 in Russell County, Kentucky, one of about 7600 people in the county then, wrapped as it was and is by the massive Cumberland River. At "six or seven" his family boarded one of the steamboats on the river he admired as a small boy and headed to west Texas, where he grew up.

Among Luther's archived papers is a document called "Statement of L.L. Bernard" (circa 1930), perhaps occasioned by junior scholars asking him for a hortatory epistle or lecture, of which only an autograph version exists (in the Bernard Papers at Penn State). It is prosaic and earnest, but concisely informative about Luther's self-understanding:

> When I was a young boy, out on the Texas prairies, I had a good deal of time to think while the cattle were grazing and not enough solid material to think with. At vacation time I had a wise old counsellor, the wife of a frontier Methodist Minister who had come to West Texas with her husband from the "bloody border" of Missouri and Kansas just after the Civil War, and with her she had brought a box of books overland in the old wagon. It was her most precious possession, and it became my greatest delight. It was composed largely of the lives of the leaders of the Southern Confederacy—men who had loved a principle and fought for it. Perhaps these lives taught me to love a principle also, and to fight for what I considered worth while. Mrs. Hawkins (that was her name) was a grand niece of Dugald Stewart and her splendid intellect was a hard taskmaster for my early years. Later I had two young high school teachers who gave me a glimpse into paradise—I mean a land of modern science, where knowledge was not forbidden and prejudice was unknown. After these experiences I was never satisfied until I finished my university course, where I became acquainted with sociology—the science of human society—through the inspiring and enthusiastic teaching of Dr. Charles A. Ellwood. He encouraged me to work for my PhD degree, which I secured in 1910 at the University of Chicago. I have now been teaching sociology—altogether in some ten colleges and universities—for twenty years.

In three and a half more pages of handwritten script, Luther explains his way of going about research: "I work concentratedly and endeavor . . . to avoid all interruptions when I am writing. I habitually write two to four hours at a stretch and sometimes longer. I habitually write 4000 to 6000 words in a day, if I am successful in avoiding interruptions." He was asked to write an encyclopedia entry (probably Bernard 1930) in 20,000 words:

> With an able assistant I prepared my material for three months. Then for thirty-three days we sat at a long table on which was piled our materials and worked for an average of eight hours a day. My assistant handed me the materials I called for and I put them together. At the end of this prolonged period we emerged with an 120,000 word manuscript. Then I proceeded to condense it to 20,000 words. That was a lot of work, but when the Editors said it was probably their most scholarly product we felt in a measure repaid for the effort.

One reasonably suspects that his "able assistant" was Jessie, his wife of a few years, vigorous research assistant, and eventual co-author. Luther then advises by example the avoidance of "all drug habits" since even coffee will disturb the scholar's equilibrium: "One cannot work and carry an extra load of nervous and body fatigues." He recommends respites through farm work, travel, and other refreshing summer activities. More importantly: "My general reading ranges all the way from astrophysics to poetry, with a strong emphasis upon the history of institutions and social psychology in between. I index all the books I read, placing numerous page references on the back fly-leaves to subjects in which I am interested." He concludes haranguing the troops with these words: "The only advice I would offer to superior ambitious students is to find something you really like to do and do that with all your might. The rest will take care of itself. But don't neglect your daily bread—I mean the commonplace tasks—while you are following the chosen bent." This self-portrait is of a hard-bitten Texan used to overcoming serious obstacles that might defeat a lesser mortal, and insistent "to the end" in pursuing goals set by himself, aimed principally at his own enlightenment.

Luther also thoughtfully wrote an abbreviated autobiography in a small, orderly cursive hand using pencil or pen that, again, exists only in his autograph version in the Penn State library (Bernard Papers, Box 10, Folders 23, 24). He filled 162 pages of conventional 8.5 x 11 stationery, the reverse of which is often nearly as informative as the clean side on which he wrote. In a version of recycling common in his time, all the sheets he used were letters from colleagues, foundations, publishers, and other professional contacts, which he regarded as dispensable, and suitable for his own note-taking and rough drafts. This was likely as much a result of growing up poor as a reflection of fiscal constraint common to the early Depression, and the poor salaries then offered to academics. He received personalized letters from The MacMillan Company, the Los Angeles Chamber of Commerce, the Governor of California, Russell Sage Foundation, Harper and Brothers, University of Washington, American Association for Labor Legislation, the National City Company (regarding the Czechoslovak State Loan of 1922), *The Survey*, Federal Council of the Churches of Christ in America, to name only those that come up early in his manuscript. And on these dispensable sheets he recorded the events of his early life, stopping in his early adolescence.

He began by remembering his mother taking him to "the old house" when he was about two years old, where she left on the mantel piece two "yellow or golden mugs that I longed for intensely," but which had belonged to his deceased siblings, John Luther and Cora Lee, both dead from diphtheria within a week of each other. Naturally, the mugs were left behind because they reminded Luther's bereaved mother "of her two infants, whom she still loved so dearly." John Luther was recalled as a "*good* baby," but Cora Lee was "perfect," amusing herself in her cradle, never clamoring for adult attention. Her ghost lingered: "The chief need of praise given one by my mother in after years, as I remember it, was that I was her best child, with the exception of Cora Lee, who ever remained the perfect one." Luther recorded hundreds of similarly domestic and familial observations, concluding with this:

> Finally, I should mention the fact that at the lower extreme north east corner of our farm there was a very satisfactory swimming hole. It was not large enough for a practiced swimmer, since it was not more than thirty by seventy feet in extent, I suppose; but it was about shoulder deep at its deepest point and it had a sandy bottom with sandy sides. It was therefore an unusually clean swimming hole for that country and the water itself was moderately clear. (162)

As one might suppose, this unpublished document gives a clear sense of Luther's youth of the *Huckleberry Finn* variety: "This was still cattle country and during my first year in Texas in this second residence I saw many droves of cattle being driven to market. The cowboy was still on the land. . ." (140). If Wordsworth was right—"The child is father of the man"—then studying Luther's Kentucky/Texas memoir should serve as the foundation to his full-blown biography.

Luther systematically participated in the self-analysis craze of the 1920s, brought on in part by the importation into U.S. intellectual circles of psychoanalysis (Freudian and Jungian) and other novel investigations of emotional life. Of many documents in his archive at Penn State which speak very frankly about his private thoughts and dilemmas, several stand out as particularly informative. One is dated September 12, 1933, entitled "Statement of Motives (To be published upon the death of L. L. Bernard from any but natural causes)." Over the course of four pages, Luther details his grave disappointment in his marriage with Jessie, which seemed doomed from the start:

> Several months ago I realized that there is probably no escape from my present unfortunate situation except by death . . . since I do not know how soon my situation will become unbearable I began this statement now, to be left in the hands of someone who will pledge me to give it to the press—some reputable magazine—when the proper time as indicated occurs.
> In 1925 (Sept. 23) I married Jessie Ravitch after a full and detailed discussion, by correspondence and in person, of the conditions of our marriage. I had known her since 1921, when at the age of 17 or 18 she became a student of mine. She professed—and I think truthfully—to admire me greatly at that time and this she continued to do thru the succeeding years. She made her admiration personal in the course of time. I was much pleased and flattered by it, but early in 1922 I came to the conclusion that our relationship should not become more personal.

The gist of the document is that at a key moment when Luther was sailing for a research trip to South America (February, 1926), Jessie announced she wanted to stay in the United States without him, and he divined that her sudden change of heart was due to her fear of disappointing her extended family for having married a non-Jew. Luther worried therefore about her apparent lack of "loyalty" to him, and her continued allegiance instead to her natal family. He had insisted prior to their secret marriage near Ithaca, NY that the marriage be "permanent":

> I told her that I couldn't afford to have any marital troubles and that she should just not marry me on any other conditions than that our marriage should be permanent and indissoluble. I asked her to think about this carefully and not to decide for marriage unless she was willing to make it final at all costs.

Jessie was 22 when they married, and was besotted with Luther, as evidenced by her letters at the time, which included her obscene drawings regarding their sexuality. Luther was 44 at the time, already once divorced, emotionally committed to another woman he had met prior to knowing Jessie, and fully engaged in a heated professional life. That he should have expected a young and inexperienced woman to commit to "permanence" seems naive, willful, even manipulative by today's standards, but at the time it served some self-therapeutic need in Luther. His passionate commitment to Hester E. McLean in Minneapolis was similarly documented in a "marriage contract" he wrote on August 14, 1922, part of which stipulates that they will "never desert the ship . . . never break the contract without the consent of the other," and so on. The marriage was prohibited by the young woman's parents in 1924, abetted by a competing suitor, their physician, and mightily contributed to Luther's eventual departure from the University of Minnesota (Bannister 1991: 49).

From these documents, and a great deal more in his archive which cannot be pursued here, we learn that Luther was very bright, limitlessly ambitious and hardworking, torn between adoration of women and perplexity at their demands on his time and attention, almost childishly manipulative of his mates in ways he would never have tolerated himself, and in general a "hard case" when it came to interpersonal conflicts. He could be very attentive and tender-hearted, and was apparently an excellent classroom teacher wherever he taught according to his students, including Jessie and others, known as a "campus legend" (Bannister 1991: 42), with students flocking to his courses. At the same time he was never easy to work or live with, as he likely would have been the first to admit.

THE PROFESSIONAL

The simplest, even if inadequate, way to approach Luther Bernard is to breeze through his major publications, leaving aside hundreds of minor ones. In 1944 he listed his "other publications" facing the title page of his final book, *War and Its Causes*, altogether fifteen titles, eight of them collaborations. The first appeared in a 1909 issue of the *American Journal of Sociology* when he was 28 years old, "The Teaching of Sociology in the United States," under the auspices of the founder of Chicago sociology, Albion Small. It is a typical product of the early "Chicago School" as it fought endlessly to legitimate the new discipline against its many critics, not to mention competing institutions. Bernard was initially a proud student of the "Chicago School," to which he longed to return as a professor, though never succeeded in doing so. The American Sociological Society at its December, 1908 meeting had invited Small to follow up on Frank Tolman's four-part series of *AJS* articles, "The Study of Sociology in Institutions of Learning in the United States" (Tolman 1902, 1903). Small and other Chicago professors delegated this large-scale task to their graduate student, Luther, which he carried out with his signature precision and energy.

By means of questionnaires mailed to "400 colleges, universities, and theological schools, and to 129 state normal schools," receiving 250 replies, then augmenting those with 167 more institutions which Luther identified by studying their course catalogues—how he procured them is not explained—a comprehensive portrait of sociology's pedagogical condition was created. The tabular and narrative detail is astonishing, as are the occasional summary remarks, for example, "Although sociology has had strong opposition in some institutions, it has had noteworthy encouragement in others. In the case of Susquehanna University [Selinsgrove, Pennsylvania] it would appear to have been developed far beyond the average. This, however, is a Lutheran institution and sociology is better received on the average by Lutheran institutions than by those of any other denomination" (211). By examining Luther's four compendious tables, the reader quickly understands exactly how, what, and where sociology was being taught in the roughly 400 institutions then offering courses under its rubric. This style of research, expertly handled by the 27-year old graduate student, stayed with Luther throughout his career. A few years later he followed a similar procedure, using an equally elaborate questionnaire, in order to write "The Teaching of Sociology in Southern Colleges and Universities" (Bernard 1918) at the behest of the National Conference of Charities and Corrections. And eventually, toward the end of his life, this mode of unmediated empiricism helped make possible the definitive *Origins of American Sociology*, co-authored with Jessie Bernard, tirty-three years after his first *AJS* article had appeared. By that time he was widely known as "the historian" of the discipline without equal.

Next, before he turned 30, his doctoral dissertation appeared, *The Transition to an Objective Standard of Social Control* (1911: 96), the subject of which became an abiding interest (see Bernard 1939). Like other doctoral students under Albion Small's guidance, Luther published the dissertation in unchanged form in three successive issues of the *AJS* (Bernard 1910–1911) prior to its formal "defense." Students today would find it difficult to fathom how or why such a document could be composed, then submitted, as a doctoral dissertation at the then leading department of sociology. Despite its brevity, the work is extremely dense from beginning to end, and required its author to make a very careful study, in several languages, of everything then known to psychologists and philosophers regarding the operation of the mind. His ultimate goal was to show that a vision of perception, cognition, conation, and every other component of human understanding is incomplete without a strong sociological—hence, interpersonal and environmental—supplementation to conventional ways of comprehending "psychological" reality. He begins vigorously, and in a tone that is sustained throughout:

> So much has been written concerning the evils of individualism and the mistakes of the hedonistic psychology and utilitarian ethics, without suggesting a satisfactory means of curing these evils or correcting these mistakes, that one is forced to believe that something is wrong with the method of attack. One reason for this failure may be that the significance of utilitarianism as a stage in the development of social theory has not yet been rightly comprehended and that we do not adequately foresee what should be the next step in our social philosophy and policy . . . we cannot escape the limitations imposed by a utilitarian ethics and by a hedonistic psychology upon our social policy until we reconstruct our system of social values, until we abandon the individual as the measure of all things social, and fix upon the group, even the widest conceivable group possessing solidarity, as the unity which lives, acts, and progresses or deteriorates . . . our current psychology and ethics . . . are essentially individualistic and hence impotent so far as contribution to a constructive sociology and social policy is concerned. (Bernard 1911: 1)

From this bold opening Luther recounts the pertinent views of Hobbes, Helvetius, Rousseau, Locke, Fourier, Proudhon, Bentham, Mill and many others, sorting out the origins of individual-based theories of ethics and perception, all of which led to modern psychology (Wundt, Hermann Lotze, McDougall, Bain, William James, Thorndike, Titchener, Sully, Höffding, Baldwin, Dewey, et al.).

He also addresses Mead, one of his professors at Chicago, in a detailed footnote that is quite characteristic of Luther's burgeoning scholarly style:

> G. H. Mead, *Journal of Phil., Psy and Sci. Methods* (March 31, 1910), 174, has attempted to remove this solipsistic character of the self of psychology by insisting upon an initially social individual (a conception which, in some form

or other, goes back at least as far as the Greek philosophers, and to Adam Smith and his contemporaries among the moderns), stating the matter, however, from the standpoint of consciousness alone and thus from the subjectivistic standpoint of the conventional psychologist. In the same article he rejects the idea that psychology should accept the *objective* definition of the social object or socius which the social sciences offer. However, the psychologists of the unconscious and relatively unconscious processes and the social psychologists, dealing with the same material, are undermining the artificial and conventional psychology of the highly conscious processes, and will assist in securing the adoption of the *objective* and social viewpoint in treating of neural and activity processes, whether conscious or unconscious. (5; emphases added)

In order to penetrate and appreciate Luther's achievement in his journeyman's labors, a vocabulary of the time must be apprehended, often without any ready terminological "synonyms" to insert when apparently desirable, since interests regarding what one might call "sociological consciousness" have so markedly changed, and shrunk, during the last century. His use, for instance, of "objective" is notable, and remote from today's understanding (see Bernard 1919).

Particularly demanding is Chapter II: "The Neural Correlate of Feeling" (10–28). A suitable primer for this material is the 68,000-word monograph called "Psychology" written by the British clergyman, lawyer, and psychologist James Ward, which he composed for the 9th, 10th, and 11th editions of the *Encyclopaedia Britannica* between 1875 and 1911 (Ward 1911). A principal argument of the time concerned differentiation between "feeling" (Ward 1911: 551, 581–586) as a large-scale category of psychological experience and "act," which comes much closer to theories later developed by Mead. Studying Luther's intense labor in this vineyard, whether or not he succeeded in "proving" the efficacy of a sociological ingredient, clearly indicates the scholarly expectations of the era, especially under the tutelage of Small and his colleagues. No source was left untouched in Luther's quest for sociological clarity, for example:

> The development of accuracy of statement has been one of delimitation and specification of the terms of correlation, arriving at a consciousness correlate in the formula of James Ward, and at a neural correlate in that of Meyer. It is proposed here to modify Meyer's statement on the basis of the neurological investigations of Herrick, Sherrington, Parker, and others, using whatever is valuable in the other statements of correlation, in an attempt to secure an adequate functional statement of the correlation of feeling modes, and thus to define feeling and to determine its relation to the act. (13–14)

For Luther the term "correlation" as partly described here took on totemic meaning throughout his dissertation, and bears no relation to the simple statistical meaning the word carries today.

Luther became a virtuoso footnote creator, not to flaunt his sharp intelligence, but because he needed these excurses to prove his argument most efficiently, as evidenced by this excerpt from a note that occupies most of an entire page:

> It appears that the similarity must be accounted for on the basis of the close connection of these sensory and activity processes with the feeling correlations in their instinctive or phylogenetic origin rather than as a matter of identity. But, even if feeling modes should be demonstrated to be only abstractions from sensory and ideational consciousness, it would not affect this theory of correlation and the resulting theory of the relativity of feeling as a criterion or valuation of activity. (20, note 38)

As one can easily imagine, any curt summary of this sort of work undercuts Luther's strenuous effort to innovate sociologically, while also giving the psychological dimension of social reality its due. His point is not to show that psychological portraits of human behavior are incorrect so much as to illustrate their inadequacy in the face of interpersonal reality—proper respect for the "socius," as he put it. To use a contemporary example: the plight of the anorexic is clearly sociological in origin, since dread of apparent fat or overeating is not mainly autogenous to the sufferer, but springs from a passionate desire to gain approval and admiration from others, even paradoxically while courting their censure. One can indeed theorize about eating disorders on the basis of individual psychopathology, but for Luther, this was incorrect at its root, and anticipates therapeutic thinking today.

How he moved from a careful dissection of psychological theories to a genuinely sociological view of "social control" does not lend itself to easy summary. His dissertation and the three articles published from it would have demonstrated Luther's theoretical acuity and energetic creativity, yet like Mead, and unlike Dewey, his rhetoric and prose style did not serve as warm invitations to most readers to join him in his expansion of sociological truth. He must have learned from this, for his later writings tended to be more "user-friendly," to use current jargon of the kind Luther would not have approved. Toward the end of the dissertation, he summarizes some of what he believes is worth concluding from his analysis:

> The less the reference is to persons conceived as mental processes, as organisms existing for hedonic or egoistic satisfactions, and the more the reference is to the society as a functioning group of persons in activity, the more the measure of social values ceases to be the individual and becomes the satisfactory functioning of the most efficient group of which he is a member. (87)

And in the formal "Conclusions and Implications," he becomes even more frank about his "domain assumptions" (to use Alvin Gouldner's expression):

> It appears that the prevailing type of sociology, especially that which has developed in American and England, is a part of the general movement for democratic gratification which had its greatest vogue in the nineteenth and the second half of the eighteenth centuries [i.e., among utilitarians]. (88)

Luther was obviously concerned about free-floating hedonism and self-realization tendencies, enemies of social solidarity and collective welfare (cf. Durkheim's relentless argument, to which Luther paid only slight attention), and believed that the "social practice for objective analysis" would "provide a social criterion based upon the relatively permanent needs of society instead of upon the changeable wants, interests, or feelings of the individual" (90).

Were it not for Luther's autobiography and his copious diary entries, it would be natural to take from his dissertation the image of a young man intently concerned about rigid social order and obedience to group norms. But that is hardly the case. In fact, the portrait one would intuit having read his early work completely opposes the life-loving, hedonistically driven character that surfaced during his 30s, between about 1911 and the early 1920s. As excellent as his dissertation was *qua* scholarly document, the Luther who surfaces in his private musings and the letters of the same period bears only the slightest similarity to the scholar-statesman of Platonic reserve and suspicion of "the masses." Perhaps he was trying hard to conform to an imagined aristocratic ethic among his Chicago professors, or was in revolt against his own basic nature, unrepentant and resistant to authority. That he found women entrancing, and they him, plays a much larger role in his private life than one would ever gather from his academic writing.

Still a junior scholar, Luther joined three others in contributing to *The Mind at Work: A Handbook of Applied Psychology* (Rhodes et al. 1914: 235), which signaled his commitment to social psychology. Writing "The Applications of Psychology to Social Problems" (207–231), Bernard evidenced a courageous forthrightness and broad scholarship that stayed with him throughout his career:

> The importance of the psychological factors in the formation and control of social phenomena has been recognized, at least in some measure, since the time of Aristotle. Systematic statements of the nature and influence of these factors have been three in number. The first and oldest of these systematizations reached its most advanced formulation in what came to be known in its later developments as Utilitarianism; the second belongs primarily to the last half century and is known in England, France, and America as Institutional or Social Psychology; while the third application of psychological facts to social

phenomena—though having its beginnings in the works of Maudsley, Kraepelin, Janet, Lombroso, and other investigators of the abnormal on the one hand, and of the practical English and German educators on the other—has reached a marked constructive efficiency only in the last decade or two. (207–208)

In the course of his chapter Bernard once again reconsiders the ideas of Helvetius, Godwin, Bentham, Mill, Spencer, Lester Ward, Hastings Rashdall, and Dewey, among many others. He shrewdly reminds his utilitarian readers that with Spencer, rational self-interest was muted in the interests of "sympathy," which much broadened the general understanding of ethics, and recalled Adam Smith's pre-sociological notions from 1759.

> Its ethical implications were seized upon by Leslie Stephen [Virginia Woolf's father] and Thomas Hill Green, and applied to such an extent that it became the agency by means of which ethics was given a distinctly social turn by these writers. Hitherto ethics had been mainly individualistic, and but slightly functional and social. (210)

He concludes his survey by pointing out that "man is not a purely intellectual animal with certain well-defined desires and sympathies which he endeavours to satisfy by the most cogent and effective reason" (230). Rather, he is shaped inescapably from beginning to end by the "conventions, fashions, fads and crazes" that constitute his society. If this seems like common sense today, it was clearly not when Luther composed his chapter for *The Mind at Work*. The American notion of frontier heroism and fierce individualism, the very cradle of Luther's own upbringing—and earnestly recorded by Max Weber when he visited the United States in 1904—has receded in the face of a broadly sociological conception of "individual-in-society," the current orthodoxy of which would probably have surprised Luther had he lived into our own era.

Following this he turned to a wide range of work including "Invention and Social Progress" (Bernard 1923), an unusual tangent for Luther, but another instance of his practical concerns regarding sociology's utility in taming postwar society during the "roaring twenties." He concludes:

> The types of inventions which are most urgently needed in these various fields are distinctly projective in character. Empirical invention will not meet the demands of consciously directed social progress in the future. We have reached the stage in social development where we must make rapid strides and long leaps. We must project our inventions from the principles and laws and formulas of science after the method described above. (33)

The quasi-Comtean social betterment commitment of the Chicago School at this time is evident in Luther's rhetoric and theorizing, just as it was prominently displayed in Mead's and Dewey's approaches to "social science."

The work which truly made his reputation and over which he struggled for years to include "everything" pertinent to the topic was *Instinct: A Study in Social Psychology* (Henry Holt & Co. 1924; 550), the main scholarly fruit of his efforts at the University of Minnesota (1917–1925). His principal goal was to demonstrate that sociology's subtle dismissal of instinct-driven human behavior was correct—not a particularly popular explanation at the time in the face of books like McDougall's *Introduction to Social Psychology* or James Drever's *Instinct in Man*:

> While at the beginning of this period no voice was to be discovered in protest against the McDougall type of interpretation, which was then dominant, in recent years numerous papers and some books have appeared controverting the older and metaphysical instinct conception. But this work has on the whole been critical rather than positive and constructively revisionary. It is now time to present a theory of habit formation which should materially assist in finding a substitute for the now largely discredited theory of instinct dominance in character formation. (19)

He was justifiably proud of this book (which he dedicated to Charles Ellwood and Max Meyer, his first sociology professors), the kind of volume sharp young scholars produce while on the rise, combining tremendous energy and fearlessness.

Given the inevitable recycling of ideas and interests within social "science," some of Bernard's concerns are echoed today as if newly discovered. Of particular interest in this regard are "The Evolution of Neuro-Psychic Traits—Habits" (87–106) and "The Evolution of Neuro-Psychic Controls—Intelligence and Language" (107–121). Modern "socio-biologists" and aficionados of everything "neural" would warm to his attention to "The Organic Bases of Action" (38–58), though he was coming at the topic from a quasi-critical point of view. Bernard's standard approach in all of his work was to travel carefully through preceding literatures, and then attempt an advance on whatever he believed had been accomplished to date. He did this in "Current Uses of the Term Instinct" and "The Classification of Instinct" (122–171). Then in almost Sorokin-like detail, he offers "Some Results of Investigation" (172–220):

> This and the preceding chapter afford some idea of the great variety of ways in which the term instinct is employed in the social sciences. In many cases it is a sort of catch-all for vague and indefinite ideas about the causes of relationships of activities. Writers, unable to account clearly for the occurrence of a particular behavioristic phenomenon on a purely objective basis, bring in the term instinct and use it as a charmed word, thus sidetracking further responsibility for an explanation. Race has been a similar term to conjure with, a stop-gap. (172)

Fully aware that there is no end to what various writers identify as "instinctually" driven behavior, and after having gone through hundreds of books in search of the extant variety, Bernard created a five-page table, "Classification of Instincts by General Groups," a product of assaying "classes," "authors," "books," and "cases" systematically. (Herbert Spencer's co-authors over many years produced similar results in *Descriptive Sociology*, and this style of comprehensive display might have inspired Luther to write the definitive study.) Then in twenty-three tables he assessed treatments of "instincts" ranging alphabetically from "The Aesthetic Instinct" to the altruistic, antisocial, disgust or repulsion, economic, ethical, and so on through "The Sex Instincts" (mentioning "Baudelaire's pathological sex instinct"!) and "The Instinct of Workmanship" (from Veblen). Finally, Bernard summarizes his findings in two master tables (217, 218) which in turn culminate in a "Grand Summary" that shows he found 5759 "classes," 412 authors, 495 books, and 14,046 "cases" (220). And this takes the reader only through nine out of twenty chapters in the book. Luther was nothing if not thorough in his pursuit of comprehensive analysis.

After detailed theoretical scrutiny of everything he could find, he offers "Some False Instincts Exposed" by means of another table, this one no less than twelve pages in length (403–414). And like all savvy didactic writers, he brings the study to its conclusion with "Some Further Misconceptions Concerning the Nature of Instinct" (416–453), finally leading to "Summary and Conclusions" where he bares his sociological soul:

> The real task before the social and educational psychologists with respect to instincts is to discover the mechanisms by means of which the child and the citizen build up their habits upon the basis of the instincts, directly or indirectly, and by means of which one habit or set of habits is transformed into another. . . . But before this change in emphasis can be brought about the inadequacy of the theory of instinctive control must be made manifest through an exposure of the current radical misconceptions regarding the nature and content of the instincts. Many sociologists have been feeling their way toward this objective for some time. It is a task which of necessity falls to the sociologist, because only he has the data regarding social organization and social pressures in sufficient mass and detail to make the error of the biological group—generally quite uninformed regarding the complexity and dynamic character of the social environment—sufficiently evident. It is not too much to say that the future control of the human race and its civilization lies not through selective breeding of the higher social qualities—although selective breeding of those traits which can be so bred—is of the greatest importance—but through their transmission by social contact and control. The overwhelming—and generally the immediate—pressures upon the character-forming process, especially in its more advanced stages, come from the accumulated psycho-social environment. (533–534)

Readers today find any suggestion of eugenics indefensible along ethical lines, and aesthetically repulsive as well, but of course in the 1920s it was still a serious undertaking, scientifically and politically. It is hard now to separate any eugenic posturing with the various ethnically driven holocausts that began with the Turkish extermination of Armenians in summer, 1915. But when Luther was writing, even right-thinking people of note took the idea seriously that human breeding could be desirable, especially if more or less commendable social goals could be attained thereby, and misery duly eliminated. It was in this context that Luther found "social control" important, not for any attachment to eugenics per se, but because the global aftermath of the First World War and the flu pandemic that followed it gave social theorists a mountain of grist for their mills, their collective goal being the creation of a new world order—yet again.

Another feature of Bernard's scope and unusual creativity as a sociologist lay in his work in Latin America, both by visiting, and by steadily reviewing works created there for his English-speaking colleagues. Luther's first recorded academic foray into this literature was a review he wrote for the *American Journal of Sociology* in 1915 of an Argentine doctoral dissertation (Bernard 1915). But it was eleven years later that his studies of the region began in earnest. On a grant "from and under the auspices of the Social Science Research Council, Inc." (Bernard 1927b) he undertook a research trip to Argentina between February 1926 and March 1927. His goal was "to study the development of the social sciences in some country and trace these sciences back to their origins in the national life and traditions and in the cultural influences, direct and indirect, operating on that country from other countries" (Bernard 1927b: 13) as a way of understanding the role environment plays in directing behavior. The immediate result of the trip was "The Development and Present Tendencies of Sociology in Argentina," which appeared in *Social Forces* in September 1927, and its sister bibliographic essay, "Topical Summaries of Current Literature: Sociology in Argentina" (Bernard 1927a), published in the *American Journal of Sociology* two months earlier. The ultimate result was career-long. The next year, Luther published two more Latin American pieces. "The Negro in Relation to Other Races in Latin America" (Bernard and Bernard 1928), which he co-wrote with Jessie, appeared in *The Annals of the American Academy of Political and Social Science* that November. "Why South Americans Fear Us" (Bernard 1928b) ran in the December issue of *The North American Review*. His answer to that question was multifold; Luther blamed everything from the Monroe Doctrine to European (especially Spanish) propaganda. Nevertheless, he laid much of the fault on the mutual ignorance South Americans and U.S. Americans have of each other. This ignorance—especially as displayed by U.S. Americans—would be a bugbear for him for the rest of his career.

Over the next twenty years, Luther wrote fifty-odd reviews of works from, or about, Latin America for publications as diverse as *Social Forces'* "Library and Bookshelf," the *American Journal of Sociology*, the newly minted *American Sociological Review*, *The Southwestern Science Quarterly*, *The Annals of the American Academy of Political and Social Science*, the *Journal of Political Economy*, and the *Journal of Philosophy*. These covered nearly 350 books overall, as well as the introductory volumes of three Argentine journals. The geographic scope of the reviewed titles was vast. They included books from Argentina, Bolivia, Brazil, Chile, Colombia, Costa Rica, Cuba, Ecuador, Mexico, Panama, Peru, "Porto" Rico, Uruguay, Venezuela, and the United States. Most were in Spanish, although (predictably) the U.S. titles all were written in English and the Brazilian titles, in Portuguese. Topically, they were comparably diverse. Luther read and reviewed histories, biographies, economic treatises, collections of government documents, travel writing, and at least one novel (*Platonia*, by a Bolivian author, Jose Aguirre), in addition to works of sociology, anthropology, and social psychology. He was generally more complimentary of the scholarship produced in Latin America than in the United States concerning Latin America; he saw most other U.S. scholars in this area as incompetent dabblers. Upon reviewing a collection of Latin-American-studies papers, for example, Luther predicted: "We are going to have some rather crude courses on Latin-American sociology in our universities, given by men seeking a 'specialty,' with a smattering of Spanish and an overnight reading of reviews of a few Spanish books in the field" (Bernard 1947a). And this was not a new complaint. His review of Frank Tannenbaum's *Whither Latin America*, ten years earlier, reads in full:

> The author is correct in saying that this sketch is not a research product in the ordinary sense. Although financed by the Brookings Institution, it might just as well have been compiled from *The Encyclopaedia of the Social Sciences* and have been called "A Latin-American Almanac." It has useful facts in it, especially about population, industry, finance, trade, transportation, education, labor, and agriculture, which might have been selected for the tired business man to read on a night when there was no good musical comedy, or for the average reader who wishes to learn all about Latin America on a Sunday afternoon. But to speak of it as a guide to the research student of Latin America (for whom it seems to have been intended) is too much of a reflection upon either the quality of the research student in this field (however poor he may be) or upon the intelligence of the research management of the Brookings Institution. (Bernard 1937)

Perhaps Luther had so little patience for those who (in his view) overestimated their knowledge of Latin America because he was so familiar with the region himself. He travelled there not infrequently. In both 1934 and 1939, he spent several weeks in Mexico; he made return trips to Argentina in 1947 (which he spent, in part, with Juan and Eva Perón) and 1949. Box 32 of the Bernard Papers at Penn State contains thirteen folders' worth of Spanish-language letters Luther received and wrote between 1926 and 1950. Some of these were to or from correspondents in Spain, but the bulk were between him and correspondents in South America, Mexico, and Cuba. Luther traded letters with academics, government officials (including national heads of education in Mexico and Ecuador and an undersecretary of foreign affairs from Bolivia), and a surprising number of *abogados*. He also corresponded with the editors of a number of Latin American journals, including Chile's *Sagitario*, the *Revista Mexicana de Estudios Historicos*, the *Revista Parlamentaria de Cuba*, and Venezuela's *Revista Juridica*. This last is not shocking, since Luther himself published in at least two *revistas*. Five of his articles appeared in the *Revista Mexicana de Sociología* in the 1940s: "La Sociología Sistematica de Mariano H. Cornejo" (1942b; an intellectual biography of a Peruvian sociologist) and "La Clasificación de la Cultura" (1942c) in 1942; in 1945, "El Nuevo Panorama del Mundo," in which Luther advocated for a pan-American union; "Las Actuales Tendencias Sociológicas en los Estados Unidos" in 1947, which articulated the major branches, questions, and methods of American sociology up to that year; and "Mito, Superstición, Hipótesis, Ciencia," which presented these as developmental stages in human explanatory thought, in 1949. Last, shortly before his death, Luther published "El Estado Paternal de Truman y la Situación Mundial" (a paean to Harry Truman's continuation of the New Deal) for the Argentine journal *Sur* (Bernard 1950).[1]

On the strength of *Instinct*, Howard Odum invited Luther to write a textbook for his "American Social Science Series" published by Henry Holt. While working briefly at Cornell, Luther's *An Introduction to Social Psychology* (1926) appeared, an encyclopedic volume of 651 pages, in which he did his best to cover a vast field while pointedly leaving his stamp on the way he believed social psychology should be carried out. Pages 591 through 636 contain a jammed bibliography by chapter-topic that, alone, constituted a major achievement, and which was supplemented with short bibliographies at the end of each of the 37 chapters. As in all his work, he did not fear taking strong positions, for example:

> An Erroneous View of Instinct—Some writers persist in speaking of these modified behavior processes as instinctive or inherited. Such usage, as is shown elsewhere, is of course untenable. Instincts must be defined in terms of their structure, since it is the biological structure only which is inherited. We cannot inherit ideas, values, or the ends of adjustment behavior processes, because these are conceptual and not structural facts. (116)

To repeat, with the eugenics movement in high gear at the time, statements such as these were reprehensible and utopian to critics of the sociological viewpoint, as Bernard well knew. His book moves from "The Organic Basis of Behavior" through environmental factors, adjustment processes, forms of consciousness, psychopathology, race, nationality, class, personality (269–410), collective behavior (including tantalizing chapters on "rational types" versus "nonrational types" of collective interaction; 438–464), culminating in chapters on leadership. There was very little about social psychology, thus broadly understood, that Bernard overlooked, as in this passage, which remains as illuminating today as it was ninety years ago:

> Phantasy—But the more seriously abnormal distortions of personality which are developed as compensations for inadequacy are purely subjective and are to be found in the subject's own consciousness. Unable to compensate for weakness by achievement of objective adjustments or by improvement of his subjective qualities and capacities, he builds up an internal world of phantasy. (197)

The relationship between this sort of "textbook" and what passes for the same nowadays is quite remote. Luther's book is a genuine scholarly achievement, and the anticipated market for it must have been small given that the American Sociological Society (A.S.S.), the predecessor in name to the ASA, numbered 1107 members, and departments of sociology were not yet numerous (Rosich 2005: 140).

Following these two substantial works, Luther joined famous colleagues in producing several collaborative volumes in quick succession. *Modern Scientific Knowledge of Nature, Man, and Society* (Cleveland 1929: 592) was jointly composed with Frederick A. Cleveland and others. *An Introduction to Sociology: A Behavioristic Study of American Society* was edited by Jerome Davis, Harry Elmer Barnes, Howard Paul Becker, L.L. Bernard, and others (D.C. Heath 1927: 926), and a companion volume, *Readings in Sociology to Accompany an Introduction to Sociology* (1,065) with the same editorial team came out simultaneously. Joining with W. F. Ogburn, A. Goldenweiser, and others, Luther appeared again during 1927 in *The Social Sciences and Their Interrelations* (Houghton Mifflin, 1927; 506). At the age of 45 he had become a writing machine and a major proselytizer for his field, chosen to collaborate with some of the leading scholars of the era. Returning to a lifelong interest, in April, 1928 he published "The Development of Methods in Sociology" in *The Monist*, reissued in book form the same year (Open Court Press).

A few months later, having moved to Tulane after a year at Cornell, he delivered "Some Historical and Recent Trends of Sociology in the United States" (Bernard 1928c), a dense thirty-page disquisition that laid the groundwork for the gargantuan treatment written with Jessie and published fifteen years later:

> The sociological storm was brewing for some decades before it finally struck our universities with a good deal of force around about 1890. . . . Sociology arose as a protest against this spirit of classicism. It preached a crusade for the study of men and their affairs rather than merely the hypothetical men of books. . . . In the next hundred years the [anti-classical] spirit of Vico entered into the minds of a host of great philosophers of history—Voltaire, Turgot, Rousseau, Montesquieu, Condorcet, Saint-Simon, Herder, Goethe, Hegel, and Comte, to mention only some of the more outstanding names. These men were forerunners of sociology. . . . The Saint-Simonian cult was largely responsible for the religio-humanitarian motivation which led to the establishment of something like one hundred and fifty experimental Owenite and Fourierian utopian colonies in this country between 1825 and 1875. (264–266)

It was in this article that Luther first drew upon the hundreds of "onion skin" autobiographies and departmental histories that he had personally solicited from every sociologist he could find to that point (268ff). Not long afterwards he elaborated on this article with another, "Schools of Sociology" (Bernard 1930a, as it was originally titled; this same article can be found archived as "An Interpretation of Sociology in the United States"), offered as a published paper in the proceedings of the A.S.S., December, 1930. Here he offered a thumbnail sketch of sociology's remote and as yet unnamed beginnings in the United States during the 1830s and 1840s, at the College of Philadelphia (University of Pennsylvania), Columbia College, Miami University of Ohio, and the University of Virginia (a course taught there by none other than W. H. M'Guffey of the *McGuffey Readers*). Sociology along Spencerian lines was taught by Sumner at Yale in 1873, and at Kansas by Frank Blackmar in 1889 in the first so-named department in the country (Sica 1980). Luther also became interested in the work of Henry Hughes of Mississippi, and of George Fitzhugh of Virginia, both of whom co-opted the term "sociology" for their own purposes. He worked on an unpublished monograph regarding Hughes and corresponded at length with informants from his home state. He also provided a tantalizing introduction to Hughes's work that he lacked the time to elaborate: "Henry Hughes, First American Sociologist" (Bernard 1936).

Meanwhile, of course, Luther wrote other chapters and articles, one of the most important being "Social Attitudes" for *The Encyclopedia of the Social Sciences* (1930b), a venue that quickly defined its topic at a high level. This was soon followed by "Attitudes and the Redirection of Behavior" in Kimball Young (ed.), *Social Attitudes* (Henry Holt 1931: 46–74). Perhaps the most telling document of this period is Luther's presidential address delivered at the 27th annual meeting of the A.S.S., in Cincinnati in December,

1932, entitled "Sociological Research and the Exceptional Man" (Bernard 1933). Given that the Depression was in full swing, and considering the expected ceremonial nature of such events, Luther's speech—theoretically offered to all 1340 members of the Society that year—revealed once again his hard-bitten approach to the business of intellectual life. His comments constitute as much a sermon on right-thinking as an inspiration for carrying out sociological research, as evidenced by his opening line: "Sociologists everywhere in this country are filled with a righteous and burning zeal for research" (Bernard 1933: 3). Almost immediately he launches into a denunciation of those colleagues who do not conform to his high standards:

> I have little sympathy with research projects that grow out of an institution's or a person's desire to get money from a foundation rather than out of some profoundly felt need for knowledge on certain points and issues. In recent years I think I have seen altogether too much money wasted on research projects made to order and carried through by individuals and groups of persons of mediocre ability who were seeking to build for themselves and their political cronies reputations as sociologists which should have been laid more securely in the mastering of knowledge already gained. I have little sympathy with research which is either mercenary or pharisaical and which aims primarily at political profit and invidious distinction. (3–4)

Imagine an ASA president today offering such a critique of grant-chasing for its own sake. One can imagine even then how certain members of the audience would have bristled at their president's sentiments, especially those who during the 1920s had learned to court the foundations for research money, and were only too glad to conform to whatever "interests" they or the government had which required "research" of the kind they could provide. He continues:

> What we need is objectively-tested fact to replace our venerable traditions; and in order that we may secure tested facts we are especially in need of research carried on by sincere and well-trained men and women who have learned to dispossess themselves of prejudices and partisanship and who seek knowledge, not for the purpose of making a showing to justify their research grants, but for the sake of the truth alone. Again, permit me to suggest that there is altogether too much so-called research undertaken today by partisans to prove their predatory creeds and "isms"; by exploiters to secure legislation or to convince public opinion of the rightness of their nefarious exploitive programs; by promoters who wish to establish research units and gain reputation for themselves; and by the merely ignorant who believe that one research project is as good as another and that all methods are equally simple and mechanical and that anyone who can turn the crank of a calculating machine and fill in a schedule is as capable of doing research as any other person. (4–5)

Much later in the lecture he says "It is entirely as possible to have moronic research as any other form of moronic thinking" (10) in case his audience to that point had not received his message in full.

Currently there is probably no better way to understand Luther Bernard's professional worldview than to remind ourselves of Alvin Gouldner's *The Coming Crisis of Western Sociology* (1970) in which he distinguishes those scholars who live "for sociology" and their antipathetic colleagues who live "off sociology":

> Just as the sharpest critics of Marxism have usually been Marxists, the keenest critics of sociology have usually been sociologists and students of sociology. Often enough the men whose rejection of such criticism is most vehement are those who live *off* sociology, while the most vehement critics are those who live *for* it. Often, but not always. (Gouldner 1970: 15; see also Gouldner's *For Sociology*, 1973)

Perhaps due to his education at Columbia University under Robert K. Merton, Gouldner's work made regular use of Weber's ideas and impetus, and in this instance he did so by "updating" these original remarks by Weber in 1919, speaking before dispirited German students and former soldiers:

> There are two ways of making politics one's vocation: Either one lives "for" politics or one lives "off" politics. By no means is this contrast an exclusive one. The rule is, rather, that man does both, at least in thought, and certainly he also does both in practice. He who lives "for" politics makes politics his life, in an internal sense. Either he enjoys the naked possession of the power he exerts, or he nourishes his inner balance and self-feeling by the consciousness that his life has *meaning* in the service of a "cause." In this internal sense, every sincere man who lives for a cause also lives off this cause. The distinction hence refers to a much more substantial aspect of the matter, namely, to the economic. He who strives to make politics a permanent *source of income* lives "off" politics as a vocation, where he who does not do this lives "for" politics. (Weber [1919] 1946: 84)

Just as remains the case today, Bernard knew that those social scientists who listened attentively to the policy demands of Congress or other governmental agencies, reshaping their requests for funds to suit whichever piper was paying at the moment, were living "off sociology" in Gouldner's (and Weber's) sense. It is utterly rational—remembering Weber's typology of social action—to pursue "external funding" single-mindedly if garnering institutional wealth and personal affluence is one's primary goal. It was not Gouldner's, nor Bernard's. Rather, they lived and worked to increase the intellectual heft and practical utility of sociology with very little support, which accounts for Bernard's detailed book on instinct and Gouldner's on Plato. Such projects did not receive lavish government funding, nor were designed to do so. The beauty of their scholarly attitude lay in a refusal to be tutored by government or foundation bureaucrats vis-à-vis how to go about social research and scholarship. They alone without intervention decided what to study and how to do it. And the results for both Gouldner's and Bernard's oeuvres were extraordinary. So it seems that about every fifty years—from Weber to Gouldner to today—it becomes necessary to invoke this now antique distinction in scholarly motivations.

Also, pertinent today is Bernard's absolute rejection of the "collaborative research model" increasingly embraced by universities in their effort to secure ever larger and more complex grants. Once again Luther goes his own way: "Let me repeat that research is primarily a highly personal operation or employment of the individual human mind and that is why it can be successfully undertaken and carried through only by the exceptional man" (Bernard 1933: 10). For the epistemological and practical foundation of his critique, he urges his audience to reconsider several of his earlier papers which he believes illustrate the legitimacy of his wide-scale attack (Bernard 1919, 1925, 1928a, 1932). Luther's bluntly stated arguments are as foreign to today's hyper-polite academic discourse as were his family's simple life in Texas compared with urbanites who work at today's major universities.

A marked change occurred when Luther added Jessie's name to the title page of a book for the first time, in February, 1934, when they published *Sociology and the Study of International Relations* (Washington University Studies 1934: 115). During their early marriage, she spent a great deal of time doing research under his stern guidance. But between 1936 and 1940, she worked in Washington and visited Paris, often staying with friends in New York City, and left Luther in St. Louis, which he protested vigorously, but to no avail. She wanted to do research on her own, but also longed to be free of his bothersome, demanding ways. He wrote to her repeatedly asking for her to return, even accusing her of having lovers she claimed not to have. While she was gone she worked at office jobs, but did excellent research along lines that fit well with Luther's work, and her own as well.

One thorn in her side was Luther's critique of "the modern woman" who did what she wished as she wished, and coupled with that, his displeasure at certain characteristics of Jews that he had difficulty countenancing. She wrote a master's thesis at Minnesota in 1924 on Jewish assimilation in the second generation. Nevertheless, she shared his dislike of "certain kinds of Jews" with whom she worked at the WPA and BLS in Washington. But in an unsigned article in *The International Journal of Ethics* (1942) she dug beneath the simple aversion to styles of interaction. Thinking of Luther's priggish insistence upon certain behavioral norms, she wrote:

> Jewish culture is sensuous—good food, fine clothing, a fine home. No theory of the depravity of human nature stands in the way of the Jew's enjoyment of

these pleasures of the flesh. He need not, therefore, be apologetic even to himself if he gloats over them. [The Protestant] might—human biology being everywhere the same—seek pleasures of the flesh, but he can never naively enjoy them, without conflict, however subtle, as Jews do. . . . If the intensely personalistic, literate, individual yet clannish, sensuous culture of the Jews produces . . . the ostentatious, spectacular, boisterous model of the new-rich sort, it produces also . . . the understanding and sympathetic model of the poet. (Jessie Bernard 1942: 443, 449–450; quoted in Bannister 1991: 71, 73)

The couple never resolved the deep-seated conflict between his intensely Protestant worldview versus her moderated midwestern Judaism, but it did give them inspiration for lengthy written commentaries, public and private.

Also in 1934 Luther edited an important volume, *The Fields and Methods of Sociology*, including chapters by thirty-three colleagues, a virtual who's-who in sociology at the time (Ray Long and Richard R. Smith, Inc.; 529). It was dedicated to "The Members of The American Sociology Society, To Which Fellowship all of the contributors to this volume belong and upon whom it is dependent for a successful reception"—surely a heterodox mode of advertising for course adoption. The book offers a soup-to-nuts portrait of sociology at the time, the first part covering seventeen different "fields" within the discipline, the second focusing on methodology within seventeen subfields. Jessie wrapped up the volume with an eight-page bibliography treating "The Sociology of Art," "The Sociology of Law," "Political Sociology," "Social Ethics," "The Sociology of Institutions," "Social Organization," "Social Control," "The Sociology of Economic Relations," "Social Pathology," and "Penology" (505–512). She is not credited within the bibliography as its compiler, but is acknowledged in the ToC. Surely she took her cue in this work from Luther, whose obsessive bibliographical labors had begun many years before at Chicago.

In August, 1939 Luther published *Social Control In Its Sociological Aspects* (Macmillan Co.: 711), a vast study designed for textbook use, but perhaps too demanding for the typical college student of the time. He dedicated the book to "My Colleagues Frank J. Bruno and Stuart A. Queen; Expert in the Techniques of Social Control," which may have amounted to a left-handed compliment. This work, along with *Instinct*, probably illustrates Luther's scholarship at its acme. His analysis betrays a deeply held suspicion about the strength of institutions to manipulate their individual members. One long section of the book is called "The Exploitive Social Controls" (force, pacification, punishment, reprisals, intimidation, fraud, intrigue, deception, repression, etc.; 51–336), while the other major part is "The Constructive Social Controls" (revolution, non-violent coercion, standardization, supernaturalism, ethics, custom and law, legislation, social reform, and education; 337–700). It differs from other treatises on social control in its unapologetic normative evaluations.

In 1942 at the age of 61, Luther brought out *An Introduction to Sociology: A Naturalistic Account of Man's Adjustment to His World* in the Crowell's Social Science Series edited by Seba Eldridge at the University of Kansas (1942a), a prestigious collection of books that transcended typical textbook pabulum (including, for example, Harry W. Laidler's masterful *A History of Socialist Thought*). The volume is 1041 pages in length, with precious few graphical interruptions to Luther's prose, the whole endeavor dedicated to "Dr. Jessie Bernard, Sociologist of Distinction, in Acknowledgment of Valuable Assistance, Useful Criticisms, and Generous Encouragement." The book is encyclopedic, including the anthropological background to modern life that at the time was considered essential to sociological understanding, in addition to discussions of climate, geography, flora and fauna, and "everything one might want to know" about a "naturalistic" understanding of social life. It likely cost Luther enormous effort.

Finally, and for historians by far the most important contribution, *Origins of American Sociology: The Social Science Movement in the United States* appeared in 1943 (also in Seba Eldridge's important series with Crowell). This time Luther and Jessie shared authorship jointly and equally. Despite writing many books thereafter, Jessie never again created a work of such lasting importance, since it literally opened and closed an entire zone of scholarly enterprise that has not been surpassed. Her work on women has been swallowed by feminist scholarship, and is acknowledged, as is that of Simone de Beauvoir, simply as a noble predecessor. But for historians of the social sciences, *Origins* remains foundational, as well it should at 866 pages of small print. Had neither of them written anything else, they would be remembered and honored for this book.

Rising to the occasion of the global conflagration, Luther tossed off his *War and Its Causes* in 1944 (479), wisely dividing the book into three sections: "War as a Social Institution" (3–200), "The Causes of War" (201–440), and "The Future of War" (441–459), to which he added his typical extended bibliography. The book is unusual in Luther's oeuvre because it is the only one he wrote aimed at pressing contemporary events. In it he succeeded in showing the utility of a sociological and historical viewpoint when viewing war "as an institution," partly in an effort to defuse the wildly emotional commitments and counter-commitments most people felt by 1944 at the height of the Second World War, with millions already dead, and no end in sight.

As easily imagined from our comments thus far, summarizing the meaning of a personal and political life as persistently fascinating, frenetic, creative, and at points annoying as Luther Bernard's is a dangerous undertaking. He came from a sociocultural background very nearly barren of any promise (except for his temperamental champion, Mrs. Hawkins, and her box of books), yet through sheer brains and unremitting effort climbed to the pinnacle of sociology at Chicago. Afterwards he produced book after innovative book, virtuoso bibliographies in many areas, expert level testimony about Latin American social science, became a gifted teacher, wrote thousands of letters and diary entries, virtually invented the history of American sociology, and drove himself and several women to the point of madness due to a monastic personality that also required female companionship of an adoring cast. If today's sociologist can learn from him, the lesson will originate as much in his several vital books—on instincts, social control, social psychology, and the origins of social science—as from his example as a rabidly dedicated scholar whose adult life entailed furthering sociology's grasp of collective reality at all costs, personal and intellectual. That he lived "for sociology" rather than "off" it cannot be forsworn, yet unlike Weber's stern Prussian self-control and scholarly projection, Luther's motivation and results were purely American in a sense widely recognized as such during the early twentieth century, when new ideas about the possibilities of social life flooded the public sphere with an optimism we can now only envy.

NOTE

1. The authors thank Andrea L. Ruiz for her help reading the Spanish-language articles.

WORKS CITED

Bannister, Robert C. 1987. *Sociology and Scientism: The American Quest for Certainty, 1880–1940*. Chapel Hill, NC: University of North Carolina Press.

———. 1991. *Jessie Bernard: The Making of a Feminist*. New Brunswick, NJ: Rutgers University Press.

Bernard, Jessie. 1942. "An Analysis of Jewish Culture." Pp. 43–63 in *Jews in a Gentile World*, edited by Isacque Graeber and Steuart H. Britt. New York: Macmillan Company.

Bernard, Luther. 1854–1961. Luther Bernard Collection (1439). Historical Collections and Labor Archives, Special Collections Library, Pennsylvania State University. 48.18 cubic feet; 48 boxes.

———. 1909. "The Teaching of Sociology in the United States." *American Journal of Sociology*, 15:2 (September): 164–213.

———. 1910–1911. "The Transition to An Objective Standard of Social Control." *American Journal of Sociology*, 16:2 (September): 171–212; 16:3 (November): 309–41; 16:4 (January): 519–37.

———. 1911. *The Transition to an Objective Standard of Social Control*. Doctoral dissertation, Department of Sociology, University of Chicago. http://hdl.handle.net2027/uc1.$b19692.

———. 1915. "[*La Sociedad Argentina. Analisis-Critica*, by Cesar Reyes]." *American Journal of Sociology*, 21:1 (July): 112–13.

———. 1918. "The Teaching of Sociology in Southern Colleges and Universities." *American Journal of Sociology*, 23:4 (January): 491–515.

———. 1919. "The Objective Viewpoint in Sociology." *American Journal of Sociology*, 25: 298–325.

———. 1923. "Invention and Social Progress," *American Journal of Sociology*, 29:1 (July): 1–33.

———. 1924. *Instinct: A Study in Social Psychology*. New York, NY: Henry Holt and Co.
———. 1925. "Scientific Method and Social Progress." *American Journal of Sociology*, 31: 1–18.
———. 1926. *An Introduction to Social Psychology*. New York, NY: Henry Holt and Co.
———. 1927a. "Topical Summaries of Current Literature: Sociology in Argentina." *American Journal of Sociology*, 33:1 (July): 110–17.
———. 1927b. "The Development and Present Tendencies of Sociology in Argentina." *Social Forces*, 6:1 (September): 13–27.
———. 1928a. "The Development of Methods in Sociology." *The Monist*, 38: 320ff.
———. 1928b. "Why South Americans Fear Us." *The North American Review*, 226:6 (December): 665–72.
———. 1928c. "Some Historical and Recent Trends of Sociology in the United States." *Southwest Political and Social Science Quarterly*. 9 (January): 264–293.
———. 1930a. "Schools of Sociology." *Southwest Political and Social Science Quarterly*, 11:2 (September): 117–134.
———. 1930b. "Social Attitudes." Pp. 305–307 in *Encyclopedia of the Social Sciences*, edited by Alvin S. Johnson and Edwin R.A. Seligman. New York: Macmillan Company.
———. 1932. "Some General Problems of Sociological Measurement." *Southwestern Social Science Quarterly*, 12: 310–20.
———. 1933. "Sociological Research and the Exceptional Man" (A.S.S. Presidential Address, 1932). *Publication of the American Sociological Society*, 27:2 (May): 3–19.
———, ed. 1934. *The Fields and Methods of Sociology*. New York, NY: R. Long & R.R. Smith, Inc.
———. 1936. "Henry Hughes, First American Sociologist." *Social Forces*, 15:2 (December): 154–74.
———. 1937. "[*Whither Latin America?* by Frank Tannenbaum.]" *American Journal of Sociology*, 43:3 (November): 518–19.
———. 1939. *Social Control in Its Sociological Aspects*. New York: The Macmillan Company.
———. 1942a. *An Introduction to Sociology: A Naturalistic Account of Man's Adjustment to His World*. New York, NY: Thomas Y. Crowell Company.
———. 1942b. "La Sociología Sistemática de Mariano H. Cornejo." ["The Systematic Sociology of Mariano H. Cornejo."] *Revista Mexicana de Sociología*, 4:2: 7–34.
———. 1942c. "La Clasificación de la Cultura." ["The Classification of Culture."] *Revista Mexicana de Sociología*, 4:3: 51–56.
———. 1944. *War and Its Causes*. New York, NY: Henry Holt and Co.
———. 1945. "El Nuevo Panorama del Mundo." ["The New Outlook of the World."] *Revista Mexicana de Sociología*, 7:2: 207–26.
———. 1947a. "[Intellectual Trends in Latin America: Papers Read Before the Institute of Latin America Studies.]" *American Journal of Sociology*, 52:5 (March): 455.
———. 1947b. "Las Actuales Tendencias Sociológicas en los Estados Unidos." ["The Current Sociological Trends in the United States."] *Revista Mexicana de Sociología*, 9:1: 23–50.
———. 1949. "Mito, Superstición, Hipótesis, Ciencia." ["Myth, Superstition, Hypothesis, Science."] *Revista Mexicana de Sociología*, 11:3: 385–408.
———. 1950. "El Estado Paternal de Truman y la Situacion Mundial." ["Truman's Paternalist State and the World Situation."] *Sur*, 185:1: 40–49.
Bernard, Luther, and Jessie Bernard. 1928. "The Negro In Relation to Other Races in Latin America." *The Annals of the American Academy of Political and Social Science*, 140:1: 306–18.
———. 1934. *Sociology and the Study of International Relations*. St. Louis, MO: Washington University in St. Louis.
———. 1943. *Origins of American Sociology: The Social Science Movement in the United States*. New York, NY: Thomas Y. Crowell Company.
Bucior, Christine, and Alan Sica. 2018. "Sociology as a Female Preserve: Feminization and Redirection in Sociological Education and Research." *The American Sociologist*. Online first: http://link.springer.com/article/10.1007/s12108-018-9395-z.

Cleveland, Frederick A. 1929. *Modern Scientific Knowledge of Nature, Man and Society.* New York, NY: The Ronald Press Company.
Drever, James. 1917/1921. *Instinct in Man: A Contribution to the Psychology of Education.* Cambridge, UK: At the University Press.
Gouldner, Alvin W. 1970. *The Coming Crisis of Western Sociology.* New York: Basic Books.
———. 1973. *For Sociology: Renewal and Critique in Sociology Today.* New York: Basic Books.
Laidler, Harry W. 1938. *A History of Socialist Thought.* New York, NY: Thomas Y. Crowell Company.
McDougall, William. 1913. *An Introduction to Social Psychology 7th edition.* London: Methuen & Company.
Rhodes, Geoffrey, ed. 1914. *The Mind at Work: A Handbook of Applied Psychology.* With contributions by Charles Buttar, E. J. Foley, and L. L. Bernard. London, UK: Thomas Murby & Co.
Rosich, Katherine J. 2005. *A History of the American Sociological Association, 1981–2004.* Washington, DC: American Sociological Assn.
Sica, Alan. 1980. "A Question of Primacy: Small at Chicago or Blackmar at Kansas?" Presented at ASA annual meeting, August, New York City.
Spencer, Herbert. 1873–1881. *Descriptive Sociology: Or, Groups of Sociological Facts* (8 volumes). New York, NY: Appleton and Company.
Tolman, Frank L. 1902a. "The Study of Sociology in Institutions of Learning in the United States. A Report of an Investigation Undertaken by the Graduate Sociological League of the University of Chicago." *American Journal of Sociology*, 7:6 (May): 797–838.
———. 1902b. "The Study of Sociology in Institutions of Learning in the United States. II." *American Journal of Sociology*, 8:1 (July): 85–121.
———. 1902c. "The Study of Sociology in Institutions of Learning in the United States. III." *American Journal of Sociology*, 8:2 (September): 251–72.
———. 1903. "The Study of Sociology in Institutions of Learning in the United States. IV." *American Journal of Sociology*, 8:4 (January): 531–58.
Ward, James. 1911. "Psychology." Pp. 547–604 in *The Encyclopaedia Britannica*, 11th edition. New York: Encyclopaedia Britannica, Inc.
Weber, Max. [1919] 1946. "Politics as a Vocation." Pp. 77–128 in *From Max Weber* edited by Hans Gerth and C. Wright Mills. New York, NY: Oxford University Press.
Young, Kimball, Ed. 1931. *Social Attitudes.* New York, NY: Henry Holt and Co.

Chapter Five

Radhakamal Mukerjee

A Regional, Social Ecological Outlook

Diane M. Rodgers

LIFE AND INFLUENCES OF RADHAKAMAL MUKERJEE

Radhakamal Mukerjee (1889–1968) was a prominent Indian sociologist who was considered one of the founding fathers of sociology in India and a pioneer in the fields of Regional Sociology and Social Ecology. He was a prolific scholar, publishing in top sociology journals and creating a substantial body of work on a range of social issues. His theoretical contributions were informed and balanced by his commitment to social justice and practical social reforms. Born into a Bengali Brahmin family in Baharampur, West Bengal, Mukerjee attended Krishnath College and subsequently was offered a scholarship to attend the prestigious Presidency College in Calcutta. Mukerjee became active in the Indian Independence movement as early as 1905 in Bengal, the birthplace of the Swadeshi movement known for its boycott of British goods. While in Calcutta, Mukerjee organized adult evening schools, as a part of the National Education movement's outreach to those who were marginalized and in poverty (Mukerjee 1997: 69). Direct involvement with the Independence movement and India's postcolonial renaissance would remain an important theme in the development of Mukerjee's social theories.

Continuing his education at the University of Calcutta, Mukerjee earned his MA in 1910 and his PhD in 1920; and also taught there from 1917–1921. He took a position at Lucknow University, becoming founder and chair of the Department of Economics and Sociology from 1921 to 1952 and later the vice-chancellor from 1955–1957 (Mukerjee 1955; Saksena 1968). In 1948 he also founded, and was director of the J. K. Institute of Sociology and Human Relations until the end of his life. Mukerjee had a distinct and long lasting influence on the department at Lucknow and Indian sociology overall with his interdisciplinary approach and focus on regional sociology: "Under the influence of Radha Kamal Mukerjee, Indian sociologists have developed the distinctive approach of the regional-ecological method in sociology which emphasizes the inter-relationship of geography, social anthropology, social philosophy and economic history (Valien 1954: 223–24). He believed in a historical comparative and institutional method, in combination with attention to the region and an interdisciplinary approach. His methods were innovative, as he himself noted: "[the] inter-disciplinary or rather trans-disciplinary method was introduced by me at Lucknow in the field of the social sciences as early as 1922" (Mukerjee 1997: 154).

Mukerjee has been viewed as one of the leaders of a distinct Lucknow School of Economics and Sociology (Joshi 1986, 1998; Singh 1955; but see Madan [2011] 2013 on whether this should be characterized as such). Visvanathan (2006) notes that, "Members of the Lucknow school of economics and sociology took a holistic view of sociology. Indeed, the very boundaries between today's economics, sociology, and political science have confined them to oblivion, for their sociology constituted, to use Albert Hirschman's term (1981), virtually 'essays in trespassing'" (243). This school of thought expanded Mukerjee's influence to many students who were trained in his regional sociological approach. Mukerjee led students in the theory and methods of regional ecology, working with "many doctorate students for more than three decades." The school engaged with the community as faculty, students and post-graduates conducted rural and urban surveys and assisted with social reforms (1997: 154). Mukerjee assessed the program based on this community work and student research:

> Year by year the best students in Economic and Sociology at the University engaged themselves in research work for MA and doctorate theses based on field investigations. In the course of thirty years of teaching about fifty students qualified themselves for the doctorate degree in Economics and Sociology—the largest number in any Indian University—having collected and collated valuable first-hand data in the vast untilled fields of Indian Economics and Sociology. (1997: 155)

In Mukerjee's inaugural lecture in 1921 he called for a "new school of economic thought and research" (1997: 152). He very clearly connected this with community involvement: "The local problems of peasants of the fields, the labourers of the factories and the artisans of the cottages must be tackled from the barren abstractions of the Colleges" (1997: 151). Previous to this Lucknow School of Economics and Sociology, Mukerjee noted that there had been an overreliance on Western textbook descriptions of social and economic issues rather than a grounding in actual Indian experiences (1997: 119). Therefore, Mukerjee conducted empirical studies of Indian villages and towns and insisted on active involvement of his students to offset the "distortion of Western deductive-abstract theorizing and formulation in the class room" (1997: 119–20). Patel describes the overall mission of the department as combining theory with practice: "the sociology constructed by the members of the group in Lucknow was visionary, analytical, empirical and interdisciplinary. It was oriented toward the present and the future and not the past. It demanded that the discipline be focused on social practice, either as social work or as social policy or as political intervention" (Patel 2002: 275).

Mukerjee's contributions were wide-ranging, assisting in the development of various disciplines in the social sciences and the practice of social reforms in India. Mukerjee founded *The Indian Sociological Review* in 1934 and organized the All India Sociological Conference (AISC) which was later merged with the Indian Sociological Society (ISS), still in existence today (www.insoso.org). He also has been credited for advancing the discipline of economics, and the field of social work in India. Hasan (2010) credits Mukerjee at Lucknow University for institutionalizing social work as a discipline:

> Under the leadership of Dr Radha Kamal Mukerjee, the father of Indian Sociology, social work was emerging as a new profession. Even though it had taken its roots in a few places—Bombay, Varanasi, and Delhi—nowhere in the world was doctoral education available in social work beyond the United States. Lucknow University initiated a PhD in social work in the late 1950s, and two MSW candidates (A. B. Bose and Hira Singh) obtained PhDs under the aegis of the J.K. Institute of Sociology and Human Relations at Lucknow University. Brij Mohan, who joined Lucknow University in 1960, obtained the first PhD degree in the Department of Social Work. (99)

Mukerjee's efforts at connecting the academy to community work and bringing sociological research to practical reforms was recognized by the Indian government. In 1962 Mukerjee was presented with the Padma Bhushan Award, which is one of India's highest awards for civilians. The Padma Bhushan award is given "for distinguished service of high order."

As influential as Mukerjee was in India, he was also well known as a sociologist and economist at a global level. He was invited to lecture in many countries and held key positions in international associations. In 1937, an invitation from Cambridge launched a six-month speaking tour in major cities throughout Europe and the United States international speaking engagements continued throughout Mukerjee's life; in 1948 he travelled to Montreal to serve on an economic committee for the International Labour Organization (ILO). From there he traveled to Harvard to present six different lectures and was also the keynote speaker at the Hindustani Students Conference at Cambridge. While there he visited with long-time colleague, Pitirim A. Sorokin. He then traveled to New York to speak at Columbia

University and NYU and then on to the London School of Economics (Mukerjee 1997: 178–79). He also served as vice-president of the International Institute of Sociology (IIS) (Madan and Gupta 2000). The IIS was created in 1893, is the "oldest continuous sociological association in existence," and still organizes a World Congress every two years (www.iisoc.org). Mukerjee had been an invited presider at the International Congress of Sociology in Paris in 1937. He also served as the editor of the *International Journal of Sociology and Social Research*. He had regular communication with other scholars internationally through his many committee positions and informal meetings (Madan and Gupta 2000).

Despite his secure place as one of founders of Indian Sociology with an international reputation, Madan (2011) argues that recognition of Mukerjee even within India has been diminished, with several books out of print and rarely featured in India's curriculum. Joshi (1986) chronicles how later generations "relegated into oblivion the rich legacy of the pioneers" of the Lucknow School. He claims that by the 1960s the Lucknow School's multidisciplinary approach fell out of fashion in the social sciences in India, giving way to increasing specialization (1456). However, Joshi's work and others such as Madan's (2013) on the Lucknow School have helped restore interest in his past contributions and a renewed appreciation for an interdisciplinary, regional approach (Sundar, Deshpande, and Uberoi 2000; Visvanathan 2006). There also are ongoing tributes, such as the Radha Kamal Mukerjee Endowment Fund that has sponsored an annual memorial lecture in his honor since 2010. Additionally, several commemorative books have been published in India on Mukerjee's work (Hasan 1971; Husain 1973; Loomba and Madan 1987; Madan 1997; Singh 1955; Thakur 2014).

Some clarifying points need to be made concerning Mukerjee being a forgotten founder. Mukerjee was an international scholar, and well known in the West. But when discussing the canon in sociology, the sources that might identify significant theorists are primarily textbooks and histories of the discipline. There has been a distinctly narrow Euro-American white, male bias, focusing on the likes of Auguste Comte, Herbert Spencer, Karl Marx, Emile Durkheim, and Max Weber from Europe, later expanding to include American sociologists such as C. W. Mills and Talcott Parsons. Not until relatively recently have women and theorists of color such as Harriet Martineau, Jane Addams and W. E. B. Du Bois been acknowledged (Deegan 1986, 1998, 2003; Wright II 2006, 2008). In most Western textbooks and histories, consideration of those outside of the West is exceedingly rare.

Mukerjee himself noted a Western bias in the social sciences: "A great defect in logical analysis in sociology arises on account of the neglect of wider cultural groups, or types which comprehend the entire life of races and regions other than the purely Euro-American and whose rich social and economic experiments have a no less significance in the evolution of world life"

(Mukerjee 1926: 22–23). His own work was not only interdisciplinary, but also framed with a critical postcolonial perspective. Both of these positions were a challenge to most of mainstream sociology and may help explain the erasure of his contributions in the Western canon. In 1938 Mukerjee provided an essay on the contributions of Indian Sociology for the second volume of *Social Thought from Lore to Science* (Valien 1954). Despite his contribution, Mukerjee was himself forgotten as a part of this history.

Aside from the Eurocentrism of the sociological canon, I argue that Mukerjee has also been forgotten because his vision of human ecology differed from the dominant conception that emerged from Park and Burgess' model of the city and their framing of human ecology. Their version of human ecology in particular has remained in the canon as an influence whereas the ideas of others, like Mukerjee, are ignored. However, his conception of human ecology is nonetheless insightful and should be acknowledged as a significant contribution to this subfield, along with many of his other theoretical works.

SUMMARY OF WORKS/CONTRIBUTIONS

Mukerjee was widely published in the top sociology journals, including *The American Journal of Sociology*, *The Sociological Review*, *Social Forces*, and the *American Sociological Review*. He also published numerous books, many with publishers in the UK and US such as *Regional Sociology* (1926); *Man and His Habitation: A Study in Social Ecology* (1940); *The Institutional Theory of Economics* (1942a); *Social Ecology* (1942b); and *The Destiny of Civilization* (1964). Mukerjee's books covered a range of topics, from economics, value systems, social psychology, regional sociology, social ecology, spirituality, art, literature and culture. He was a pioneering thinker in many of these areas. His first book *The Foundations of Indian Economics* (1916) was written when he was 27 years old; the introduction was provided by the well-known Scottish sociologist, ecologist and urban planner Patrick Geddes (Madan [2011] 2013). Many of Mukerjee's books were well received and reviewed by prominent sociologists, for instance, E. A. Ross wrote the preface for *Regional Sociology* and Robert E. Park reviewed it in *AJS* (1926). Park claimed that, compared to others, Mukerjee provided empirical data to back up his theory:

> [M]an's relation to his environment have been subjected to a searching analysis by the professor of economics and sociology in Lucknow University, India, Radhakamal Mukerjee. On the basis of this analysis he has constructed a program for systematic studies which he has called regional sociology. Mukerjee's regional sociology outlines, in fact, a program of scientific studies more

comprehensive than anything else that has yet been attempted in this field. (489)

In his work Muukerjee addressed a broad range of topics, but here I will provide a short summary of the major areas he contributed to that relate directly to sociological theory and concepts. He also wrote extensively on spirituality, which I do not address in this chapter. I will instead summarize five main areas of Mukerjee's contributions to theory: Regional Sociology, Comparative Economics, Culture, Values, and Social Ecology.

Regional Sociology

Regional Sociology (1926) was one of Radhakamal Mukerjee's major theoretical books. His regional theory was grounded in empirical data he had gathered over eight years. In 1918 Mukerjee embarked on three months of field research and a lecture tour in South India focusing on "the social effects of industrialisation and the unsettlement of the village communities" (1955: 9). From his time observing the communal organization of villages and towns in South India Mukerjee claimed, "It was here that the conceptions of Regionalism in Sociology and the distinctive regional pattern of Rural Communalism in Economics were clearly defined in my mind" (1955: 9). His approach incorporating geography into socioeconomic considerations was influenced by region, although not in a deterministic manner. As he cautioned,

> a merely geographical classification of peoples according to the regions which they inhabit will be too superficial and shallow, though the regional influences, of course, enter as a valid formative factor in the form of economic tradition into the evolution of peoples and their zones. The geographical explanation must not be carried too far. For man can overcome geographical facts in a way to which the rest of the animal world has no parallel. (1926: 94)

One aspect of Mukerjee's regionalism was a focus on sustainability and local, technological alternatives. This was in contrast with the dominant Western idea of modernity and development at the time. Mukerjee felt that the Western model of development was unsustainable and exploitative, contrary to the goals of regional planning: "Regional planning would not accept only the pecuniary valuation of technology and economy but recognises human values as the ultimate product of the regional adjustment" (Mukerjee 1942b: 317). He proposed that by understanding regional differences, the management of resources might be better tailored to unique needs, rather than abstract generic, technological solutions:

> Regionalism aims at a continuity of this vast current of resources, energies and services for the permanence of the community through conservation and implementation, not through exploitation, and the transformation of these resources, energies and services into higher and higher values furnishing a permanent dynamics for human culture, free from the artificiality and emptiness of the technological society. (Mukerjee 1942b: 317–18)

The historical comparative method was used by Mukerjee for theory building (similar to many other founders), and Mukerjee incorporated his extensive knowledge of Eastern and Western economics and sociocultural differences to understand the significance of regions. He felt that India's pattern of communal socioeconomics did not fit into Western economic schemes, stating that: "This was characterised by me as Rural Communalism that I differentiated from Capitalism or Socialism of the West" (Mukerjee 1955: 9). Despite the idea of regionalism originating from his study of Indian rural communalism, the theoretical concept was one that was also meant to be applied to other countries. Mukerjee saw the village model as offering potential for blending rural-urban planning. He was not alone in understanding the generalizability of this theory, for instance the American sociologist H. W. Odum recognized Mukerjee's influence in his own 1938 book, *American Regionalism*. During Mukerjee's 1937 speaking tour, Odum introduced Mukerjee's talk at Columbia University on "The Ecological Movement in Sociology" (Mukerjee 1997: 172–73). Robert E. Park rightly noted that Mukerjee's idea of regional sociology not only dealt with geography and human relations but also provides a larger ecological theoretical perspective. As Park (1926) said of Mukerjee's work:

> To the studies of plant and animal communities, arising out of the characteristic conditions of a natural region, the new science of regional sociology proposes to add the study of the human community. Just as plant formations and animal communities are determined not merely by their physical environment but by their relations to one another—by their 'collective co-operation,' as Mukerjee calls it—so the human community is determined not merely by physiology and climate, but by the plant and animal communities which with it constitute the regional complex. In other words, the geographical region and the web of life within that region has been made the subject of a new division of the social sciences. (489)

The theoretical concept of region underpinned much of Mukerjee's vast contribution to the sociological and economic literature.

Regional Economics

Mukerjee considered himself to be on the "borderlands" of economics, due to his critique of the field and as a proponent of a new multi-disciplinary approach (Mukerjee 1925). He insisted on a "comparative and regional economics" as a way to accurately capture the social and cultural aspects of economics. He cites as an influence in developing this approach the Indian philosopher Brajendra Nath Seal due to his use of the comparative method combined with an interest and expertise in many fields (1955: 15). Consulting with Seal on earlier book drafts, Mukerjee published *The Foundations of Indian Economics* (1916). In 1917 Mahatma Gandhi presided over a lecture by Mukerjee, and afterwards commented on his agreement with the principles and necessary practices of economic regionalism that Mukerjee had presented (Mukerjee 1997: 123).

Mukerjee proposed the idea of economic Institutionalism, yet distinguished this from what was known as American Institutionalism at the time. As he stated, "The methods of Indian Institutionalism are largely comparative and sociological, rather than historical and statistical" (Mukerjee 1997: 130). Mukerjee also rejected an individualist model of economics and felt that economics was moving toward a more holistic approach: "More and more Institutionalism, Regionalism and Cooperativism are asserting themselves in Indian economic thought and planning for both the theoretical framework and practical economic direction and guidance" (1997: 133).

Underlying social issues that are still relevant today had been critically explored by Mukerjee early on. Papola (2015) claims that Mukerjee's *The Indian Working Class* (1945), based on two decades of fieldwork in India, still stands the test of time. In that work, Mukerjee explained that the reason for his focus on economics and the working class stemmed from a concern with inequalities and his own history in forming adult evening classes for the working classes of Calcutta (Mukerjee 1945: xi). From 1954 to 1955, Mukerjee and Baljit Singh conducted extensive socioeconomic surveys of Gorakhpur, a medium sized town, and Lucknow, the second largest city and capital of Utter Pradesh at the time. These surveys were funded by the Research Programmes Committee of the Planning Commission and were conducted by a team of field workers, supervisors and statisticians, some of whom were post graduates of the Lucknow School of Economics and Sociology. The findings were published in *Social Profiles of a Metropolis* (Mukerjee and Singh 1961). The end results of Mukerjee's theories were meant to improve quality of life for marginalized people, rather than being simply abstract formulations: "The basic aim of social science that emerged and that urged me in all separate social investigations was the planning and building up of the Indian society and institutions and the mitigation of Indian social and economic ills—unemployment, poverty, casteism, and illiteracy—all at that time felt to be basically connected with imperialism" (Mukerjee 1997: 68–69).

Social reforms were a focus of his work throughout Mukerjee's life as he sought to use social theories to help mitigate the social problems brought on by poor planning for the needs of inhabitants of towns and cities. He edited a volume, *Social Sciences and Planning in India*, from a conference that he organized in 1965 on the topic. He believed that insights from the full range of the social sciences had been left out of planning, and that urban/rural planning was tilted toward a skewed understanding of economic/industrial advance. Instead, "planning has to accept and implement such norms and standards of justice, equality and self-clarity for economic decisions and policies. Accordingly, the impact of the entire range of social sciences on planning and planners cannot but be democratizing and equalizing" (Mukerjee 1970: 10).

Planning for socioeconomic equality in Mukerjee's work included an emphasis on cooperative organizations as a solution to social and economic problems: "Where resources of organized community life are lacking in a region, a good deal may be accomplished by a rational mode of coöperative organization, as seen in the movements of school consolidation and church federation, agricultural coöperation and coöperative production and use of electric and other power in the countryside" (Mukerjee 1926: 206–7). Chauhan (1997) said of Mukerjee that, "His enthusiasm and hope relating to the Cooperative movement seems . . . rooted in the dignity of man and its innate capability for collective betterment of life" (237). This was not a utopian idea but one rooted in the cooperative movement that was flourishing in post-independence India. Mukerjee himself was very involved in this movement, as he describes of his time in 1910 in Bengal, where he took on the role of "Honorary Organiser of Co-operative Societies for the District and started a network of village banks with an agricultural demonstration plot and an evening school at the headquarters of the Co-operative Union" (1955: 7). Mukerjee used this experience to push for reforms through the creation of "experiments with co-operatives for village rehabilitation, starting agricultural supply and cattle improvement societies for which new bylaws were drafted for approval and sanction by Government" (1955: 7).

While most of Mukerjee's work was informed by his experiences during the Indian post-Independence period, he also insisted on the global generalizability of his theories, viewing his economic theories as providing a model that allowed for specific cultural differences and adaptions but providing economic justice on an international scale: "If I have deviated from the well-trodden path of the classical economists, and seem to strike an idealistic note in my insistence on social and communal values as decisive and determining factors of economic organisations, it is only as a part of the contribution of Indian culture to the world-scheme of life, which cannot be fulfilled without the confluence of such tributaries from the various streams of life. . . . I seek to outline a scheme of cooperative internationalism consistent with regional self- determination in the world-distribution of capital, labour and industry" (Mukerjee 1921: xxv). Mukerjee's work here has been recognized in the area of institutional economics and he stayed true to his synthesis of sociological and spiritual concerns: "The Theory of Institutions is a tool for economic and non-economic facts, values and institutions and the unity of social sciences are basic in my theoretical systems" (Mukerjee 1997: 131).

Value Systems

The concern with values also was interwoven in Mukerjee's theories and elaborated specifically in several lectures and publications compiled in his *The Social Structure of Values* (Mukerjee 1949). Some scholars compared this work with Talcott Parsons's *The Social System* (1951), while noting the significant differences. Manuel Gottlieb maintained of Parsons's and Mukerjee's theories on values: "It is of course accidental that at approximately the same time two of the most creative figures in the contemporary social sciences should have attempted systematic expositions of their theoretical systems" (1955: 96). Gottlieb claims that both approaches have their strengths, but with Parsons's work missing the ecological, regional perspective provided by Mukerjee. Gottlieb also noted that value systems had long been a concern for both theorists: "The common stress on value-orientations and on social man as a valuing creature was already prominent in the writings of the two men in the Thirties. Both authors employ a tripartite breakdown of value-orientations. But Mukerjee's breakdown—into values, ideals and norms—is both very persuasively argued and appears to weave a richer fabric of meaning" (Gottlieb 1955: 96). Saramma Thomas also made a theoretical comparison of the two theorists, claiming that "Mukerjee's idea as to how to build a theoretical system is almost contrary to Parsons'[s]. His work is comprehensive in range and distinguished by its generalizations. . . . On the whole Mukerjee's work shows a rich generalization with broad learning. His works also show a rare combination of first-hand observation of social reality and skillful use of theoretic literature" (1971: 3). Another difference that becomes apparent can be found in the roots of Mukerjee's theory of values as more spiritual than biological or psychological as evident in Parsons's theory. Writing in the Preface to his *The Destiny of Civilization* (1964), Mukerjee makes a similar point:

> Contemporary social science in dealing with society and civilization is deflected by the archaic premises and presuppositions of both biology and psychology. It exaggerates man's drive and tension-reduction and opportunistic adjustment at the bio-social dimension, and neglects value-seeking and value-experience. It altogether overlooks the emergent multi-dimen-

sional character of his adjustment and values and his native oneness with life, society and cosmos. (1964: vii)

The recognition of Parsons as part of the sociological canon while Mukerjee is largely forgotten appears to be based on the social location of the theorist. Social theorists have referred specifically to an East/West dichotomy to explain different worldviews; however, it is important to take into account the extent to which these have also been distorted or exaggerated. Mukerjee himself addressed the East/West social location distinction many times as part of his historical comparative and regional method. There is also an existing literature on the idea of "styles" of science as opposed to a universal way of doing science (Abend 2006; Graham and Kantor 2006; Harwood 1987). However, there is not always a simple division based on style alone and differences must be explained in a more complex sociohistorical fashion. Charles Camic (2008) and Neil Gross (2008) have both promoted such an approach in their historical research on the development of theoretical ideas. In this vein Joshi (1986) explains that the "roots of the Lucknow School and its founders alike were deep in anti-colonial national awakening which expressed itself in the intellectual and cultural as well as political spheres" (1457).

Although well-versed in sociological theories of the West, Mukerjee was also steeped in Eastern thought. He challenged Western writers on their characterization of the East, bringing a decidedly postcolonialist viewpoint to his thinking. Yet, Mukerjee was by no means a cultural relativist and believed there were common human values and the possibility for universal and "transcendent evolution." In *The Destiny of Civilization* (1964) he described what he calls a new science of "Geo-civilization" where he connects his ideas of regional sociology to larger shared values:

> [Geo-civilization] will reject the one-sided, Western unilinear view of the development of mankind that postulates each civilization as a discrete stage or phase in the historical series. It will adopt instead the multilinear view of cultural evolution in which the major civilizations are envisaged as maturing and developing on parallel lines, historically and logically. Civilizations become divergent, due to the manifold, accumulated forces of region, race and history, but show a common trend. In the broad march of human history each major civilization contributes in its own manner toward universal values and experiences. (1964: 113)

Mukerjee's ideas of evolution incorporated Indian spiritual beliefs and he promoted a humanism that was influenced by an Eastern perspective as found in his major book on the subject: *The Way of Humanism, East and West* (1968).

Culture, Art, and Literature

It is clear that Mukerjee's theories were in many ways ahead of their time. For instance, he published several books and articles on the sociology of art, which has only recently become a subfield in sociology (Foster and Blau 1989; de la Fuente 2007; Tanner 2003; Zolberg 1990). Mukerjee's work has rarely been mentioned in these works; however, Foster and Blau, in their reader on the topic, cite him four times including in a section devoted to writings on sociology of the arts worldwide. Mukerjee is mentioned there in one line as: "Interest in the sociology of art in India goes back at least forty years to the work of Radhakamal Mukerjee." This quotation suggests that Mukerjee's contribution was merely on the art of India, but the book of his that is referenced, *The Social Function of Art*, formulates a sociological theory that is meant to explain art as a universal phenomenon. Tanner's (2003) reader on the subfield cites theorists such as Marx, Weber, Simmel, Durkheim, Habermas, Bourdieu, Parsons, and others, but ignores Mukerjee altogether. An interesting way to understand this absence is through the social construction of the canon offered by Zolberg (1990) on the subfield's emergence in the 1980s:

> Considering the ubiquity and omnipresence of the arts in all known human societies and the varied individual and social functions they seem to serve, it is strange that until relatively recently sociologists, and American ones in particular, have not incorporated them into the center of their intellectual concerns. The reasons for this gap have a great deal to do with the development of sociology in the United States because for various reasons, some circumstantial, others arguably systemic, American sociology came to dominate sociology as a whole for several decades. Examining the scholarly foundations on which sociology came to be modeled reveals how the arts ended up being virtually excluded from its purview. (1990: 29)

Foster and Blau (1989) also state that American sociology ignored art from the 1920s onward, and then appears to conflate this with the entire field of sociology. Ironically, when Mukerjee embarked on outlining his conception of the sociology of art as a social function in his book on the topic in 1948, and also in earlier articles, he noted:

> A fruitful, but neglected approach to art is the sociological. The sociology of art brings under its purview the social relations of forms and motifs of art. Artistic activity is dominated by the sense of norms and values, and these are largely of social origin. On the other hand, art as individual creative expression clarifies and in some measure reshapes and determines social values. As one manifestation of human aspiration and experience, art is woven into the scheme of values and general pattern of collective living and culture of the people. Art also remoulds the prevailing thought processes, values and ideals of society. (Mukerjee 1948: 30)

In addition to his prolific career of publishing in academic outlets, Mukerjee was also involved in what was termed "proletariat literature." He was editor of the Bengali magazine, *Upasana*, and wrote articles on the consciousness of the masses. He also wrote a novel and a play in this vein of literature as well (Mukerjee 1955: 7). Offering a translated passage of a book he had written on modern Bengali literature, Mukerjee describes the need to "rescue art from the emptiness and artificiality of a Western drawing room atmosphere, expand and deepen it so that it can renew and be renewed by the sympathetic resonance of the multitude" (Mukerjee 1955: 8). This concern for social reform, including outreach to the public through non-academic writing, is similar to other previously forgotten theorists, such as Charlotte Perkins Gilman and W. E. B. Du Bois. Writing for a popular audience in the service of a social cause has at times been a reason for overlooking these theorists in the sociological canon. Yet the idea of a public scholar has become more accepted currently, and these theorists fit this model. All three were editors and authors of literary works that spoke to social movements of their time. Mukerjee recounts his involvement with these movements in India:

> A whole host of new writers in Bengal in the post-Rabindra Nath [*sic*] period have shown a poignant sympathy for the have-nots, a profound sense of social justice and compassion as well as a capacity to deal with the new social scenes and situations from the under-world. A proletariat literature is now emerging in Bengal. As the Editor for many years of the North Indian Bengali monthly "Uttara," I welcomed this development in many articles. (Mukerjee 1955: 8)

Mukerjee's theoretical ideas were innovative and had a broad influence in both academia and the public sphere. Also, he joins with other previously forgotten scholars whose work addressed everyday struggles and larger social issues.

Social Ecology

Mukerjee viewed himself as one of the early founders of human ecology, which he also referred to as social ecology to encompass an expanded understanding of this concept:

> Social Ecology, as it is now being more rigidly demarcated, is an infant discipline. It is essential, therefore, that usable concepts of plant and animal ecology under which certain types of social phenomena may be classified, and by means of which these may be brought together in a series that may indicate specific social trends, should be precisely defined. Several works have suffered owing to the absence of adequate knowledge and loose use of ecological notions. (Mukerjee 1940: vii)

To further establish himself as one of the founders of this subfield he traces his previous work in this field in his 1942 book, *Social Ecology*:

> Social Ecology is a vast and virgin field orienting social phenomena on the basis of the give-and-take between life, mind and region. It may be permissible to refer to three previous works of mine in which some aspects of Social Ecology will be found treated in greater detail than here. In my *Regional Sociology* (1926) I defined Human Ecology as the study of social behaviour with reference to conditioning environmental circumstances and indicated the social psychology of regionalism. (1942b: xv)

Mukerjee continued by discussing other works, such as *The Regional Balance of Man: An Ecological Theory of Population* (1938); *Man and His Habitation: A Study in Social Ecology* (1940). He also claimed that the book *Social Ecology* would, "contribute to a scientific classification of social-ecological concepts and to the development of a methodology according to which Social Ecology may form the basis of a new functional and quantitative Sociology" (1942b: xv). Guha (1994) said of the distinct approach developed by Mukerjee:

> In a series of books and articles written in the interwar period, Mukerjee fleshed out his theory of "social ecology." . . . He drew fascinating parallels between ecological influences on the plant, animal, and human worlds respectively. While eschewing ecological determinism, he illuminated the influence of the "web of life" on human economic, political and social relations. Finally, Mukerjee tested his theoretical ideas through empirical studies of different geographical regions. (12)

In James A. Quinn's 1940 summary of the human ecology literature, Mukerjee's work is included as significant. However, the sociological canon has since focused almost solely on Park and Burgess, claiming that the first mention of the concept was in their *Introduction to the Science of Sociology* (1921). Park subsequently developed the idea further, particularly to describe urban settings. It is interesting to note that Park visited Mukerjee in Lucknow to discuss Human Ecology, and Mukerjee used Park's office at the University of Chicago when he was there as a visiting lecturer and Park was away on leave (Mukerjee 1955; 1997). Also, during a speaking tour of the United States, Mukerjee visited the University of Chicago and met with Burgess, Faris, Ogburn, Shaw and McKay. He described his reaction to a seminar held with students on Human Ecology: "I did not at all conceal my surprise that the Department of Sociology was pre-occupied with social pathological problems, giving little attention to the normal community structure and process" (Mukerjee 1997: 174). Mukerjee went on to detail the fundamental differences between American Human Ecology and his own:

> The lines and methods of human ecological investigation adopted by me have been somewhat different. These include of course the analysis of patterns of spatial distribution of population and of social and economic classes and occupations. . . . But I have laid greater stress on the broader scientific aspects of Social Ecology as the comprehensive science of the vital balance and solidarity of the region. The laws, structures and processes of population have subserved the more comprehensive laws of ecologic balance and inter-change. (1997: 210–12)

Mukerjee claimed that his view of social ecology was more concerned with "ecological complexity and conservation" than the American human ecologists, and by comparison he probably had more in common with the Chicago Ecology group of the time. In his 1937 six-month speaking tour in the United States and the United Kingdom, he met with W. C. Allee and other ecologists at the University of Chicago as well as other significant ecologists in the UK (Gross 2004; Mitman 1992; Worster 1985). It is Mukerjee's wider conceptual use of ecology that makes his theory more significant for understanding current environmental concerns and sustainable solutions.

Mukerjee's Social Ecology and Sustainability

I would argue that overall Radhakamal Mukerjee's theories have continued relevance and can be successfully applied to many contemporary issues. I would, however, maintain that his theory of Social or Human Ecology, just described, is especially timely, and that his unique approach incorporates his related concerns with culture, region and values.

Mukerjee's theory of social ecology can be applied to a broad range of contemporary issues including the disappearance of farmland, the impoverishment of rural areas, environmental degradation, and a need for sustainable solutions to address global environmental crises such as climate change. His theory shifts the sociological perception of human ecology to fit more closely with current critical human ecologists such as York and Mancus (2009). Accepting Mukerjee's conception into the canon in the subfield of human ecology would provide a tradition to draw from for theorists who wish to incorporate the significance of the natural environment for understanding human society. This is not the typical theoretical version of human ecology that employs the concept of nature in a merely metaphorical fashion, such as the notion of "natural areas" to characterize sections of the city. This overly narrow urban-centered approach to human ecology provided only a limited explanation to describe the relationship between humans and their actual natural environment according to Mukerjee: "A fresh drawback in American ecology arises from the American pre-occupation with urban settlements and communities. There is a wide gap between the ecological approach to wild nature in the U.S.A." (1955: 17). Mukerjee felt that the discipline's decision to ignore the significance of nature in understanding societies leads to a serious imbalance:

> Social science hardly comprehends that human life and welfare in a long vista are interlocked in a subtle, ramifying web of relations with earth and organic nature or that man himself is part and parcel of the process by which the balance of the region is maintained and shifted, and the process is ever continued in see-saw fashion, now in favour of man, now definitely against him. Ecology guides and warns human culture in the long perspective of its prosperity and ruin, its exploitative outburst and recurrent defeat. Often has mankind's unwise, short-sighted and exploitative land-water culture led to disaster and extermination in the hands of revengeful nature. Civilization even in a scientific age is heedless in its ignorance, selfishness and improvidence. (1955: 17–18)

From 1922 to 1930, Mukerjee lectured at universities and governmental committees on the issue of sustainability and the need for agricultural reform, including "cooperative irrigation, agricultural cooperation" and "forestry and river conservancy" (1997: 155). He addressed both the need for forest reserves to save farm land from desertification and the plight of farmers displaced by socioeconomic pressures of the land system (1997: 156–57). Mukerjee's idea of regional ecological sociology maintains the need for local indigenous diversity and a belief that humans should live in closer balance with the natural environment. More than simply appreciating the natural environment, Mukerjee called for sustainable practices in regard to planning for human societies, claiming that societies needed to "apply the synthetic ecological principles for building up a new social economy based on a more scientific, practical and humane utilization of the environmental and human resources, if civilization is not to be weighted down by perpetual want and the recurrence of natural and agricultural calamities" (1955: 18). Mukerjee understood the neglect of the rural as a valid ecological area of study to be a modern Western bias (Mukerjee 1926, 1940), relegating his conception of regional sociology to the status of being the rural stepchild of urban sociology. However, he defended his regional social ecological approach as a superior model for shaping both urban and rural areas into more sustainable societies and ensuring that rural communities could thrive: "Applied social ecology today demands the utilisation of the culture and traditions of the rural community, which are now wasted and destroyed by the urban community" (Mukerjee 1940: 278–96).

Mukerjee also was an advocate of "rurbanization," a concept developed by Charles Galpin in 1918 to reflect a blending of the urban and rural that results when urban populations are dispersed into rural areas. Mukerjee goes further and calls for regional planning that emphasizes rural areas over urban ones. Although critical of technology and communication systems under modern capitalism, Mukerjee argues that these could be employed in a less exploitative way. Similar to the urban planning of Patrick Geddes, Mukerjee did not envision a return to a time without technology. Rather, he advocated for technology to be distributed in a more equitable fashion and to be more sustainable through a regional approach: "Regionalism is essentially the art of linking ecological, technological and cultural development in terms of stability and survival of resources, community and culture" (1942b: 316–17).

Mukerjee was interested in viewing humans as a part of the larger environment alongside plants and animals, with an eye toward conservation of resources and sustainable city planning. Having been involved in the Indian independence movement and concrete urban reforms, Mukerjee saw his regional social ecological approach to be a vital part of a broader attempt to suggest remedies for a variety of social ills, including conservation of the environment (Joshi 1998):

> Co-operation, scientific and broad-minded, with the ecologic forces which have stamped the region with a unity and individuality ought to be the keynote of the future. The conservation of soil, water and food, the economy of man's food and energy circulation, the protection of the earth's mantle of trees and grasses, the selection and crossing of crops, trees and animals, the biological control or eradication of diseases, pests and parasites, the utilization of all kinds of organic wastage, permanent agriculture, the conservation of water supply and the training and management of rivers and water courses, a nicely adjusted occupational balance which may best utilize the resources and possibilities of different sections of the region and the skill and aptitudes of the people—all this is social ecology. (1942b: 352)

Reading Mukerjee induces a shock of recognition at the relevance of his work for understanding the social conditions experienced in contemporary society. It is not only his pioneering vision on social ecology that calls for bringing Mukerjee back into the theoretical canon, but also his ideas on region, economics, values and culture. Radhakamal provided a critical, yet hopeful and practical, theoretical perspective that deserves to be reconsidered.

WORKS CITED

Abend, Gabriel. 2006. "Styles of Sociological Thought: Sociologies, Epistemologies, and the Mexican and U.S. Quest for Truth." *Sociological Theory* 24: 1–41.
Alihan, Milla A. 1938. *Social Ecology: A Critical Analysis.* New York: Columbia University.
Bulmer, Martin. 1985. "The Chicago School of Sociology: What Made it a 'School'?" *History of Sociology* 5 (2): 61–77.
Camic, Charles. 2008. "The History of Sociology as a Bi-Focal Project (Part 1)." *Timelines* 12: 1–2.

Chauhan, D. S. 1997. "Homage to Professor Radhakamal Mukerjee" Pp. 229–36 in *India: The Dawn of a New Era* by Radhakamal Mukerjee (posthumously). New Delhi: Radha Publications.

Deegan. Mary Jo. 1986. *Jane Addams and the Men of the Chicago School 1892–1918.* New Brunswick, NJ: Transaction Books.

———. 1998. "Theory and Methods in Historical Sociology: Changing the Canon." *American Sociological Association.* San Francisco, CA.

———. 2003. "Textbooks, the History of Sociology, and the Sociological Stock of Knowledge." *Sociological Theory* 21 (3): 298–305.

de la Fuente, Eduardo. 2007. The 'New Sociology of Art" Putting Art Back into Social Science Approaches to the Arts." *Cultural Sociology* 1 (3): 409–425.

Foster, Arnold W., and Judith R. Blau, eds. 1989. *Art and Society: Readings in the Sociology of the Arts.* Albany, NY: SUNY Press.

Gottlieb, Manuel. 1955. "Parsons and Mukerjee: An Essay on Ecological Analysis in Social Thought." Pp. 96–114 in *The Frontiers of Social Science: In Honour of Radakamal Mukerjee*, edited by Baljit Singh. London: Macmillan & Co.

Graham, Loren, and Jean-Michel Kantor. 2006. "A Comparison of Two Cultural Approaches to Mathematics: France and Russia, 1890–1930." *The History of Science Society* 97: 56–74.

Gross, Matthias. 2004. "Human Geography and Ecological Sociology: The Unfolding of a Human Ecology, 1890 to 1930—and Beyond." *Social Science History* 28 (4): 575–605.

Gross, Neil. 2008. *Richard Rorty: The Making of an American Philosopher.* Chicago: University of Chicago Press.

Guha, Ramachandra. 1994. "Introduction." In *Social Ecology*, edited by Ramachandra Guha. Delhi: Oxford University Press.

Harwood, Jonathan. 1987. "National Styles in Science: Genetics in Germany and the United States between the World Wars." *Isis* 78 (3): 390–414.

Hasan, Saiyid Zafar. 1971. *Research in Sociology and Social Work: Radhakamal Mukerjee Memorial Volume.* Lucknow: Department of Sociology and Social Work, University of Lucknow.

———. 2010. "Brij Mohan: The Evolution of a Social Scientist." *Journal of Comparative Social Welfare* 26 (2–3): 99–106.

Hawley, Amos. 1950. *Human Ecology: A Theory of Community Structure.* New York: Ronald Press.

Husain, Ishrat Z. 1973. *Population Analysis and Studies: Radhakamal Mukerjee Commemoration Volume.* Tunbridge Wells: Abacus Press.

Jayaram N. 2014. "Against Fragmentation: Radhakamal Mukerjee's Philosophy of Social Science." *Sociological Bulletin* 63 (1): 4–20.

Joshi, P. C. 1986. "Founders of the Lucknow School and Their Legacy: Radhakamal Mukerjee and D. P. Mukerji: Some Reflections." *Economic and Political Weekly* 21 (33): 1455–1469.

———. 1998. "Lucknow School of Economics and Sociology and Its Relevance Today: Some Reflections." *Sociological Bulletin* 35: 1–28.

Lengermann, Patricia Madoo, and Gillian Niebrugge-Brantley. 1998. *The Women Founders: Sociology and Social Theory 1830–1930, A Text Reader.* New York: McGraw-Hill.

Loomba, Ram Murti, and Gurmukh Ram Madan. 1987. *Society and Culture: In Honour of Late Dr. Radhakamal Mukherjee.* Ahmedabad, India: Allied Publishers.

Madan, Gurmukh Ram. 1979. *Western Sociologists on Indian Society: Marx, Spencer, Weber, Durkheim, Pareto.* London/Boston, MA: Routledge & Kegan Paul Ltd.

———. 1997. "Preface" pp. 13–20 in *India: The Dawn of a New Era* by Radhakamal Mukerjee (posthumously). New Delhi:Radha Publications.

Madan, Gurmukh Ram, and V. P. Gupta, eds. 2000. *Integral Sociology: An Anthology of the Writings of Prof. Radha Kamal Mukerjee. Vol. 1–4.* New Delhi: Radha Publications.

Madan, T. N. 2011. *Sociological Traditions: Methods and Perspectives in the Sociology of India.* New Delhi: SAGE Publications.

———. [2011] 2013. "Radhakamal Mukerjee and His Contemporaries: Founding Fathers of Sociology in India." In *Readings in Indian Sociology: Volume X: Pioneers of Sociology in India*, edited by Ishwar Modi. SAGE Publishing India.

———. 2013. *Sociology at the University of Lucknow: The First Half Century (1921–1975)*. Oxford University Press.
Mitman, Gregg. 1992. *The State of Nature: Ecology, Community, and American Social Thought, 1900–1950*. Chicago: University of Chicago Press.
Mukerjee, Radhakamal. 1916. *The Foundations of Indian Economics*. London: Longmans, Green.
———. 1921–1922. *Principles of Comparative Economics*. London: P.S. Ling & Son.
———. 1925. *Borderlands of Economics*. London: George Allen & Unwin Ltd.
———. 1926. *Regional Sociology*. New York: The Century Co.
———. 1932. "The Ecological Outlook in Sociology." *American Journal of Sociology* 38 (3): 349–55.
———. 1938. *The Regional Balance of Man*.
———. 1940. *Man and His Habitation: A Study in Social Ecology*. New York: Longmans, Green, and Co.
———. 1942a. *The Institutional Theory of Economics*. London: MacMillan & Co.
———. 1942b. *Social Ecology*. London: Longmans, Green, and Co.
———. 1945. *The Indian Working Class*. Bombay: Hind Kitabs Ltd.
———. 1948. *The Social Function of Art*. Bombay: Hind Kitabs Ltd.
———. 1949. *The Social Structure of Values*. London: Macmillan & Co.
———. 1955. "Faith and Influences." Pp. 3–20 in: *The Frontiers of Social Science: In Honour of Radakamal Mukerjee*, edited by Baljit Singh. London: Macmillan & Co.
———. 1964. *The Destiny of Civilization*. London: Asia Publishing House.
———. 1997. *India: The Dawn of a New Era*. New Delhi: Radha Publications.
———. 1968. *The Way of Humanism: East and West*. Bombay, New Delhi: Academic Books.
———. 1970. *Social Sciences and Planning in India*. London: Asia Publishing House.
Mukerjee, Radhakamal, and Baljit Singh. 1961. *Social Profiles of a Metropolis*. Bombay: Asia Publishing House.
Odum, H. W. 1938. *American Regionalism*. NY: Henry Holt and Co.
Papola, T. S. 2015. "Radha Kamal Mukerjee and The Indian Working Class: Seventy Years in Retrospect." *Indian Journal of Labour Economics* 58 (1): 99–117.
Park, Robert E. 1926. "Review." *American Journal of Sociology* 32 (3): 486–90.
Park, Robert E., and Ernest W. Burgess. 1921. *Introduction to the Science of Society*. Chicago: University of Chicago Press.
Parsons, Talcott 1951. *The Social System*. Glencoe, IL: Free Press.
Patel, Sujata. 2002. "The Profession and its Association: Five Decades of the Indian Sociological Society." *International Sociology* 17 (2): 269–84.
Quinn, James. 1940. "Topical Summary of Current Literature: On Human Ecology." *American Journal of Sociology*. 46 (2): 191–226.
Saksena R. N. 1968. "Radha Kamal Mukerjee [1189–1968]." *Sociological Bulletin* 17 (2): ii–iv.
Singh Baljit, ed. 1955. *The Frontiers of Social Science: In Honour of Radakamal Mukerjee*. London: Macmillan & Co.
Smith, David A. 1995. "The New Sociology Meets the Old: Rereading Classical Human Ecology." *Urban Affairs Review* 30 (3): 432–57.
Sundar, Nandini, Satish Deshpande, and Patricia Uberoi. 2000. "Indian Anthropology and Sociology: Towards a History." *Economic and Political Weekly* 35 (24): 1998–2002.
Srivastava, H. C. 1967. "Radhakamal Mukerjee's Inter-Disciplinary Method and Frame of Reference in Social Science." *Indian Journal of Social Research* 8: 33–38.
Tanner, Jeremy, ed. 2003. *The Sociology of Art: A Reader*. London: Routledge.
Thakur, Manish. 2014. *The Quest for Indian Sociology: Radhakamal Mukerjee and Our Times*. Rhashtrapati Niwas, Shimla: Indian Institute of Advanced Study.
Thomas, Saramma. 1971. "Parsons and Mukerjee: A Comparative Analysis." MA thesis, North Dakota State University.
Valien, Preston. 1954. "The Status of Sociology in Independent India." *Social Forces* 32 (3): 222–25.

Visvanathan, Shiv. 2006. "Official Hegemony and Contesting Pluralisms." Pp. 239–58 in *World Anthropologies: Disciplinary Transformations Within Systems of Power*, edited by Gustavo Lins Ribeiro and Arturo Escobar. Berg: Oxford University Press.

Wright II, Earl. 2008. "Deferred Legacy! The Continued Marginalization of the Atlanta Sociological Laboratory." *Sociology Compass* 2 (1): 195–207.

———. 2006. "W.E.B. Du Bois and the Atlanta University Studies on the Negro, Revisited." *Journal of African American Studies* 9 (4): 3–17.

Worster, Donald. 1985. *Nature's Economy: A History of Ecological Ideas* Cambridge: Cambridge University Press.

York, Richard, and Philip Mancus. 2009. "Critical Human Ecology: Historical Materialism and Natural Laws." *Sociological Theory* 27 (2): 122–49.

Zolberg, Vera L. 1990. *Constructing a Sociology of the Arts.* Cambridge University Press.

Part II

Other Neglected Social Theorists

Chapter Six

Pitirim A. Sorokin

Integral Science, Global Culture, and Love

Lawrence T. Nichols

BIOGRAPHICAL SKETCH

In the rural far north of Russia, in early 1889, Pitirim Sorokin was born to an artisan Russian father and a peasant Komi mother.[1] The family soon disintegrated. Pitirim's mother died when he was quite young, and subsequently he, along with older brother Vassily and younger brother Prokopy, separated from their still grieving, alcoholic and occasionally abusive father, Alexander. Pitirim and Vassily plied their father's craft in a semi-nomadic life, visiting briefly in local villages to paint and gild churches and their sacred ornaments.[2] Pitirim's formal education was likewise irregular until he was accepted, with scholarship assistance, into the elementary school in Gam, and then, as a young teen, into the Khrenovo Teachers Seminary run by the Holy Synod of the Russian Orthodox Church. There, like many idealistic adolescents, he entered a deeply religious phase, finding inspiration in hagiographic "lives of the saints" and dreaming of an ascetic life of prayer. But gradually he was swept up in the political turmoil of the day, shed his religious views, and became passionately involved in efforts to end tsarist autocracy and create a European-style democracy.[3] Sorokin thus experienced a personal transition from what he would later term an "Ideational" to a "Sensate" culture mentality based on secularism, positivism, socialism and an ideology of linear progress. His political activism led to the first of several arrests, and to his expulsion from the Seminary.

Still imbued with revolutionary fervor, Pitirim pursued the new role of an itinerant evangelist of change and joined a major political party on the left, the peasant-based Social Revolutionaries.[4] As the authorities closed in, he left his native region in 1907 and journeyed to Saint Petersburg, Russia's cultural capital, attending night school in order to qualify for university study. There he entered the privately operated Psycho Neurological Institute, which housed Russia's first department of sociology led by Maxim M. Kovalevsky and E. De Roberty.[5] However, in order to avoid the military draft, he transferred to state-run Saint Petersburg University and its faculty of jurisprudence, where he was strongly influenced by legal scholar Leon Petrazhitsky [6] and also by Ivan Pavlov's researches on conditioned reflexes.

Meanwhile he continued his political activism and became an editor of a Social Revolutionary newspaper, *Narodnaya Volya* ("The People's Will"). Sorokin was elected to the recently established national legislature, the Duma, and in 1917, at age 28, he became a staff member of the Provisional Government (as personal secretary to prime minister Alexander Kerensky), the nation's first democratic governing body, which came into power following the abdication of Tsar Nicholas II. His career in politics came to an abrupt end, however, when the October Revolution swept away the Provisional regime and placed the Bolsheviks at the head of the world's first self-proclaimed "workers' state," the Union of Soviet Socialist Republics.

As he pursued doctoral work in sociology, teaching and publishing empirical research, Sorokin also became involved in subversive activities. Eventually, aware that he was wanted by the Soviet authorities, he turned himself in and was informed that he would be shot as a counter-revolutionary—the same fate that befell his brother Vassily and innumerable others. Fortunately, politically influential former students interceded on his behalf, and after several anxious weeks behind bars and awaiting execution, Sorokin received a reprieve from Vladimir Lenin ([1918] 1971), on the condition that he renounce politics for science.[7]

Several years later, Sorokin took advantage of the government's offer of voluntary emigration and banishment, joining a large stream of highly educated persons who fled to Europe. From 1922 to 1923, he lived in Prague, Czechoslovakia, where he taught social science at Charles University. He then sailed to the United States in order to explore the possibility of an academic career there, leaving behind temporarily his wife, Elena Petrovna Baratynskaya, a university-educated cytologist.[8] Sorokin found a temporary position at Vassar College and subsequently gave public lectures on the Russian revolution at the Universities of Wisconsin and Illinois that were arranged by prominent sociologists Edward A. Ross (Nichols 1996) and E. C. Hayes.[9]

In fall 1924, at age 35, he joined the faculty of the University of Minnesota, whose department of sociology was prominent nationally, with F. Stuart Chapin as its chair and Luther L. Bernard and Edward A. Sutherland among its faculty.[10] There Sorokin also met rural sociologist Carle C. Zimmerman, who would become a coauthor, long-term colleague, and (later) next-door neighbor. During the next several years, Sorokin (now reunited with Elena) poured out a series of important books, most of which have never gone out of print.[11] In the spring of 1929, Sorokin gave invited lectures at Harvard University that had been arranged by economist-sociologist Thomas Nixon Carver,[12] and in September of that year President A. Lawrence Lowell offered him Harvard's first full, tenured professorship in sociology.

Sorokin joined the Harvard faculty in 1930, teaching for a year in Economics, and then chairing the newly established Department of Sociology (where Zimmerman joined him a year later).[13] In 1937, Sorokin published the first three volumes of his major work, *Social and Cultural Dynamics*, which generated widespread and intense controversy, and proved to be a turning point in Sorokin's career in the United States (Nichols 1989). Many U.S. sociologists and other academics rejected Sorokin's diagnosis of non-linear change ("trendless fluctuations") as well as his assertion that the West was at an extraordinary crossroads ("the crisis of our age"), and his prediction that contemporary culture would give way to a more spiritual worldview. Consequently, Sorokin became increasingly alienated from the sociological profession and stopped attending professional conferences.[14] At Harvard, he was succeeded as chair by Talcott Parsons, who led a successful effort to form an interdisciplinary Department of Social Relations (1946–1972) that reduced Sociology from a department to what members called a "wing" of the new unit (Johnston 1986; Johnston 1995).[15]

Sorokin then devoted himself to the study of altruism. Having received a large grant from the Eli Lilly Foundation, he launched the Harvard Center for Research in Creative Altruism, edited two symposia, introduced an undergraduate course on social solidarity and altruism, and published a series of related works, among which *The Ways and Power of Love* (1954b) is most noteworthy.[16] In 1959, Sorokin reached the mandatory age of retirement at Harvard, becoming emeritus. But in 1961 he entered a new phase as president of the recently established International Society for the Comparative Study of Civilizations (ISCSC), delivering an address in Mexico City that condemned the escalating nuclear arms race shortly before the 1962 Cuban Missile Crisis. Two years later, Sorokin reappeared at Harvard for a teach-in against the expanding U.S. war in Vietnam, which he condemned.

Meanwhile, in 1963, he had unexpectedly been elected president of the American Sociological Association, following a write-in campaign to place his name on the ballot (Johnston 1987), and he subsequently gave a presidential address (in 1965) on "The Sociology of Yesterday, Today and Tomorrow." At about the same time, a series of *festschrift* volumes in his honor began to appear, first in the United States (Allen 1963; Tiryakian 1963) and then in India (Hallen and Rajeshwar 1972), along with work in England by historian Frank Richard Cowell (1970) that promoted Sorokin's values-based approach.[17] In 1966 he published his final important work, *Sociological Theories of Today*, a review of the preceding forty years.

Pitirim Sorokin died at his home in Winchester, Massachusetts, in February 1968, at the age of 79, almost exactly fifty years after his reprieve by Lenin. By any measure, this was an extraordinary life, rich in adventure and scholarship, a life that has generated an enduring legacy. The end of the Soviet era (during which his works were banned) led to a rediscovery of Sorokin by scholars in his former homeland (e.g., Kravchenko and Pokrovsky 2001; Doykov 2008; Zyuzev 2010) and during the past two decades there have been many commemorative events, culminating in the official rededication of Syktyvkar State University (Komi Republic) "in the name of Pitirim Sorokin," along with a newly sculpted life-size statue.[18] Similar future events, including a conference in fall 2019 in Syktyvkar, are also being organized. In this way, the slogan worn by dissident sociologists at the 1969 American Sociological Association (ASA) annual conference has been proven true, not only in the United States but also internationally, "Sorokin lives!"

MAJOR WORK/CONTRIBUTION

Sorokin's published output, spanning more than half a century, is unusually extensive, and therefore selecting the key contributions presents a challenge—all the more so as many of the early works were written in Russian and have not been translated into English. Given, however, that Sorokin focused more on monographs than on journal articles, it is possible to simplify the task by emphasizing what seem the most important books.

Sorokin's first monograph, in Russian, *Crime and Punishment, Heroism and Reward* (1914), was a significant achievement for a twenty-five-year-old scholar. This study dealt with both negative and positive deviance, and the book's twin themes of social control and pro-social behavior would remain central in Sorokin's later work. The inclusion of these polarities is an early expression of Sorokin's dialectical outlook, a perspective strongly influenced by philosopher Vladimir Solovyov's *Philosophical Principles of Integral Knowledge* ([1877] 2008) and similar Russian writings in the "Slavophile" tradition, though Sorokin was also well versed in the Hegelian-Marxist perspective and was acquainted with some ancient texts such as Confucian writings on dialectical harmony.

In 1920, Sorokin published a highly ambitious treatise, *A System of Sociology* (two volumes), again in Russian. This genre, introduced by earlier, founding generations, included Auguste Comte's writings on "positive philosophy" (Martineau 1853), Herbert Spencer's widely influential *Principles of Sociology* (1898) and, in America, Franklin Giddings's *Principles of Soci-*

ology (1896) and Lester F. Ward's *Static and Dynamic Sociology* (1895). Like some of his predecessors, Sorokin divided sociology into social statics and social dynamics, and tried to create a conceptual framework for each—an approach that might also be characterized as "integral." A significant contribution in the *System* was a classification of organized social groups as "uni-bonded" or "multi-bonded" (reflecting Sorokin's training in chemistry) along with the ideas of "social space" and "social time" and the concept of a "multiplicity of selves" corresponding to the number of organized groups to which an individual belongs.

Living through dramatic, often violent change, Sorokin introduced a new genre he would later designate as "the sociology of calamity." This embraced especially the traumatic phenomena of war, revolution, famine and natural disasters. In 1922, during the fierce "Reds versus Whites" civil war that followed the Bolshevik seizure of power, Sorokin produced a monograph on *Hunger as a Factor in Human Affairs*, based partly on his own observation of people near starvation. The Soviet authorities, however, seized the plates of the book, and it only appeared a half-century later (Sorokin 1975), in a posthumous English translation by Pitirim's widow Elena. Sorokin was thus limited to presenting the analysis as an "oral publication" (Merton 1980, 1994) in his university courses (Sorokin 1963).

Meanwhile, Sorokin worked on a path breaking study, *The Sociology of Revolution*, largely from a biosocial perspective that reflected the emphasis of Pavlov. He smuggled the Russian-language manuscript to Czechoslovakia, and it appeared in English in 1925, Sorokin's second year at Minnesota. Earlier scholars, notably Herbert Spencer, had written much about warfare and "militant" societies, and Edward A. Ross had published a recent book on *The Russian Bolshevik Revolution* (1921). But Sorokin's wide ranging historical and conceptual analysis was new, and this specialty—along with his unique experience as a member of the Provisional government—was what initially distinguished Sorokin within American sociology.

In 1927, having settled into his new homeland and professorship, Sorokin brought out his most widely accepted and, one might say, "most American" book, *Social Mobility*. This theoretical and empirical study examined not only stratification or the levels of social organization, but also upward and downward movement by individuals and groups in "social space." It built upon existing sociological literature but broadened the conceptualization significantly, and it was widely adopted as a reading in sociology programs. The key term, "mobility," resonated with the American Dream, suggesting the hope of a better life for recent immigrants like Pitirim and Elena, as well as for future generations, which would soon include their sons Peter and Sergei. *Mobility*, like *Revolution*, had an important historical component, as Sorokin examined the varying height and shape of societal pyramids, and he noted the recurrence of socialist style movements when the gap from top to bottom became extreme.

A year later, Sorokin published *Contemporary Sociological Theories*, a wide ranging treatise that organized sociological writings of the preceding fifty years into a series of "schools," including the mechanical school (e.g., Pareto), the sociologistic school (e.g., Durkheim), the psychologistic school (e.g., Tarde and E. A. Ross), and so forth. The European-style encyclopedism of this survey, with more than a thousand references, including some ancient and medieval writings, again set Sorokin apart from his professional peers. Employing a metaphor based on his own experience as a gardener who would win awards for his azealea and rhodondendron hillside, Sorokin spoke of the need to remove unscientific "weeds," but also to accept many varieties of "flowers." This approach is again "integralistic," and it accords with more recent usage such as George Ritzer's description of sociology as "multi-paradigmatic."[19]

In the late 1920s and early 1930s, Sorokin's works on *The Principles of Rural-Urban Sociology* (with Zimmerman) and *A Systematic Sourcebook in Rural Sociology* (with Zimmerman and C. J. Galpin) did much to promote this special field. It is again noteworthy that these authors (Zimmerman [1973] would later write of a "Sorokin-Zimmerman school of sociology") framed the subject-matter dialectically, in terms of both rural and urban, implying that these phenomena could only be properly understood in conjunction with one another. This approach was more intellectually ambitious than its urban-centric counterpart at the University of Chicago, which was then approaching the peak of its influence (Faris 1967).

At Harvard, Sorokin (with funding from the Rockefeller Foundation that allowed him to hire specialist researchers) labored for seven years to produce the first three volumes of his major work, *Social and Cultural Dynamics* (1937).[20] This study addressed a problem usually explored in anthropology (e.g., in Ruth Benedict's work) rather than sociology, namely, "the integration of culture," and then presented a vast, content analytic study of fluctuations over more than two millennia in the main components of European and American culture, including art, architecture, ethics, law, literature, music, philosophy, religion, science and technology. These were understood as expressions of two contrasting "culture mentalities," namely, the Ideational (spiritual, non-materialistic) and the Sensate (secular, materialistic).[21] The third volume focused on fluctuations of social relations ("familistic, contractual, compulsory"), with emphasis on civil disturbances, wars and revolutions, which erupted more frequently during transitional phases between the dominance of the two major mentalities—a finding that accords with the "anomie" tradition dating back to Durkheim. *Dynamics* featured the idea of "sociocultural systems and supersystems," approaching these as meaningful, causal and functional sets of relations. Its broad historical sweep, epistemological sophistication and focus on culture again reflected Sorokin's background as a Russian and European style scholar (Nichols 2012b).[22]

In 1941, Sorokin brought out the final, theoretical and explanatory volume of *Dynamics*, which emphasized especially the idea of "immanent causation." In contrast to the then dominant model of external causation ("social forces") the immanent approach asserts that systems change mainly as a result of their own operations, aided or hindered by external factors. Thus, systems of culture, whether Ideational or Sensate or Mixed (e.g., Idealistic), begin with creative possibilities that their makers and members explore, leading to particular types of knowledge and invention. But, over time, these possibilities are gradually exhausted, and the cultures become less creative, stagnant or "over-ripe"—a pattern that Sorokin conceptualized in terms of "the principle of limit"—and this prepares the way for their dialectical replacement by another culture mentality. Sorokin's emphasis was thus on "agency," and his formulation accords with the well-known Marxist principle that human beings "make their own history." It likewise agrees with Marx's view that new social orders (e.g., socialism) are nurtured "in the womb of" preceding orders (e.g., capitalism). The volume also introduced the idea of Integral epistemology that would remain central during the final quarter-century of Sorokin's work.

In 1941 Sorokin also published *The Crisis of Our Age*, a summary of *Dynamics* for non-academic readers that was based on lectures in Boston under the auspices of the Lowell Institute for popular education. Here Sorokin asserted that Western culture, including all its major components, was in the throes of an extraordinary ordeal as the dominant supersystem of the preceding five centuries broke down amid global economic depression and the unprecedented violence of two world wars. Previous notions of truth, of beauty and of goodness had largely disappeared as relativism increased and people became strangers and enemies, and "might made right." The only possible solution was the creation of a new sociocultural order based on Ideational and Idealistic values that would reassert the sacred quality of human life and turn science and technology away from destructive purposes, while holding national governments and economic elites accountable. *Crisis* marked Sorokin's turn toward "public sociology" (Burawoy 2004), a genre Sorokin had earlier practiced in Russia with the "Notes of a Sociologist" column in *Narodnaya Volya* (Sorokin 2000; Nichols 1999).[23]

Importantly, both *Dynamics* and *Crisis* implied that sociology needed to undergo a fundamental change, away from its "sensate," materialistic and deterministic premises—a "prophetic" view (Friedrichs 1970) that Sorokin's peers mostly rejected. Yet even those who could not embrace Sorokin's proposed remedy articulated similar critiques. Robert Lynd, famous as the coauthor (with Helen Merrell Lynd) of *Middletown* (1929), raised the fundamental question of *Knowledge for What?* (1940). C. Wright Mills, rebelling against the mainstream of his profession, called for a reorientation that would link "the biographical and the historical" in *The Sociological Imagination* (1959). Alvin Gouldner (1970), in a prophetic voice reminiscent of Sorokin's, proclaimed *The Coming Crisis of Western Sociology*. Jonathan Turner and Stephen Turner examined sociology's dysfunction in *The Impossible Science* (1990). And, as the new millennium approached, Irving Louis Horowitz (1994) traced *The Decomposition of Sociology* and proposed an alternate path.

Sorokin's volumes *Man and Society in Calamity* (1942) and *Sociocultural Causality, Space and Time* (1944b) attracted relatively little attention from academics and the general public still preoccupied by warfare. But *Russia and the United States* (1944a) gained a more widespread and favorable response. Here Sorokin—anticipating the Cold War of 1945 to 1991—asserted that there were no fundamental conflicts between the two nations and wartime allies, and that they had much in common. Indeed, he argued that sociologists could discern an important macro-level process of "convergence" through which each system began to acquire the other's characteristics. Thus, the United States was no longer a land of unbridled, nineteenth-century-style capitalism, especially since Franklin Roosevelt's "New Deal," while the U.S.S.R. had been moving away from strict state socialism since Lenin's New Economic Plan. *Russia*, along with *Crisis*, again followed the example of Lev Tolstoy—a major influence on Sorokin—of "writing for the people" (Nichols 1998).

Sorokin's first postwar book, *Society, Culture and Personality* (1947), was a major, synthetic treatise—arguably unparalleled—that might be considered his mature reworking of the earlier, two-volume *System of Sociology*. This work incorporated much of his earlier published research on social structure, on stratification and mobility, on rural and urban societies, on fluctuations of cultural systems, and on war and revolution. It engaged an enormous body of sociological work in Europe and the United States, and is Sorokin's fullest statement of "the science of sociology." Significantly, it anticipated the model of "interpenetrating systems" of society, culture and personality that would shortly be featured in Harvard's newly formed Department of Social Relations as articulated by Talcott Parsons and Edward Shils (1951) and their collaborators in the influential programmatic work, *Toward A General Theory of Action*.

At the time that *Society* appeared, U.S. sociologists mostly ignored the idea of "culture," focusing instead on "interaction." But Sorokin, in accord with the German "verstehen" tradition epitomized by Max Weber and also the American approaches of social psychology and symbolic interactionism, held that human social interaction required meaningfulness, that it was thus always "sociocultural." Today, the model of society-culture-personality is mainstream and is featured in virtually all introductory sociology textbooks.

Meanwhile, Jeffrey Alexander (2003) and others (e.g., Hall, Grindstaff and Lo 2012) have built up a contemporary field of "cultural sociology" that has also generated one of the largest sections of the American Sociological Association. In a related development, Judith Blau (2001), Charles Camic and Neil Gross (2001) and others have created a literature in the "sociology of ideas."

Sorokin's treatise also presented an unconventional, four-level model of human personality including: (1) the biological unconscious; (2) the biological conscious; (3) the sociocultural conscious; and (4) the superconscious. In part, this was a critical response to the increasingly popular Freudian model that emphasized unconscious forces (id, eros, thanatos) and biology. The distinctive idea of the "superconscious"—comparable to earlier concepts about "the soul" from Plato and Aristotle through Aquinas and nineteenth century Russian and German philosophy—would also feature prominently in Sorokin's subsequent works.

A year later, in 1948, Sorokin brought out a programmatic work, *The Reconstruction of Humanity*, that criticized as inadequate a broad series of proposed remedies for social problems, and asserted that the only foundation of positive, enduring change was the altruization of individuals and groups. *Reconstruction* met with widespread criticism as an exercise in preaching and prophesy, rather than science, and there are again interesting parallels with Lev Tolstoy, especially his 1896 work, *The Kingdom of God Is Within You*.[24] But *Reconstruction* also became the basis for a decade of scholarly work by Sorokin on the sociology of love and pro-social behavior in which he always sought empirical evidence, though at times from unconventional sources. Interestingly, this hearkened back to the writings of Auguste Comte on altruism, as well as to the writings and praxis of Jane Addams and her Hull House circle on "the neighborly relation" (Addams [1910] 2008). Indeed, Sorokin's 1950 book, *Altruistic Love*, was subtitled *A Study of Good Neighbors and Christian Saints*

Although grounded in sociology, Sorokin began to look beyond his discipline, which he believed had largely failed to understand major historical forces and trends. He therefore promoted the creation of a new field called "amitology" that would feature work across a broad range of scholarly disciplines, including biology, psychology, sociology and philosophy, on "the mysterious energy of love." Sorokin made a successful start by editing symposium volumes, *Explorations in Altruistic Love and Behavior* (1950b) and *Forms and Techniques of Altruistic and Spiritual Growth* (1954a), that included contributions by psychologist Gordon W. Allport, anthropologist Ashley Montagu and French cardiologist Dr. Therese Brosse, among others.

The most important publication of this altruism period was the 1954 book, *The Ways and Power of Love*, which deserves to be regarded as one of Sorokin's major works. Its main focus is on how society might create more "love energy." *Ways and Power* also presents a five-dimensional conceptualization of love, details its biological, psychological and social benefits, and links it closely with the idea of the "superconscious" as a source of creativity.

The 1956 volume *The American Sex Revolution* pursued a theme Sorokin had articulated since the 1920s after observing the sexual licentiousness of the revolutionary era in Russia. Events such as the launch of *Playboy* magazine strengthened his conviction that western "Sensate" culture was approaching an extreme that would ultimately generate a strong counter-reaction. In the manner of the traditional Russian "intelligentsia" who served as moral teachers, he appealed for "sexual sanity." Among critics, this work added to Sorokin's reputation as a preacher rather than a serious scientist, though Lewis Coser (1977), writing in the decade after Sorokin's death when pornography became mainstream, assessed Sorokin's view as "remarkably prescient." Since that time, multiple "waves" of the feminist movement have condemned (heterosexual) pornography as the objectification of, and violence against, women, while psychologists and physicians have recognized dependence on pornography as a type of "addiction." Were Sorokin somehow to reappear, he might assert that the dramatic spread of sexually transmitted diseases, along with the deadly AIDS epidemic, have vindicated much of his *Sex Revolution*.

In 1959, Sorokin and Walter Lunden (a graduate student of his at Minnesota) published a political work, *Power and Morality: Who Shall Guard the Guardians?* Beginning with the famous question from Plato's *Republic*, this volume presented a systematic indictment of governments as the most criminal type of human group, responsible for the oppression and slaughter of innumerable innocent persons. This view accords with more recent scholarship on "state-corporate crime" (Michalowski and Kramer 2006) and the emergence of the field of "genocide studies" (Bloxham and Moses 2010). Sorokin and Lunden argued that a new type of government was needed if a devastating third world war was to be avoided, one composed not of power hungry politicians but rather of "scientists, sages and saints."

In 1964 Sorokin brought out a short volume for popular audiences, *Basic Trends of Our Times* that extended major themes dating back to *Dynamics*. Assuming a global perspective, Sorokin noted the diminishing hegemony of European culture and the resurgent creativity of Asian societies. He promoted the ideal of inter-civilizational dialogue and expressed the hope that East and West would cooperate in building a new Integral international order.

Sorokin's final major work, *Sociological Theories of Today* (1966), provided an overview of major intellectual developments in general sociology during the preceding forty years. Though in a sense a companion volume to his 1928 *Contemporary Sociological Theories*, it dropped the earlier "schools" approach for a new classification. As always, Sorokin sharply criticized aspects of the surveyed approaches that he regarded as erroneous.

And yet, possibly more than any other scholar of the era, he also sought to reconcile diverse views, taking what seemed valid from each and combining them all in an Integral sociology. For Sorokin, the ultimate truth, in a classic Latin phrase he often cited, was the *coincidentia oppositorum*, that is, the coincidence of opposites, the transcendence of contradictions.

APPLICATION TO A CURRENT SOCIAL ISSUE/PROBLEM

Altruization of Society. Since Sorokin's path-finding efforts, the study of altruism has spread widely across academic fields, especially psychology and evolutionary biology. Ironically, however, considering that the sociological treatment of altruism dates back to Comte, sociologists have until recently done comparatively little in this area. Robert K. Merton and Paul Lazarsfeld (1954) wrote about "friendship as a social process," and Merton and Thomas Gieryn (1978) examined "institutionalized altruism" in the professions. In the late 1970s, Kay Bierwiler (1978) did a doctoral thesis on Sorokin's altruism studies at the State University of New York, Albany. Samuel and Pearl Oliner (1988) later brought out *The Altruistic Personality*, and Vincent Jeffries published an article on "virtue and the altruistic personality" (1998). Jay Weinstein (2000) appealed for a restoration of Sorokin's program of applied altruism. I myself once taught a course on Sorokin's altruism works for the Peace Studies program at Boston College. There were, thus, sporadic efforts, but American sociologists generally focused on other issues.

In the most recent decade and a half, however, interest in altruism has spread within sociology. A substantial professional literature has appeared, including a vision statement by several scholars (Jeffries et al. 2006), research by Paul Schervish and Keith Whitaker (2010) on philanthropy, and an analysis of "the paradox of generosity" by Christian Smith and Hilary Davidson (2014). Jeffries (2014) edited a *Handbook* of specialized contributions, including the evolution of altruism (Turner 2014), identity theory and altruism (Stets and McCaffree 2014), religious altruism (Lee 2014), "the sociology of love" (Nichols 2014) and "Sorokin's heritage" (Krotov 2014). Sociologists have also drawn on Stephen Post's work (2003) on "unlimited love." The Templeton Foundation provided financial support for some of these efforts.

Jeffries also led a successful effort to establish a section on Altruism, Morality and Social Solidarity in the American Sociological Association, and that section now actively promotes and recognizes both scholarship and teaching in this area. Altruism has sometimes also been emphasized in regional associations in the United States, such as in the presidential addresses of Lawrence Nichols (2012a) and Lissa Yogan (2015) at the North Central Sociological Association. Meanwhile Robin M. Williams, a former student of Sorokin's and a president of the American Sociological Association, introduced a course on altruism and cooperation at the University of California at Irvine, and Matthew Lee, a president of the North Central Sociological Association, taught a similar course on love and pro-social behavior at the University of Akron.

Prosocial Behavior. For much of its history, sociology has focused largely on what was formerly called "social pathology." There has been a consistent preoccupation with a range of social ills, including poverty, violent crime, inequality, prejudice and discrimination, family breakups, war, suicide, pollution, etc. From the late nineteenth to the mid-twentieth centuries, sociologists framed these in terms of evolution, modernization, urbanization, social disorganization or dysfunction. More recently, sociologists have applied conflict lenses, including Marxism (and its derivatives, "critical theory" and World Systems Theory), along with varieties of feminism and queer theory—all of which, as "liberation" sociology" (Feagin and Vera 2001) implicitly or explicitly assume that self-interest and a "will to power" control all human interaction. There is no talk of love, and little, if any, celebration of goodness.

Sociology's situation is arguably comparable to that of medicine in its earlier, "disease fighting" era. Presently, however, medicine is transitioning to an alternative approach, variously known as "holistic" (Mincolla and Siegel 2015) or "integral" medicine (Dacher 2006), or the "wellness model" (Weil 2004). Medical people do not deny the reality of disease, but they no longer make it the defining feature of their field. In a similar way, contemporary psychologists have created the approach of "positive psychology" that does not deny pathology, but that focuses primarily on such issues as developing "character strengths" (Peterson and Seligman 2004), "flourishing" in "the life well-lived" (Keys and Haidt 2003) and attaining "authentic happiness" (Seligman 2004). Sorokin's work on altruism offers a model of how to build, on a scientific basis, an analogous "positive" sociology that includes mutual aid, compassion, generosity, forgiveness, reconciliation and love. This accords with the "communitarian" approach lately developed under the leadership of Amitai Etzioni (1998) and others.

While always maintaining a deep concern for human suffering, and the ways in which social orders inflict and perpetuate suffering, sociologists can also choose to celebrate all that is good in the social world, just as Sorokin did by lauding the lives of exemplary altruists. For it is only the good that provides the resources—including mutual aid, courage and perseverance, inspiration, hope and even joyfulness—that are necessary to overcome the pathological. A sociology rooted in anger will inevitably experience, as a field, the characteristic self-destructive effects of anger against which Buddhist monk and peace activist Thich Nhat Hanh (2002) has provided an eloquent warning. In recent decades, sociologists and professional associations in the field have often designated justice or "social justice" as, in effect, the highest ideal. But though a primary value, justice can, and often does degenerate into vindictiveness, vengeance and violence. Therefore justice must be integrated with other basic values, especially love, the highest ideal. The ultimate challenge for sociologists, as Sorokin's work implies, is to move beyond the mere study of love in order *to practice sociology with love*, in teaching, in research, and in public service (Nichols 2012a).

Spirituality. From its earliest days as a product of the European Enlightenment, sociology has been largely anti-religious but has developed a countervailing tradition of what might be termed secular spirituality and secular salvation. Comte famously asserted that the era of theological knowledge was over, but he advocated for a new Religion of Humanity rooted in altruism (Martineau 1853). Marx ([1843] 1970) tried to unmask organized religion as a popular anesthetic and a tool of ruling groups, but he promoted the development of a true consciousness that would build a just world. Durkheim ([1912] 1999) claimed that society was actually "worshipping itself," but he nonetheless supported the phenomenon of "the sacred" in human groups. Weber ([1922] 1964) could not accept the transcendental claims of religious creeds, but he seemed to support an "innerworldly" religiosity and has sometimes been called "sociology's last Puritan." Subsequently, in the United States, many early sociologists likewise broke away from organized religion, especially Protestant Christianity, but they nevertheless embraced the Social Gospel rooted in that faith (Vidich and Lyman 1985; Villadsen 2018).

Sorokin took a somewhat different stance, though one that has strong affinities with the Social Gospel. Beginning with a long-term view of the sociology of knowledge and culture, he asserted that sociocultural systems based on religious doctrines deserved to be respected as legitimate adaptations that captured some of the truth of human life. "Ideational" cultures and social systems, he argued, were especially creative with regard to non-material elements of life, producing variants of the Golden Rule of treating others with compassion and love. At the same time, by articulating sacred, absolute values they dialectically corrected for the excessive relativism of Sensate orders. Deeply shaped by his Christian upbringing in Russia, Sorokin was not an orthodox believer, but more a Transcendentalist, though in the mold of Tolstoyism and the Sermon on the Mount, rather than American Protestantism or Unitarian Universalism.[25]

In recent decades, the terms "spirituality" and "soul" have reappeared across a wide and growing range of fields, including not only academic disciplines but also medicine, popular education and even the business sector. Thus, entrepreneur and ecological activist Tom Chappell (1996), in partnership with his wife Kate Chappell, published *The Soul of a Business* about building a successful enterprise on Christian and Buddhist values. Popular psychologists and spiritual development authors Thomas Moore (2016) and Wayne Dyer (2003) brought out *Care of the Soul* and *There's a Spiritual Solution to Every Problem*. Meanwhile medical researchers published empirical research that explored the effects of prayer on healing (Astin 2000; Andrade and Radhakrishnan 2009).

Others promoted the idea and practice of "mindfulness." Thus, American Buddhist nun Pema Chodron recorded public lectures on loving kindness, including *The Fearless Heart: The Practice of Living with Courage and Compassion*, while Vietnamese Buddhist monk Thich Nhat Hanh (1997) published *Living Buddha, Living Christ*, and the Dalai Lama spoke on American college campuses. Dr. Jon Kabat-Zinn (2006) documented the benefits of meditation in pain management. Within sociology, Janine Schipper (2012) advocated for a Buddhist approach.

In a similar way, other popular authors promoted the idea of "consciousness." Dr. Deepak Chopra published a series of best sellers ranging from "mind-body health" (2001) and "quantum healing" (2015) at the personal level to a new cosmology of "how consciousness became the universe" (Chopra and Penrose 2017). The emergence and influence of the "Big Bang" theory of the origin of the physical universe also facilitated the spread of a new, more spiritualized outlook. Even the informal naming of the Higgs boson (which may give mass to matter) as "the God particle" (Lederman and Teresi 1993) suggests a shift in attitudes.

Such developments have strong affinities with Sorokin's discussion of the "superconscious" dimension of human personality, a discussion with deep roots in the Russian tradition of Intuitionism (Nichols 2012b). Indeed, Sorokin (1954b) pointed to intuition, rather than logical reasoning, as the main source of creativity in human societies. Recently, intuition has gained an array of advocates, partly in conjunction with the increasing "feminization" of diverse fields, including even the formerly hyper-masculine world of business via the movement, or "megatrend" (Aburdene 2007) of "conscious capitalism" (Mackey and Sisodia 2013).

Chopra (2003) has also been an influential proponent of "miracles," in a non-church-based movement partly inspired by Dr. Helen Schucman's "self-study spiritual thought system," entitled "A Course in Miracles." Popular writers such as Marianne Williamson elaborated the ideas of the "Course" in public lectures and books that included *A Return to Love* (1996) and *Age of Miracles* (2008). Critics who took a self-proclaimed "biblical" stance denounced many of these events as anti-Christian and "occult," but the "miracles" movement brought this religiously grounded and previously discredited idea back into popular discourse. Other pop spirituality writers meanwhile produced a new literature on angels (Virtue 2007; Eckersley and Quinn 2008; DeStefano 2012), understood as divine messengers and life guides.

There were also significant developments in what came to be called the field of "thanatology," that is, the study of death and dying largely inspired by the path breaking work of Dr. Elizabeth Kubler Ross. In 1975, Raymond Moody published a landmark study of *Life After Life* that detailed "out of body" accounts of persons who had come close to dying. Such narratives featured recurrent elements, including the "tunnel" experience of leaving the body, the life review, a sense of joyfulness and peace, and an overwhelming encounter with an unearthly light or a Being of Light. Since then similar stories of such paranormal events have emerged. In 1994 Betty J. Eadie published a best-selling account, *Embraced by the Light*. More recently, Dannion Brinkley (2009) brought out *Secrets of the Light: Lessons from Heaven*. Physician Mary Neal (2012) reported the experience of drowning, witnessing her own death, being transported to a spiritual realm and ultimately returning to earth. Dr. Eben Alexander (2012) likewise published a memoir, *Proof of Heaven: A Neurosurgeon's Journey into the Afterlife*. Thanatologist David Kessler (2011) published *Visions, Trips, and Crowded Rooms: Who and What You See Before You Die* that reported communication between deceased persons and those nearing death. Anita Moorjani (2014) brought out *Dying to Be Me: My Journey from Cancer, to Near Death, to True Healing* that reported an encounter with her deceased father. Such accounts and personal testimonies have led to the formation of the International Association for Near Death Studies.

The near-death experiences (NDE) literature as a whole asserts the existence—indeed, the priority—of a reality beyond everyday sensory perception. Significantly, these "new revelations" did not emanate from organized religious groups, some of which rejected their messages as inconsistent with established theology. Widespread acceptance of NDE-based views would reverse the modern "disenchantment of the world" and would radically redefine the universe and the place of human beings within it.

From Sorokin's perspective, such events point toward the obsolescence of the materialist or Sensate premise, and to an important approaching change in culture and psychology. He would regard these data as indications of a big story in the making, one that sociologists have largely ignored, due to their lingering commitment to obsolescent Sensate premises, whether rooted in Comtean positivism, Marxist dialectical materialism or other secularist traditions.

Sorokin would likely see the emerging discourse of spirituality also in the popularity of recent writings by religious and fantasy authors such as J. R. R. Tolkien, voted "author of the century" for his epic *Lord of the Rings*. Christian apologist C. S. Lewis's retelling of salvation history as a space trilogy is comparable. Joseph Campbell published studies of mythologies around the world, and lectured about these on a popular television program. Former British Catholic nun Karen Armstrong, once an atheist, became a leading scholar of religion who published influential volumes on *A History of God* (1994) and *The Case for God* (2010). J. K. Rowling's enormously popular "Harry Potter" stories and popular films of good and evil magic also seem to answer a widespread desire for something beyond the material realm.

And Sorokin would also note that, despite the ongoing secularization of Europe, there has been a persistence or even a dramatic spread of religion elsewhere, including an Islamic revival on several continents, a growth of Catholicism and Lutheranism in Africa, a great increase in evangelical Protestantism in South Korea, a surge of Pentecostalism in Latin America, and a greater tolerance of religion in nations with formerly militant secularist or atheistic regimes. A recent instance is provided by the construction of a large Orthodox Christian cathedral, with public funding, in Romania. There are likewise many faith-related developments in China, including the spread of Christian "house churches," the persistence of strong Islamic beliefs among minorities such as the Uighurs, and a grassroots revival of traditional Taoism and Confucianism (Osnos 2015). As two reporters from the European *Economist* news magazine put it, "God is back, and "the global revival of faith is changing the world" (Micklethwait and Wooldridge 2009).

Sorokin would likewise recognize the spread of 'the new atheism," as articulated in *The God Delusion* by evolutionary biologist Richard Dawkins (2008), as well as in Christopher Hitchins's best seller, *God Is Not Great* (2009). He would note that the world's most famous physicist, Stephen Hawking, maintained an atheistic stance to the end, even though his best-selling book, *A Brief History of Time* (1998), on the "Big Bang," provided material for theists, including creationists and "intelligent design" advocates (Dembski 2002; Leisola and Witt 2018). Sorokin would interpret these oppositions in terms of the macro-level process of "positive and negative polarization" that recurs in times of great change. And he might be particularly interested in the conversion of formerly atheistic natural scientists, including Antony Flew, who published *There Is A God* (2008), and distinguished geneticist Francis S. Collins (2007) who articulated his faith in the best seller, *The Language of God: A Scientist Presents Evidence for Belief*.

But, again, he would regard all these developments having to do with religion and spirituality as a big story that sociologists generally—not merely sociologists of religion—need to address and to illumine from an Integral perspective. Though sometimes cast as a pessimist, Sorokin believed that once "the crisis of our age" had run its course, a new, richer and nobler sociocultural order would emerge. There would be, he predicted, "crisis, catharsis, charisma and resurrection" (Sorokin 1941).

Integral Epistemology and Science. Sorokin's major work, *Dynamics*, was deeply involved with the validity of knowledge, an issue that had been raised most influentially by Karl Mannheim ([1929] 1954) in *Ideology and Utopia*. Anthropologists had likewise grappled with the same problem, and had moved strongly in the direction of cultural relativism as championed by Margaret Mead (1935). The stances of Mannheim and Mead implied, first, that there was no absolute knowledge, and, second, that knowledge was limited to the membership of particular groups and cultures, and was, in effect, "for members only." These intellectual positions have recently reappeared in a variety of relativistic paradigms, including ethnomethodology, neo-Marxism, constructionism, feminism, deconstructionism, post-structuralism, postmodernism and queer theory—all of which advocate some version of "standpoint epistemology," which views knowledge as "for members only" or "for believers only."

Sorokin adopted a different stance in *Dynamics* and subsequent works, one that affirmed the possibility of valid knowledge that would escape the endless regress of relativism. This was a dialectic of complementarity in which opposites act as checks and balances on each other. Thus, the externalistic understanding of a scientifically trained observer could be combined with the experiential perspective of group members. Such an approach would not entirely reject traditional science, but would not grant the sort of privilege that science previously enjoyed.

A case can be made that an approach such as Sorokin's is needed, if sociology is to maintain credibility as a scientific discipline, that is, as a field generating knowledge that is not mere ideology and mere political partisanship. A sociology that denies the possibility of such knowledge has no future. Nor does a sociology whose findings are simply derivatives of ideological dogmas, in which the answers to all important questions are, in effect, known in advance. Sociologists must observe, but always ethically and with deep respect for the life-worlds of those they study. And sociologists must continue to make genuine discoveries, including inconvenient facts that go beyond or even contradict ideological formulas.

Integral Sociology. The contemporary field of sociology is sharply divided, even fragmented, and intellectual differences have often spilled over into interpersonal conflicts within academic departments and into factional battles within professional associations. There is much mutual avoidance and "encampment" (Crawley 2019), even between groups such as "critical theorists" and feminists who otherwise have much in common. The increasing "feminization" of sociology (DiFuccia et al. 2007; Stephen Turner 2014; Bucior and Sica 2019), while redressing previous inequities, has also resulted in significant patterns of self-segregation that sometimes border on separatism. In response, Jonathan Turner (2016) has interpreted sociology's "big divide" as "differentiation without integration," and has proposed a split into two coexisting working groups of those who are more politically or more scientifically oriented.

Sorokin's Integralism offers a framework in which at least some of the more serious differences might be reconciled (Jeffries 1999; Rhodes 2017).

In some respects, such an Integral approach would be highly compatible with the influential fourfold model advocated by Michael Burawoy that is usually (and mistakenly) referred to only as "public sociology" (Nichols 2011). For Burawoy, both applied ("policy") sociology and politically oriented ("public") sociology must be deeply rooted in scientific ("professional") sociology. In other words, something akin to what Robert Merton (1942) called "the ethos of science" must be preserved if sociology is to survive and prosper (Calhoun 2010). Sorokin's Integral model, which advocates the unification of "the true, the beautiful and the good," offers a means of doing science without abandoning ethical values, especially creativity, love and non-violence, to which Sorokin was deeply committed.

NOTES

1. The Komi are not Slavs, but belong to the Ugro-Finnish ethnic group.
2. The biographical sketch presented here is based mainly on Sorokin's autobiographical works, including *Leaves from a Russian Diary* (1924), and *A Long Journey* (1963).
3. Pitirim was sixteen at the time of the Russian Revolution of 1905, a major upheaval that resulted in a movement away from absolutism toward constitutional monarchy, including an elected legislature to be called the Duma (based on the Russian word for deliberation).
4. The Socialist Revolutionary Party, founded in 1901, promoted a program of agrarian socialism under a federal government. At the time of the 1917 Revolution it was the largest socialist political organization in Russia, and some of its members allied themselves with the Bolsheviks, only to see their party officially suppressed following the Civil War of 1917 to 1922.
5. After serving as a professor of sociology at the Psycho Neurological Institute, Kovalevsky (1851–1916) was appointed professor of legal history at the University of Saint Petersburg. He was especially known for his researches on the legal institutions of Caucasian highland peoples. A political liberal, he was a founder of the Progressist Party and a member of the Duma, who had also lived abroad and met both Karl Marx and Friedrich Engels. Kovalevsky served as vice president and president of the International Institute of Sociology, and he was elected into the Russian Academy of Sciences. Evgeni Valentinovich De Roberty (1843–1915) was known for his "hyper positivism," and had written on ethics and economics, publishing works in both Russian and French.
6. Petrazhitsky (1867–1931) was a child of the Polish gentry in the eastern Russian Empire, who earned a doctorate in 1896 at the University of Saint Petersburg, and who was a professor of the philosophy of law at that institution from 1897 to 1917. Sorokin was especially influenced by Petrzhitsky's idea of two-sided "law-norms," which, he believed, were fundamental binding forces in all organized social groups. See his 1947 treatise, "Society, Culture and Personality" for a detailed discussion of law-norms.
7. Sorokin's experience is somewhat resembles that of Fyodor Dostoyevsky, who was arrested for participating in a "subversive" discussion group (the "Petrashevsky Circle") as a young man. Dostoyevsky was actually led, along with other condemned prisoners, to the place of execution, where they received an unexpected last-minute reprieve. Subsequently, Dostoyevsky was exiled to Siberia, where he wrote the famous early work *The House of the Dead*. Interestingly, Edward Tiryakian, who was Sorokin's teaching assistant at Harvard, published an article (1988) on Sorokin as "sociology's Dostoyevsky." Also interestingly, Sorokin himself had a strong interest in Dostoyevsky, and he published two short articles in 1921 on the famous author, including one on Dostoyevsky as a sociologist.
8. This family name suggests that Elena was from a higher status group than was Pitirim.

9. Both Ross (1914-1915) and Hayes (1921) had been presidents of the American Sociological Society. Ross (1866-1951) trained in economics at Johns Hopkins, but switched to sociology and published influential articles on "social control" in the *American Journal of Sociology* edited by Albion Small. Hayes (1868-1928) had studied divinity and had actually been a pastor. Ross was a large figure in his day, best known as a social psychologist but also considered an early criminologist, who dined at the White House at the invitation of President Theodore Roosevelt. Having also visited Russia at the time of the 1917 Revolution, Ross developed a fairly extensive correspondence with Sorokin in the 1920s and was very supportive of Sorokin's early work, though he later rejected Sorokin's "Dynamics." See L. T. Nichols, "Intergenerational Solidarity in Social Science: The Ross-Sorokin Correspondence, 1921-1931."

10. Like other departments from about the turn of the twentieth century through the 1930s, the sociology department at Minnesota had a close relationship with social work. F. Stuart Chapin (1888-1974), president of the American Sociological Society (1935), served simultaneously as chair of Sociology and as director of Minnesota's School of Social Work. He had earlier served as director of the School of Social Work at Smith College. It is possible that this affiliation affected Sorokin's later resistance to the proposed combination of sociology and "social ethics" at Harvard during the 1930-1931 academic year.

11. In a memorial lecture, Elena commented that Pitirim had "an exceptional capacity for hard work," and in a letter from the late 1920s, Edward Ross told Sorokin, "I hear you are killing yourself with work."

12. Carver (1865-1961) came from a Midwestern rural background, and had studied economics at Johns Hopkins and Cornell (where he received a doctorate). After teaching economics and sociology (largely based on Herbert Spencer's works) for several years at Oberlin College, Carver accepted an appointment in Harvard's Department of Economics in 1900. In selecting Carver, Harvard President Charles William Eliot intended not only to bolster economics but also to fill the gap in sociology created by the resignation of Edward Cummings, who held Harvard's first professorial (at assistant professor rank) position in sociology during the late 1890s, within Economics. Interestingly, Harvard might have brought in Edward Ross, following his forced departure from Stanford for holding controversial political views on the use of cheap Asian labor. Ross gave a series of invited lectures, sponsored by Economics and arranged by the department's most prominent figure, Frank W. Taussig. But Harvard let Carver, rather than Ross, be its main sociologist for the next three decades, until Lowell brought in Sorokin.

13. The Department of Sociology had very few permanent staff, and the impact of the Great Depression made expansion very difficult throughout the 1930s. The former chair of the Department of Social Ethics, Richard Clarke Cabot, as well as associate professor James Ford, moved into sociology; but Sorokin and Zimmerman held the only tenured lines in sociology until Talcott Parsons received a permanent appointment in 1939. Harvard supported the department by designating "interdepartmental" faculty who taught in the unit, including Carver along with social psychologist Gordon W. Allport, social historian Arthur Schlesinger, Sr., physiologist Lawrence J. Henderson, criminologist Sheldon Glueck and vital statistician E. B. Wilson. In 1934, the department proposed hiring Robert M. MacIver of Columbia, but President James B. Conant rejected the recommendation. Instead, Conant allowed the department to bring in a series of prominent sociologists on a visiting basis, including W. I. Thomas, Robert Park, Leopold von Wiese, Corrado Gini, E. Wight Bakke and Read Bain. Junior faculty included Parsons, Paul Pigors, Edward P. Hutchinson and Edward Y. Hartshorne, as well as Robert K. Merton and George C. Homans. Despite its limitations (e.g., white males), it was an extraordinarily rich intellectual environment, and many of its faculty and graduate students became presidents of the American Sociological Society (later Association) or held other prominent positions. For a more detailed account, see Barry V. Johnston, "Pitirim A. Sorokin: An Intellectual Biography."

14. In 1940, at the annual conference of the American Sociological Society, held in Chicago, Sorokin delivered a paper entitled "The Nature of the Challenge" that was highly critical of the field. Alfred McClung Lee, who chaired the publicity committee, released the paper to the local press. This led to an intense debate about sociology's image that can be found in the

American Sociological Review, including the argument by Howard P. Becker that sociology should "censor" papers like Sorokin's rather than further damage itself.

15. Sorokin was so infuriated by the reorganization, from which he had been largely excluded, that there followed what became known in Harvard College as "the second Russian Revolution." In response, Dean Paul Buck, a major supporter of the Social Relations experiment, considered bringing the matter to a formal disciplinary hearing.

16. There is an interesting historical parallel between Lilly's support and earlier donations by Alfred Tredway White, a New York City housing developer and philanthropist, which funded much of the work of the Reverend Francis Greenwood Peabody and the Department of Social Ethics (1906–1931) that he founded at Harvard. Sorokin's Center can be considered a continuation of the social ethics tradition at Harvard, although he felt strongly that sociology should not reduce itself to mere moralizing.

17. See also Palmer C. Talbutt, *Rough Dialectics: Sorokin's Theory of Value*.

18. This is known locally as "the fisherman statue," because Sorokin is portrayed with his hands spread as though describing a fish he had just caught in Lake Memphremagog, just north of Vermont, where he purchased a summer cottage (what the Russians like to call a "dacha") in the late 1930s.

19. As an undergraduate sociology student at Temple, Robert K. Merton was enormously impressed by *Contemporary Sociological Theories*, and it played a major role in his decision to enter Harvard in 1931 as one of the first doctoral students in the Department of Sociology. President A. Lawrence Lowell also cited the work as a major reason why he decided to offer Sorokin Harvard's first tenured appointment in sociology.

20. At Harvard, funds from the Rockefeller Foundation were distributed via a Committee on Research in the Social Sciences, of which Sorokin was a member. William Buxton (1996) has called attention to the role of private foundations in setting agendas for social science research, and has examined the question of why the self-interest of such groups might lead them to favor an approach like that of Talcott Parsons over Sorokin's.

21. Robert K. Merton, who did an MA thesis and doctoral dissertation under Sorokin's direction, and who coauthored two journal articles with Sorokin, has claimed credit for suggesting the term "sensate" in place of the term "sensuous" that Sorokin originally intended to use. Merton also did much of the empirical fact gathering for the discussion of fluctuations of scientific discoveries in *Dynamics*. For an affectionate memoir of the sometimes difficult Sorokin-Merton relationship, see Robert K. Merton, "The Sorokin-Merton Correspondence on 'Puritanism, Pietism and Science,' 1933–34," *Science in Context* 3(1): 291–98.

22. Joseph B. Ford recalled a conversation with Sorokin (then retired from Harvard) in California, in which Sorokin praised Oswald Spengler as greater than himself or historian Arnold J. Toynbee, whom Sorokin otherwise admired. It therefore seems likely that Spengler's *Decline of the West* was a particular inspiration for Sorokin's later *Dynamics*. And this also helps to account for critical responses to *Dynamics* in the United States, where some readers found the work to reflect a Spenglerian pessimism at odds with the emerging "American century."

23. Sorokin's columns have been collected in a Russian-language volume, *Zametki Sotsiologa*, edited by O. A. Boronoyev, and published by Aleteya, Saint Petersburg, 2000.

24. This work made a profound impression on Mohandas Gandhi as well as Jane Addams, who journeyed to Russia and visited with Tolstoy and then wrote about his philosophy for several decades.

25. The Sermon on the Mount, given by Jesus of Nazareth, is reported in chapters five to seven of the Gospel of Matthew. It contains the Beatitudes (i.e., "blessed' or "happy" are the poor of heart, the meek, etc.) as well as the doctrine of loving one's enemies.

WORKS CITED

Aburdene, Patricia. 2007. *Megatrends 2010*. New York: Hampton Roads.
Addams, Jane. [1910] 2008. *Twenty Years at Hull House*. Mineola, NY: Dover.

Alexander, Eben. 2012. *Proof of Heaven: A Neurosurgeon's Journey into the Afterlife*. New York, NY: Simon and Schuster.
Alexander, Jeffrey C. 2003. *The Meanings of Social Life: A Cultural Sociology*. New York, NY: Oxford.
Allen, Philip, ed. 1963. *Pitirim A. Sorokin in Review*. Durham, NC: Duke University Press.
Andrade, Chittaranjan and Rajiv Radhakrishnan. 2009. "Prayer and Healing: A Medical and Scientific Perspective on Randomized Controlled Trials," *Indian Journal of Psychiatry* 51, 4 (October–December): 247–53.
Armstrong, Karen. 1994. *A History of God*. New York, NY: Ballantine Books.
———. 2010. *The Case for God*. New York, NY: Anchor.
Astin, John. 2000. "The Efficacy of 'Distant Healing': A Systematic Review of Randomized Trials," *Annals of Internal Medicine* 132 (June): 903–10.
Bierwiler, Kay. 1978. *Pitirim Sorokin's Research into Altruism*. Doctoral Dissertation, State University of New York, Albany.
Blau, Judith R., ed. 2001. *The Blackwell Companion to Sociology*. New York, NY: Blackwell.
Bloxham, Donald and A. Dirk Moses, eds. 2010. *The Oxford Handbook of Genocide Studies*. New York, NY: Oxford.
Brinkley, Dannion. 2009. *Secrets of the Light: Lessons from Heaven*. New York: Harper.
Bucior, Christine and Alan Sica. 2019. "Sociology as a Female Preserve: Feminization and Redirection in Sociological Education and Research." Forthcoming in *The American Sociologist* 43.
Burawoy, Michael. 2004. "For Public Sociology." *American Sociological Review* 70(2): 4–28.
Buxton, William. 1996. "Sociological Snakes and Ladders: Parsons and Sorokin at Harvard." Pp. 31–43 in *Sorokin and Civilization: A Centennial Assessment*, edited by Joseph B. Ford, Michel Richard and Palmer C. Talbutt. New Brunswick, NJ: Transaction Publishers.
Calhoun, Craig, ed. 2010. *Robert K. Merton: Sociology of Science and Sociology as Science*. New York, NY: Columbia University Press.
Camic, Charles and Neil Gross. 2001. "The New Sociology of Ideas." Pp. 236–49 in *The Blackwell Companion to Sociology*, edited by Judith R. Blau. New York, NY: Blackwell.
Chappell, Tom. 1996. *The Soul of a Business*. New York, NY: Bantam.
Chodron, Pema. 1996. *Awakening Loving-Kindness*. Boston, MA: Shambhala Publications, Inc.
———. 2010. *The Fearless Heart: The Practice of Living with Courage and Compassion*. Series of public talks, recorded on CD. Available from Boulder, CO: Shambhala Audio Publications.
Chopra, Deepak. 2001. *Perfect Health: The Complete Mind-Body Guide*. New York, NY: Three Rivers Press.
———. 2003. *The Spontaneous Fulfillment of Desire: Harnessing the Infinite Power of Consciousness to Create Miracles*. New York, NY: Random House.
———. 2015. *Quantum Healing: Exploring the Frontiers of Mind/Body Medicine*. New York, NY: Bantam.
Chopra, Deepak and Roger Penrose. 2017. *How Consciousness Became the Universe: Quantum Physics, Cosmology, Neuroscience, Parallel Universes*. New York, NY: Science, Publishers.
Collins, Francis. 2007. *The Language of God*. New York, NY: Free Press.
Coser, Lewis. 1977. *Masters of Sociological Thought*, 2nd ed. New York, NY: Harcourt.
Cowell, Frank R. 1970. *Values in Human Society: The Contributions of Pitirim A. Sorokin to Sociology*. Boston: Porter Sargent.
Crawley, Sara L. 2019. "Reality Disjunctures and Epistemological Encampment: Addressing Relevance in Constructionist Perspectives on Social Problems." Forthcoming in *The American Sociologist* 43.
Dacher, Elliott S. 2006. *Integral Health: The Path to Human Flourishing*. New York, NY: Basic Health Publications.
Dawkins, Richard. 2008. *The God Delusion*. New York, NY: Mariner Books.
Dembski, Willam A. 2002. *Intelligent Design: The Bridge Between Science and Theology*. New York, NY: IVP Academic.

DeStefano, Anthony. 2012. *Angels All Around Us*. New York, NY: Image.
DiFuccia, Maria, Pelton, Julie, and Alan Sica. 2007. "If and When Sociology Becomes a Female Preserve," *The American Sociologist* 38(3): 3–22.
Doykov, Y. V. 2008. "Pitirim Sorokin: A Man of All Seasons," *Biography*, 1.
Durkheim, Emile. [1912] 1999. *The Elementary Forms of Religious Life*. New York, NY: Free Press.
Dyer, Wayne. 2003. *There's a Spiritual Solution to Every Problem*. New York, NY: Quill.
Eadie, Betty J. 1994. *Embraced By The Light*. New York: Bantam.
Eckersley, Glennyce S., and Gary Quinn. 2008. *Everyday Angels*. New York, NY: Random House.
Etzioni, Amitai, ed. 1998. *The Essential Communitarian Reader*. Lanham, MD: Rowman and Littlefield.
Faris, Robert E. L. 1967. *Chicago Sociology: 1920–1932*. San Francisco: Chandler Publishing.
Feagin, Joe and Hernan Vera. 2001. *Liberation Sociology*. Boulder, CO: Westview.
Flew, Antony. 2008. *There Is A God*. New York, NY: Harper.
Friedrichs, Robert W. 1970. *A Sociology of Sociology*. New York, NY: Free Press.
Giddings, Franklin. 1896. *The Principles of Sociology*. New York, NY: Macmillan.
Gouldner, Alvin. 1970. *The Coming Crisis of Western Sociology*. New York, NY: Basic Books.
Hall, John, Laura Grindstaff, and Ming-cheng Lo, eds. 2012. *Handbook of Cultural Sociology*. New York, NY: Routledge.
Hallen, G. C., and P. Rajeshwar, eds. 1972. *Sorokin and Sociology*. Agra, India: Satish.
Hanh, Thich Nhat. 1997. *Living Buddha, Living Christ*. New York, NY: Riverhead Books.
———. 2002. *Anger: Wisdom for Cooling the Flames*. New York: Riverhead Books.
Hawking, Stephen. 1998. *A Brief History of Time*. New York, NY: Bantam.
Hitchins, Christopher. 2009. *God Is Not Great*. New York, NY: Twelve.
Horowitz, Irving Louis. 1994. *The Decomposition of Sociology*. New York, NY: Oxford.
Jeffries, Vincent. 1998. "Virtue and the Altruistic Personality," *Sociological Perspectives* 41: 151–66.
———. 1999. "The Integral Paradigm: The Truth of Faith and the Social Sciences," *The American Sociologist* 30, 4 (Winter): 36–55.
———, ed. 2014. *The Palgrave Handbook of Altruism, Morality and Social Solidarity*. New York, NY: Palgrave Macmillan.
Jeffries, Vincent, Barry V. Johnston, Lawrence T. Nichols, Samuel Oliner, Edward P. Tiryakian, and Jay Weinstein. 2006. "Altruism and Social Solidarity: Envisioning a Field of Specialization," *The American Sociologist* 37, 3 (Fall): 67–83.
Johnston, Barry V. 1986. "Sorokin and Parsons at Harvard: Institutional Conflict and the Origin of a Hegemonic Tradition," *Journal of the History of the Behavioral Sciences* 22 (April): 107–27.
———. 1987. "Pitirim Sorokin and the American Sociological Association: The Politics of a Professional Society," *Journal of the History of the Behavioral Sciences* 23, 2 (April): 103–22.
———. 1995. *Pitirim A. Sorokin: An Intellectual Biography*. Lawrence, KS: University Press of Kansas.
Kabat-Zinn, Jon. 2006. *Coming to Our Senses: Healing Ourselves and the World Through Mindfulness*. New York, NY: Hachette Books.
Kessler, David. *Visions, Trips and Crowded Rooms: Who and What You See Before You Die*. 2011. New York, NY: Hay House.
Keys, C. I., and J. Haidt. 2003. *Flourishing: Positive Psychology and the Life Well-Lived*. Washington, DC: American Psychological Association.
Kravchenko, S. A., and Nikita E. Pokrovsky, eds. 2001. *The Return of Pitirim Sorokin*. Moscow: Kondratieff International Institute.
Krotov, Pavel. 2000. "Pitirim Sorokin's Autobiography as a Reflection of His Altruistic Transformation," *Sociology*, 1.
———. 2014. "Pitirim Sorokin's Heritage: From Core Ideas to Syntheses of Theory and Practice." Pp. 123–47 in *The Palgrave Handbook of Altruism, Morality and Social Solidarity*, edited by Vincent Jeffries. New York, NY: Palgrave Macmillan.

Lederman, Leon M., and Dick Teresi. 1993. *The God Particle*. Boston: Houghton Mifflin.
Lee, Matthew. 2014. "The Essential Interconnections among Altruism, Morality and Social Solidarity: The Case of Religious Altruism." Pp. 311–31 in *The Palgrave Handbook of Altruism, Morality and Social Solidarity*, edited by Vincent Jeffries. New York, NY: Palgrave Macmillan.
Leisola, Matti and Jonathan Witt. 2018. *Heretic: One Scientist's Journey from Darwin to Design*. New York, NY: Discovery Institute.
Lenin, Vladimir I. [1918] 1971. "The Valuable Admissions of Pitirim Sorokin." Pp. 57–64 in *V. I. Lenin, Selected Works in Three Volumes*, Vol. 3. Moscow: Progress Publishers.
Lynd, Robert. 1940. *Knowledge for What? The Place of Social Science in American Culture*. Princeton: Princeton University Press.
Lynd, Robert and Helen Merrell Lynd. 1929. *Middletown: A Study in Modern American Culture*. New York, NY: Harcourt, Brace.
Mackey, John and Raj Sisodia. 2013. *Conscious Capitalism*. Cambridge, MA: Harvard Business Review Press.
Mannheim, Karl. [1929] 1954. *Ideology and Utopia*. New York, NY: Harcourt.
Martineau, Harriet. 1853. *The Positive Philosophy of Auguste Comte*. London: Chapman.
Marx, Karl. [1843] 1970. "A Contribution to the Critique of Hegel's Philosophy of Right." Pp. 3–129 in *Marx/Engels Collected Works*. New York, NY: International.
Mead, Margaret. 1935. *Sex and Temperament in Three Primitive Societies*. New York, NY: Morrow.
Merton, Robert K. 1942. "A Note on Science and Democracy," *Journal of Legal and Political Sociology* 1: 115–26.
———. 1980. "On the Oral Transmission of Knowledge." Pp. 1–35 in *Sociological Traditions from Generation to Generation: Glimpses of the American Experience*, edited by Robert K. Merton and Matilda White Riley. Norwood, NJ: Ablex Publishing.
———. 1994. "A Life of Learning: Charles Homer Haskins Lecture." *Occasional Paper No. 25*. Washington, DC: American Council of Learned Societies.
Merton, Robert K., and Paul Lazarsfeld. 1954. "Friendship as a Social Process: A Substantive and Methodological Analysis." Pp. 18–66 in *Freedom and Control in Modern Society*, edited by Monroe Berger, Theodore Abel and Charles Page. New York, NY: Van Nostrand.
Merton, Robert K., and Thomas Gieryn. 1978. "The Uses of Institutionalized Altruism: The Case of the Professions." Pp. 309–44 in *Sociocultural Change since 1950: Essays in Honor of Carle C. Zimmerman*. Bombay: Vikas Publishing.
Michalowski, Raymond J., and Ronald C. Kramer, eds. 2006. *State-Corporate Crime: Wrongdoing at the Intersection of Business and Government*. New Brunswick: Rutgers University Press.
Micklethwait, John and Adrian Wooldridge. 2009. *God Is Back: How the Global Revival of Faith is Changing the World*. New York, NY: Penguin Books.
Mills, C. Wright. 1959. *The Sociological Imagination*. New York: Oxford University Press.
Mincolla, Mark and Bernie S. Siegel. 2015. *Whole Health: A Holistic Approach to Healing for the 21st Century*. New York, NY: Tarcher Perigee.
Moody, Raymond. 1975. *Life After Life: The Investigation of a Phenomenon—Survival of Bodily Death*. New York, NY: Harper.
Moore, Thomas. 2016. *Care of the Soul*. New York, NY: Harper.
Moorjani, Anita. 2014. *Dying to Be Me: My Journey from Cancer, to Near Death, to True Healing*. New York: Hay House.
Neal, Mary. 2012. *To Heaven and Back*. New York, NY: Waterbrook.
Nichols, Lawrence T. 1989. "Deviance and Social Science: The Instructive Case of Pitirim Sorokin." *Journal of the History of the Behavioral Sciences* 25(4): 335–55.
———. 1996. "Intergenerational Solidarity in the Creation of Science: The Ross-Sorokin Correspondence, 1921–1931," *Journal of the History of the Behavioral Sciences* 32, 2 (April): 135–50.
———. 1998. "Sorokin, Tolstoy and Civilizational Change." Pp. 33–38 in *Rough Dialectics*, edited by Palmer C. Talbutt. Amsterdam, Netherlands: Rodopi Press.

———. 1999. "Science, Politics, and Moral Activism: Sorokin's Integralism Reconsidered," *Journal of the History of the Behavioral Sciences* 35(2): 139–55.
———. 2011. "Burawoy's Holistic Sociology and Sorokin's Integralism: A Conversation of Ideas." Pp. 27–46 in *Handbook of Public Sociology*, edited by Vincent Jeffries. Lanham, MD: Rowman Littlefield.
———. 2012a. "Renewing Sociology: Integral Science, Solidarity and Loving Kindness," *Sociological Focus* 45(4): 262–73.
———. 2012b. "Sorokin as Lifelong Russian Intellectual: The Enactment of an Historically Rooted Sensibility." *The American Sociologist* 43(4): 374–405.
———. 2014. "Modern Roots of the Sociology of Love: Tolstoy, Addams, Gandhi and Sorokin." Pp. 149–75 in *The Palgrave Handbook of Altruism, Morality and Social Solidarity*, edited by Vincent Jeffries. New York, NY: Palgrave Macmillan.
Oliner, Samuel P., and Pearl I. Oliner. 1988. *The Altruistic Personality*. New York, NY: Free Press.
Osnos, Evan. 2015. *Age of Ambition: Chasing Fortune, Truth, and Faith in the New China*. New York: Farrar, Straus and Giroux.
Parsons, Talcott, and Edward Shils, eds. 1951. *Toward A General Theory of Action*. Cambridge, MA: Harvard University Press.
Peterson, Christopher and Martin Seligman. 2004. *Character Strengths and Virtues*. New York, NY: Oxford University Press.
Post, Stephen. 2003. *Unlimited Love*. West Conshohocken, PA: Templeton Press.
Rhodes, Colbert, ed. 2017. *Renewal: The Inclusion of Integralism and Moral Values into the Social Sciences*. Lanham, MD: Hamilton Books.
Ross, Edward A. 1921. *The Russian Bolshevik Revolution*. New York, NY: Century.
Schervish, Paul G., and Keith Whitaker. 2010. *Wealth and the Will of God: Discerning the Use of Riches in the Service of Ultimate Purpose*. Bloomington, IN: Indiana University Press.
Schipper, Janine. 2012. "Toward a Buddhist Sociology: Theories, Methods, and Possibilities," *The American Sociologist* 43, 2 (June): 203–22.
Seligman, Martin. 2004. *Authentic Happiness: Using the New Positive Psychology to Realize Your Potential for Lasting Fulfillment*. New York, NY: Atria Books.
Smith, Christian and Hilary Davidson. 2014. *The Paradox of Generosity*. New York, NY: Oxford.
Solovyov, Vladimir. [1877] 2008. *The Philosophical Principles of Integral Knowledge*, translated by Valeria Z. Nollan. Grand Rapids, MI: Erdman.
Sorokin, Pitirim A. 1912. *L. N. Tolstoy as a Philosopher*. Petrograd: Kolos.
———. 1914. *Crime and Punishment, Service and Reward* (Russian title: *Prestuplenie i Kara, Podvig i Nagrada*). St. Petersburg: Dolbushev.
———. 1920. *A System of Sociology*. Petrograd: Kolos.
———. 1921a. "Dostoyevsky's Legacies," *Artistic Affairs* 17–120: 4–7.
———. 1921b. "Dostoyevsky as a Sociologist," *Annals of the Palace of Literature* 1: 7.
———. 1924. *Leaves from a Russian Diary*. New York, NY: Dutton.
———. 1925. *The Sociology of Revolution*. Philadelphia: Lippincott.
———. 1927. *Social Mobility*. New York, NY: Harper.
———. 1928. *Contemporary Sociological Theories*. New York, NY: Harper.
———. 1927–1941. *Social and Cultural Dynamics*. New York, NY: American Book Co.
———. 1941. *The Crisis of Our Age*. New York, NY: Dutton.
———. 1942. *Man and Society in Calamity*. New York, NY: Dutton.
———. 1944a. *Russia and the United States*. New York, NY: Dutton.
———. 1944b. *Sociocultural Causality, Space and Time*. Durham, NC: Duke University Press.
———. 1947. *Society, Culture and Personality*. New York, NY: Harper.
———. 1948. *The Reconstruction of Humanity*. Boston: Beacon Press.
———. 1950a. *Altruistic Love: A Study of American Good Neighbors and Christian Saints*. Boston: Beacon Press.
———, ed. 1950b. *Explorations in Altruistic Love and Behavior: A Symposium*. Boston: Beacon Press.

———, ed. 1954a. *Forms and Techniques of Altruistic and Spiritual Growth*. Boston: Beacon Press.
———. 1954b. *The Ways and Power of Love*. Boston: Beacon Press.
———. 1956. *The American Sex Revolution*. Boston: Beacon Press.
———. 1963. *A Long Journey*. New Haven: College and University Press.
———. 1964. *Basic Trends of Our Times*. New Haven, CT: College and University Press.
———. 1966. *Sociological Theories of Today*. New York, NY: Harper and Row.
———. 1975. *Hunger as a Factor in Human Affairs*, translated by Elena P. Sorokin. Gainesville, FL: University of Florida Press.
———. 2000. *Zametki Sotsiologa (The Notes of a Sociologist)*, edited by A. O. Boronoyev. Saint Petersburg: Aleteya.
Sorokin, Pitirim A., and Walter Lunden. 1959. *Power and Morality: Who Shall Guard the Guardians?* Boston: Beacon Press.
Sorokin, Pitirim A., and Carle C. Zimmerman. 1928. *Principles of Rural-Urban Sociology*. New York, NY, NY: Henry Holt.
Sorokin, Pitirim A., Carle C. Zimmerman, and C. J. Galpin. 1930–1932. *A Systematic Sourcebook in Rural Sociology*, 3 volumes. Minneapolis: University of Minnesota Press.
Spencer, Herbert. 1898. *The Principles of Sociology*. New York, NY: Appleton.
Stets, Jan E., and Kevin McCaffree, 2014. "Linking Morality, Altruism and Social Solidarity Using Identity Theory." Pp. 333–51 in *The Palgrave Handbook of Altruism, Morality and Social Solidarity*, edited by Vincent Jeffries. New York, NY: Palgrave Macmillan.
Talbutt, Palmer C. 1998. *Rough Dialectics: Sorokin's Theory of Value*. Amsterdam, Netherlands: Rodopi Press.
Tiryakian, Edward A., ed. 1963. *Sociological Theory, Values and Sociocultural Change: Essays in Honor of Pitirim A. Sorokin*. New York, NY: Free Press.
———. 1988. "Sociology's Dostoyevksi: Pitirim A. Sorokin," *The World and I* (September): 569–80.
———. 2001. "Pitirim A. Sorokin: My Teacher, Prophet of Advanced Modernity." Pp. 47–63 in *The Return of Pitirim Sorokin*, edited by S. A. Kravchenko and Nikita E. Pokrovsky. Moscow: Kondratieff International Institute.
Tolstoy, Lev N. [1896] 1961. *The Kingdom of God Is Within You*. New York, NY: Farrar, Straus and Cudahy.
Turner, Jonathan H. 2014. "The Evolution of Affect: Sociality, Altruism and Conscience in Humans. Pp. 275–301 in *The Palgrave Handbook of Altruism, Morality and Social Solidarity*, edited by Vincent Jeffries. New York, NY: Palgrave Macmillan.
Turner, Jonathan H. 2016. "Academic Journals and Sociology's Big Divide: A Modest But Radical Proposal," *The American Sociologist* 47(2–3): 289–301.
Turner, Stephen P. 2014. *American Sociology: From Pre-Disciplinary to Post-Normal*. New York, NY: Palgrave Macmillan.
Turner, Stephen P., and Jonathan H. Turner. 1990. *The Impossible Science: An Institutional Analysis of American Sociology*. Newbury Park, CA: Sage.
Vidich, Arthur J., and Stanford M. Lyman. 1985. *American Sociology: Worldly Rejections of Religion and Their Directions*. New Haven: Yale University Press.
Villadsen, Kaspar. 2018. "Jane Addams' Social Vision: Revisiting the Gospel of Individualism and Solidarity," *The American Sociologist* 49(2): 218–41.
Virtue, Doreen. 2007. *How to Hear Your Angels*. New York, NY: Hay House.
Ward, Lester F. 1895. *Static and Dynamic Sociology*. Boston: Ginn.
Weber, Max. [1922] 1964. *The Sociology of Religion*, translated by Ephraim Fischoff. Boston: Beacon Press.
Weil, Andrew. 2004. *Natural Health, Natural Medicine: The Complete Guide to Wellness and Self-Care for Optimum Health*. New York, NY: Mariner Books.
Weinstein, Jay. 2000. "Creative Altruism: Restoring Sorokin's Program of Applied Sociology," *Journal of Applied Sociology* 17: 86–117.
Williamson, Marianne. 1996. *A Return to Love: Reflections on the Principles of A Course in Miracles*. New York, NY: Harper.
———. 2008. *Age of Miracles*. New York, NY: Hay House.

Yogan, Lissa. 2015. "Positively Teaching Positive Sociology," *Sociological Focus* 48(1): 1–15.
Zimmerman, Carle C. 1973. "My Sociological Career." *Revue Internationale de Sociologie* 9(1–2): 89–117.
Zorbaugh, Harvey W. 1929. *The Gold Coast and the Slum: A Sociological Study of Chicago's Near North Side*. Chicago: University of Chicago Press.
Zyuzev, Nikolai F. 2010. *Pitirim Sorokin's Philosophy of Love*. Syktyvkar: ESKOM.

Chapter Seven

Gregory P. Stone's Contributions to Urban Sociology, Social Psychology, and the Sociology of Sport

Harvey A. Farberman

Gregory P. Stone (1921–1981) is well known for his major contributions to the fields of urban sociology and social psychology but less so for his intellectual and organizational contributions to the development of the sociology of sport as a professional, social scientific, sub-discipline of sociology. My aim in this chapter is to (1) provide a brief sketch of Stone's career, (2) present his contributions to urban sociology, social psychology, and the sociology of sports, and (3) apply his insights to better understand why professional football teams (and their star athletes) have become agents of protest and social change.

A BIOGRAPHICAL SKETCH

Stone began his academic career as an undergraduate at Hobart College, located in the Finger Lake Region of Geneva, New York. Hobart is a private, liberal arts institution with an historical affiliation to the Episcopal Church. There, he came under the influence of sociologist Leo Srole (1908–1993) and worked with him on a community survey that assessed the impact on small town life of the Japanese attack on Pearl Harbor. Srole was called into military service in WWII before the project was completed and replaced by the political scientist Ithiel de Sola Poole (1917–1984) but Stone remained with the project until he was graduated from Hobart in 1942.

In April 1943, Stone also was called into military service. In 1944, he was placed into a Turkish language certification program at Princeton University in preparation for some sort of intelligence work. After achieving certification, however, Stone's entire unit was posted to the European Theatre of Operations and integrated into a mortar company. For 180 consecutive days, Stone saw intensive combat in the Battle of the Bulge. His two closest friends, one a poet, the other a mathematician, were both killed; one during an enemy artillery barrage, the other when American bombers missed their coordinates and unloaded ordnance on front-line American positions. Stone survived these events and on April 12, 1945, as part of the combined effort of the 104th US Infantry Division and the 3rd Armored Division participated in the liberation of the Nordhausen/Dora-Mittelbrau concentration camp located in the Harz mountains north of the town of Nordhausen in Thuringia, Germany. Stone was discharged from military service on December 8, 1945. His pre-war ambition to become an Episcopal priest did not survive his wartime experiences.

Throughout his military service, Stone carried along, and studied, three books. The first was The *Collected Poems of Kenneth Fearing*. Fearing (1902–1961) was a two-time Guggenheim Fellow, a co-founder of the *Partisan Review*, and a novelist who wrote about the plight and alienation of the lower and middle working classes. The second was an excursus on Marxist political economy by Harvard trained economist and co-founder of the left-leaning *Monthly Review*, Paul Sweezy (1910–2004), entitled *Theories of Capitalist Development*. And the third was a treatise on the sociology of knowledge by Karl Mannheim (1893–1947), the Hungarian-born social philosopher and sociologist, entitled *Ideology and Utopia*. Stone described these books respectively as easy, logical, and incomprehensible. In a handwritten, unpublished, autobiographical fragment, he reports "what attracted me to Chicago [University] was the brute fact that I did not understand the orgiastic chiliasm of the Anabaptists discussed in Karl Mannheim's book" (Stone n.d.a).

Stone was a student in the sociology department at the University of Chicago from January 1946 to September 1949, and was awarded a Master's Degree in 1952 and a PhD in 1959. In the sociology department, he encountered established scholars such as William Ogburn (1886–1959), Ernest Burgess (1886–1966), Louis Wirth (1897–1952), Everett Hughes (1897–1983) and Herbert Blumer (1900–1987); young instructors including Herbert Goldhammer (1907–1977) and Nelson Foote (1916–2012); and fellow students including Erving Goffman (1922–1982), Anselm L. Strauss (1916–1996), Howard S. Becker (1928–), and Robert W. Habenstein (1915–2011), among many others. He also was influenced by the work of other Chicago faculty outside of the sociology department including Lloyd Warner (1898–1970), from the Committee on Human Development, Robert Redfield (1897–1958) in anthropology, and Frank Knight (1885–1972) in economics. Lloyd Warner, along with Everett Hughes, were co-chairmen of Stone's doctoral dissertation committee.

Stone held teaching positions at Michigan State University (1949–1955), the University of Missouri at Columbia (1956–1958), Washington University in St. Louis (1959–1960) and the University of Minnesota, Minneapolis where he spent the remainder of his academic career. At Minnesota, he held a joint appointment in the American Studies Program (where, from time to time, he lectured on the history of city planning) and an adjunct appointment in the Department of Home Economics (where, on occasion, he lectured on the social psychological importance of clothing in everyday life).

In 1965, Stone attended a meeting in Warsaw, Poland of primarily European sport sociologists and became a full member of the Executive Board of the International Committee for Sport Sociology. In 1967, under the auspices of the Committee of Sport Sociology, Stone, in collaboration with Gunther Luschen, originally from West Germany and subsequently a faculty member in the sociology department at the University of Illinois, Urbana-Champagne, organized a "methodological working seminar" hosted by the University of Illinois and sponsored by both the departments of sociology and physical education. In 1974, Stone became co-chair of the Steering Committee for the founding of the Society for the Study of Symbolic Interaction (SSSI), and in 1977 became the Society's first president. Upon his passing, his wife, Dr. Gladys Ishida Stone established a trust fund to underwrite an annual SSSI Stone Symposium. With the passing of Carl J. Couch (1925–1994), also a co-founder and president of the SSSI, relatives and friends set aside additional funding in honor of Couch that led to the re-naming of the symposium, now known as the SSSI Couch-Stone Symposium.

URBAN SOCIOLOGY

Stone's contributions to urban sociology may be grouped under two major concepts: *non-ranked status aggregates* and *personalization*. When he arrived at the University of Chicago, Stone came under the wing of Lloyd Warner who had been conducting a decade-long empirical study of stratification systems in Newburyport, Massachusetts, a small, New England community (The so-called Yankee City Series). There, Warner had adopted a Weberian (as opposed to a Marxian) approach to the study of societal organization. Whereas Marx had argued for the precedence of economics (and for the analysis of economic class struggle) over politics and sociability, Weber (1946), in his examination of class, status, and party, had argued for the relative autonomy of social, political, and economic institutional orders and for the analysis of status politics. Following Weber, but ignoring the political and economic side, Warner focused exclusively on *status groups* and their usurpation and distribution of status and honor as a way of understanding how communities were organized. Based on extensive empirical research,

Warner developed a rank-ordered model of social stratification. While he did not pursue an analysis of the structure of political power and economic class in the grand European sense, he did incorporate a *hierarchical* approach to the development of a model of the social order.

C. Wright Mills (1942) leveled a critique of Warner's work, given its neglect of political and economic matters, and provoked a debate between Marxists and Weberians over which network of elites, (social, political, or economic) controlled the country. Form and Stone (1957) came to the conclusion that the debate was fruitless and that attention should focus on whether Weber's original conception of status group itself was adequate for an analysis of social order and whether it should be tied into an exclusively hierarchical model of that order. Stone's answer was no, on both counts. In general, he believed that a vertical model of any sort, whether of the social, political, or economic orders, was unable to capture the richness, flexibility, and nuance of sociocultural reality and, in fact, had hobbled the development of sociological theory. In particular, he believed that the notion of hierarchically ordered status groups should be replaced by that of non-ranked status aggregates.

Non-Ranked Status Aggregates

Stone came to this view after having conducted considerable quantitative empirical research. For example, Stone had used Warner's Index of Status Characteristics in an ongoing six-year study of *clothing* that began in 1950 and was sponsored by the (then) Michigan State College Agricultural Experiment Station and carried out by members of the university's sociology and anthropology departments. The research team had used Warner's instrument for describing and discriminating status in a community survey of Vansburg, Michigan, and came up with a very different picture of the social organization of that small, south central, county seat of 10,000 than that anticipated by Warner's model.

Stone, and his collaborators did not find a system of vertically ranked status groups, or a community ecology that reflected such a system; rather, they found that the broad middle range of the community had no discernible status reputation at all, and that there actually was an ongoing *status war* at the very top of the community between an old line local elite and an invading horde of newcomers who recently had descended upon the community when the national corporations that they worked for located some branches of their companies in a nearby area in order to take advantage of Vansburg's supply of cheap labor. Indeed, the new cosmopolitan elite identified with national level culture and fashion and began to set trends for the rest of the community. The status war that broke out between the old and new elites spread throughout the entire community and made a shamble of what, at an earlier time, may well have been a settled status order. Instead of a vertical order, what Stone found was a configuration that looked more like a "Y," that is, a community bisected at the top with reverberations reaching down the bottom.

To interpret this situation, Stone introduced the concept of *status aggregate* and distinguished it from status groups. He thought it more useful for analysis because, for the large middle range of the population, it did not presuppose either frequency of contact or communality among members but rather occasional, episodic, encounters characteristic of middle-class, urban society. Nevertheless, *status aggregates* still refer to agglomerations of individuals who enjoy the same amount and kind of honor in a community and who tend toward a limited degree of social closure or exclusiveness. This distinctiveness, however, comes to them more by default than design; subordinate groups emulate them. Unlike status groups, *status aggregates* maintain only a loose monopoly over their symbols of distinctiveness so that individuals who are not objectively part of the aggregate may appropriate its symbols and render them unreliable as indicators of actual social position. People may learn and copy the lifestyle of a status aggregate without being part of it.

In consequence, in the anonymous situations that are typical of an urbanized lifestyle, and were now infiltrating small towns and small cities not to mention large ones, the dignity and honor of a status aggregate might be borrowed by those who are not objectively entitled to it. Indeed, individuals may misrepresent themselves and pass without disclosure. This may be taken to the extreme in larger urban communities, where bars, department stores, and consumer situations provide anonymous stages upon which individuals may assume identities and play roles that are outside their normal, everyday life. Stone refers to these situations as *status platforms* or *status transformers*.

Stone's research led him to believe that there was more instability than stability in the status arrangements of the average community. He was impressed enough with the phenomenon of *status instability* that he theorized about three of its possible modes: *horizontal competition* among groups, *vertical polarization* between groups, and totally *unranked groups*. The evidence from his own empirical work led him to elaborate more fully on the last of these where he pointed out that unranked groups usually voluntarily withdraw to a marginal position on the outskirts of a community and see themselves as independent of the appraisals of mainstream groups. They adopt and display esoteric symbols of expressive, intrinsic value, cultivate their own sense of taste, maintain internal solidarity, and rebuff the intrusion of outsiders. They typically place a higher value on *status sentiment* than on *economic interest* and often set trends and display symbols that other groups eventually appropriate. At the extreme, these groups often are the bohemian artists and intellectuals who other groups first revile and then imitate.

Stone's identification of at least three status configurations that either reflect or precipitate community instability was a self-conscious attempt to counter the conservative image associated with studies of social status as compared to the radical image associated with studies of economic class. He asserted that there are powerful dynamics for change inherent in status conflicts and discrepancies. For example, groups that are unable to achieve an esteemed position in the overall social organization of a community, nevertheless, as Mannheim had suggested, may continue to regard themselves with dignity and solidarity by looking toward a future with the hope of eventual redemption and fulfillment. And, when there is a wide discrepancy between a group's low objective position and its subjective claim to a higher position, the condition exists for what Everett C. Hughes (1949) called *status protest*. And this may well produce a powerful challenge to a community's structure. Therefore, while it may be permissible to say that the status arrangements of communities tend toward a structure of hierarchy, it would be a mistake to underestimate the dynamic for change embedded in status instabilities especially in mass, urban environments where anonymity, ethnicity, and race magnify such instabilities.

Stone was quite clear in recognizing, however, that, even at the extreme, status instability and status protest are not the same as, and do not lead to, class struggle. To the contrary, as Thorsten Veblen's (1899) turn-of-the-century examination of the nature of conspicuous consumption had shown, status groups jockey for position through *emulation* of those above them and *exclusion* of those below them. And they do this mainly through displays of consumption. People do not so much resent their betters as look up to, envy, and wish to be like them, or, at least, to have some of what they have. And this is the case, perhaps, even more so, with status aggregates.

This insight was compatible with David Riesman, Nathan Glazer, and Reuel Denny's (1950) mid-century examination of the profound structural transformation of the United States, from a middle-class to a middle-mass society; from an inner-directed, producer-oriented to an, other-directed, consumer-oriented society. The long-term effects of rapid and pervasive industrialization and urbanization when combined with explosive demographic growth had culminated in a people who had become susceptible to external manipulation and had surrendered to consumerism. What Veblen (1857–1929) had identified as the ornate, consumption rituals of turn-of-the-century elites, Riesman and his colleagues saw as the animating spirit of middle-mass America.

Based on his own research, and the sociohistorical perspectives provided by Veblen and Riesman, Stone began to envision the specter of a middle-mass society held together in loosely organized status aggregates filled with individuals animated by consumer desires. While he could not turn his back on the data and the findings and was impressed and influenced by the powerful way in which both Veblen and Riesman had dramatized their respective historical epochs, he did not like the specter that was implied and emphatically believed that there was more to be said. For example, if industrialization, urbanization, and population growth had resulted in massification and anonymity, then more than anything else, Stone surmised that this would produce a counter reaction, a quest for personalized relationships, social identity, and a sense of being integrated into one's own community.

Stone had learned much from Srole and Warner about quantitative research methodology but he went his own way in developing a theoretical framework. Following Warner, Stone ignored the economic and political side of community life and focused on the social. However, he rejected Warner's hierarchical view of the distribution of social status and social honor and, instead, began to develop a conception of local community organization based on a model of *non-ranked status aggregates*, albeit leaving the door open to alternatives. He believed that it made more sense to approach the topics of how communities were organized and what the quality of life was like in them as empirical questions to be answered by research, rather than by ideological assertions that were in the service of Marxian or Weberian ideas. The emphasis should be on discovering the conditions under which possible options might become actual realities. This means avoiding an a priori acceptance of a hierarchical model of community organization and searching for the anomalies and negative cases that might stimulate further theoretical speculation.

Stone's effort to confirm Warner's model put him at odds with it; instead of status groups with clear-cut definitions and well-defined boundaries, he found amorphous aggregates; instead of a uniform, pyramidal, hierarchy, he found a "Y" formation that bisected the community at the top and reached down with separate legs toward the bottom; instead of order, he found instability. While this model grew out of Stone's research in small towns and cities, it fit neatly into the larger interpretive understanding that Veblen presented of the early twentieth century and Riesman presented of the middle twentieth century. In sum, the succession of historical epochs was a story of *status instability, bisected communities, amorphous aggregates, and conspicuous consumption.*

Louis Wirth (1938), under the influence of Georg Simmel, summed up a whole generation of work on the sociology of city life when he characterized urban communities as an array of anonymous situations in which warm, intimate, primary relationships were being replaced by role-specific, secondary contacts; as a habitat in which an admixture of different ethnic, racial, and linguistic groups lived cheek-by-jowl in social heterogeneity and physical density. In an environment characterized by anonymity, impersonality, and antipathy, how and where might individuals establish personal relationships that would enable them to distinguish, for themselves, and others, just exactly who they are and how they fit into the community?

Stone rose to the challenge by undercutting what he saw as a romantic, anti-urban bias pervasive in the work of both Simmel and Wirth. To do so, he pursued some of the leads that Herman Schmalenbach had developed in his critique of Ferdinand Toennies's distinction between *Gemeinschaft* and *Gesellschaft*. Indeed, Stone (1956) was able to go beyond Schmalenbach in the re-conceptualization of Toennies's principal ideas, as he had become thoroughly acquainted with Toennies via the lectures and writing of Wirth (1926). He also became intimately familiar with the work of Schmalenbach, when, in fulfillment of his doctoral language requirement at the University of Chicago, he followed up on an intriguing footnote about Schmalenbach penned by Edward Shils (1951). In fact, in 1961 Stone undertook the first English language translation of one of Schmalenbach's key essays, titled *The Sociological Category of Communion*.

Schmalenbach (1961) had introduced the concept of *communion* to fill a gap that existed between Toennies's ideal-typical constructs of community (*Gemeinschaft*) and society (*Gesellschaft*). Communion characterizes the type of relationship where people get caught up in a sentiment that may well encompass both love and hate, joy and despair; in other words, a sentiment that goes beyond mere positive emotion (friendship is one example). These relationships typically occur in, or lead to, the formation of a *Bund*, or primary type group, similar to that described by Charles H. Cooley. Moreover, this kind of relationship may emerge out of even the most mundane, routine, or incidental encounters.

Going beyond Schmalenbach, Stone realized that relationships, whether based on the economic and juridical rationality of the marriage contract (behind which society stands); or the rights, duties, privileges, and obligations that members of a family owe each other (behind which community stands); or the unpredictable, volatile, ecstasies of a love relationship (behind which communion stands), all have an antinomian quality that goes beyond the bi-polar imagery implied by Tonnies ([1887] 1957), that is, each can become the other. The violence of passion may become the sweet reasonableness of compassion or the other way around. Each contains latent countertendencies or incipient potentials that, under the right conditions, allow them to undergo profound and radical transformations. Even the most mundane, routine, incidental encounter may become the basis for communication, consensus, and solidarity. Indeed, as Schmalenbach argues, "there are forms of community that can be sustained [even] between the salesman and the customer in shops that one frequents with some regularity" (1961: 332).

Personalization

To Stone, this was a clarion call that led him right to the heart of the beast; to the driving force of the city, the market economy itself, to see if some urban dwellers, in their consumer behavior, established relationships with sales personnel in retail stores that became *personalized* and, in some manner, bound them to the larger community. Thus, he began to study exchanges of value to see if they became valued exchanges; to see if economic interest gave way to social sentiment, a transformation first foretold long ago by Adam Smith in his *The Theory of Moral Sentiments* ([1759] 2005), and, after various incarnations, more recently theorized by Tamotsu Shibutani in his *Society and Personality: An Interactionist Approach to Social Psychology* (1961).

This audacious quest led Stone (1954) to analyze survey data from 150 women who lived on Chicago's Northwest Side and who were asked to evaluate shopping centers and retail stores and to indicate what they expected of sales personnel. With surprising frequency, many women stated that their shopping behavior included a personal dimension. After closer analysis, Stone discerned four different types of consumers and shopping orientations: "economic" (33 percent) where price was the only thing that counted; "personalizing" (28 percent) where an individual touch and a degree of closeness with the service personnel was more important than price or variety of goods; "ethical" (18 percent) where there is a sense of moral obligation to shop at local stores rather than the larger chain or department stores; and "apathetic" (17 percent) where they did not care nor give much thought to where they shopped. As it happens, the combination of personalizing and ethical shoppers, who see price as secondary to other more important noneconomic issues, constitute 46 percent of all respondents.

To explain this finding, Stone entertained the possibility that these shoppers merely were carrying over, into an urban market place, shopping styles that they had learned at earlier stages of their lives in small town rural environments. A closer look into respondents' background data indicated that, in fact, most of the sample were native Chicagoans within each consumer category. The only differentiating background variable was that the ethical shoppers tended to be third generation Chicagoans. The only interpretation that made sense, then, was that the personalization and moralization of shopping originated in the heart of the city. That was not supposed to happen, given Wirth's view: ethical shoppers patronize local stores in the best interests of the store owners, and personalizing shoppers enter the market place open to the possibility of building some sort of relationship with sales personnel. But why should this be the case? If it was true that a significant segment of born and bred urban consumers put matters of social and moral sentiment above economic interest, what else about them might make sense of this?

Using Warner's Index of Status Characteristics that contained both subjective and objective measures of community identification, and running tests of statistical significance on a host of variables, Stone drew up social profiles of each type of consumer and identified some of the conditions that probably went into shaping their shopping orientations. Economic consumers, for example, tended to be young, have small children, be upwardly mobile, and on their way to other more prestigious residential areas of the city. They were cost conscious, detached from the local neighborhood, and were instrumentally oriented. Personalizing shoppers had spent their early married years outside the local area, were cut off from most of their long-time friends, were of lower social status, and had either very few or very many children. They did not participate in community activities but, nevertheless, identified strongly with the local community and expressed no desire to move. Ethical consumers were long-time area residents of high social status, and unhappy with the rapid business development going on in and around their local community. They shopped at local stores as a protest against an unwanted change in their way of life. Apathetic shoppers were older, settled into the local area, reconciled to unfulfilled upward mobility aspirations, and enjoyed strong ties with other locals. They did not look to their shopping activity for social ties; the consumer arena was of no special interest to them.

So, ethical and apathetic consumers were long-time area residents, while economic and personalizing shoppers were more recent arrivals. The variables that discriminated among them seem to be aspiration, marginality, and degree of success. High aspiration newcomers adopt an economic orientation; low aspiration newcomers tend toward personalization; successful, long-time residents display an ethical orientation; and unsuccessful long-timers are apathetic. What remains as an apparent anomaly is why low status, low aspiration, recent arrivals, who do not participate in any community activities and are not objectively integrated into the local community, still report strong subjective identification with it.

By way of explanation, Stone advanced the following hypothesis: subjective identification with local area was a latent function of the personalization of market relations. Stone thought that these shoppers compensated for their social losses by developing quasi-personal relationships with store personnel who were at the same status level. To test this hypothesis, Stone singled out the personalizing shoppers and assessed their degree of embeddedness in the community based on a cumulative score on four indices of objective integration: (a) less than six years of residence in the neighborhood, (b) over 29 years of age at entry into neighborhood, (c) moved into the local neighborhood from a completely different location, and, (d) left the majority of their close friends in the old neighborhood, outside the local area. Those indicating all four were interpreted as having "no apparent basis," in terms of objective integration, for their reported subjective identification with the local community. Those with three had "little apparent basis," those with two, "some apparent basis," and those with one, "apparent basis." After applying tests of statistical significance, Stone concluded that personalizing shoppers, when compared to all other types of shoppers, established subjective identification with the local area, with very little or no apparent objective basis. Consequently, the hypothesis that personalization fulfilled the latent function of establishing community solidarity for some city residents should not be rejected.

In line, then, with a generally Weberian approach, Stone acknowledged the multidimensional nature of societal stratification, and its transformation into functionally autonomous social, political, and economic orders. In line with Veblen, Stone focused on status symbolism as emblems of consumption that delineated social boundaries and acted as a medium through which groups and aggregates signaled their emulation and exclusion of one another. Following Riesman, Stone believed that consumption had replaced production as the central institution of American society and sought the bases of personal and community integration initially within the sphere of consumer interaction and later within the sphere of recreation. In response to Warner, Stone offered an empirically grounded non-hierarchical model of community status arrangements. He also noted that the analysis of stratification could occur on societal, communal, institutional, and interpersonal levels and that it might incorporate both subjective and objective dimensions. And while his own work focused on the community level and blended both subjective and objective elements, he also believed that it had implications for the societal and interpersonal levels.

SOCIAL PSYCHOLOGY

Stone's contributions to social psychology can be grouped under the concepts of (1) *universe of appearance* and (2) *identity*. Despite some success in demonstrating that the city contained situations and settings in which some urban dwellers might establish quasi-personal relationships either to compensate for their lack of general integration elsewhere, or to protect their way of life against unwanted incursions, Stone could not but acknowledge that in the city, most social encounters are segmented and fleeting, and that participants are strangers who are unable to evaluate each other in the context of their family, work, or residential history. Also, that they appraise each other based on appearance rather than reputation, and that appearance could be crafted by the clever manipulation and display of symbols. Urban dwellers bestow status and social position on each other because of appraisals and inferences concerning one another's symbols. This is in contrast with the way people assess each other in small towns and rural areas. There, they evaluate each other over time, in repeated encounters, in the context of membership in family networks, churches, occupations, and civic associations. And, in consequence, they constitute and reconstitute a consensually agreed upon order of reciprocal rights, duties, privileges, and obligations. Symbols are merely surface emblems or symptoms of deeper lying status arrangements. People know the social order and evaluate the appearance of symbols against it. In the city, people appraise the symbols and from them infer the order. Whether the symbols are authentic (or not), and the inferences from them correct (or not), there is not much by way of alternative. Thus, several pertinent questions arise: (a) Do urbanites rely on a particular type of symbolism? (b) Is there agreement on this symbolism? and (c) Can inferences from these symbols be tested?

Universe of Appearance

Form and Stone (1957) began an effort to answer these questions by drawing on Goffman's (1951) understanding of status symbols as having both personal-expressive and social-categorical significance. Goffman's approach is premised on Weber's (1946) observation that status groups tend toward commensal and connubial exclusiveness, and on Speier's (1952) declaration that, for status and honor to exist at all, there must be bearers, bestowers, and observers. The primary question is: what signs and symbols do urbanites use to appraise the social position of anonymous others? For example, Chicagoans who resided adjacent to the downtown central business district indicated, in response to a sample survey, that style of appearance, social identity (that is, occupation, education, or group affiliations), image of appearance, physical appearance, and attitudinal references, in that order, all come into play, but that style and substance of appearance (and taste as it might be revealed in that appearance) was most important. For example, all agreed that down-and-outers at the bottom of the social order could be distinguished by shabby dress, slovenliness, obscene language, and excessive drinking. Members of the working class could be recognized by their hands, teeth, hair, shoes, occupational uniforms, and lunch buckets. Members of high society stood out because of their manners, conversation, dress, jewels, clothing, and limousines. Although it was less easy to be sure of who was middle class, appraisals usually focused on apparent indicators of income, occupation, education, and family. So, what stood out across the board were dimensions of the style and substance of appearance. And based on such apparent symbols, city dwellers discern each other's social location and bestow status.

Reliance upon apparent symbolism to place an anonymous stranger in social space, so that a fleeting encounter may proceed, obviously gives way to a more in-depth inspection and test of that person's status when some sort of long-term commitment to that individual is on the horizon. When the bestowal of status implies permanence, such as accepting someone into the family via marriage, then it proceeds based on an evaluation of that person's reputation in the larger scheme of things and questions concerning the style and substance of appearance recede into the background. But the question remains as to how the individual's status claims are tested or validated and the answer is, in the conventional manner. Information is sought about family, job, affiliations, etc., either in direct conversation with the individual or through queries of friends and mutual acquaintances. And, more important than all the rest is information about family.

Thus, human transactions occur within a matrix of appearances composed of gestures, posture, dress, language, settings, and any number of other situationally relevant variables that enable participants to identify and empathize with each other, and thereby to underwrite the meaning, value, and sentiment of their interactions. Indeed, as Stone and Farberman (1970) declare in the opening sentence of their article on appearance and the self, "Appearance means identification of one another" and the question is whether identification follows any discernible order or pattern.

Following George H. Mead who rejected a Freudian, psychologistic, approach to the self, in favor of a transactivist, social behavioral model, Stone sought the meaning of appearance within the field of interaction and transaction, especially in the responses that appearances call out or mobilize in others. Stone focused on appearance to counteract what he took to be a linguistic or discursive bias in Mead's work. Stone reasoned that, before people spoke, they appeared, and that appearance formed the silent, pre-text of subsequent dialogical interaction. And, it had to have some effect on the discourse to follow.

Stone returned to the Vansburg data to study talk about that dimension of appearance provoked by clothing and was aware of other dimensions of appearance including tattooing, face painting, body scarring, lip stretching, ear piercing, and nose rings, as well as that special manner of talk which was more for (status) "show" than for (conversational) "tell," which he labelled "apparent discourse." In any event, Stone focused on talk about clothing and generated his data from a proportional stratified sample of 100 married couples who were presented with a battery of four interview schedules plus a series of drawings formatted as a Thematic Apperception Test. Each subject was visited twice for an average of three hours per total interview. All sessions were tape recorded. In response, the sample gave rise to 8,682 statements about appearance. Stone focused on two modes of response: "reviews" (or responses made by other about the wearer's clothes), and "programs" (responses the wearer made about his or her own clothes). Stone (1959) also identified a third response category in his doctoral dissertation, namely, the wearer's imagination of others' response, an important dimension of interaction.

Stone asserted that when the statements made by wearers about their own clothes coincide with statements made by others, then the self of the wearer has been validated. When there is no coincidence of response, the self of the wearer has been challenged. Personal appearance thus provokes either validation of, or challenge to, the self; it establishes the individual as a social object; it gives the person an identity or, in Mead's terminology, it produces a "me." It also invests the individual and others with expectations about possible future activity.

Moreover, to the degree people appraise or make judgments about individuals based on their appearance, they impute a value to the individual that leaves the person who makes the imputation with a certain feeling toward the individual. In Stone's words, *The meaning of appearance . . . is the establishment of identity, value, mood, and attitude.* To forestall confusion, Stone reminds us that identity is not to be equated with the self nor is it a replacement for self but rather indicates what and where a person is in social terms; it situates individuals in the social landscape by their membership in certain social circles. Identity becomes a meaning of the self as a result of individuals announcing who they are in social terms, and a corroborating placement, in social terms, by those to whom the announcement is addressed. Often, this coincidence of announcement and placement is triggered, at the outset, by apparent symbols. And, one consequence of socially situating individuals is to bind them to some people while setting them apart from others. To have an identity is to be a part of, and apart from, certain others.

Identity

In line with the work of Simmel, Toennies, and Schmalenbach concerning the various forms or styles of association, Stone suggests that there are four types of identity based upon four types of social relations. And, to enter a particular type of ongoing transaction, an individual must establish the appropriate type of identity. Thus, participation in basic human relations requires the establishment of such *universal identities* as age and gender; entry into interpersonal relations require an exchange of *interpersonal identities* involving names or nicknames; involvement in structural relations requires exchange of *structural identities* such as taking on a title and giving up a name, and entry into mass relations requires an *anonymous identity*. Stone theorized that, since interpersonal identities outlast structural identities, in that one's name usually stays the same even though one's organizational affiliations change, it constitutes one possible basis for continuity of personal identity.

But, if a relationship is to endure beyond that of a fleeting encounter, the identities of the parties to that interaction must become elaborated beyond the establishment of what each in social terms. In everyday interaction, for example, people normally express their pleasure at seeing each other and then proceed to ask one another how they feel. This almost ethological, ritual exploration of each other's feeling-tone or mood aims at a quick assessment of the other's state of ease or dis-ease, anxiety or security, boredom or rapture, torpor or excitation, and appears to be a prerequisite for the rest of the encounter. Stone and Farberman (1970) theorize that mood sets a tone for what is to come; it guarantees that the participants are braced properly and attuned to each other. It's as if one tunes up an instrument to insure a concerted and decorous interactional performance. If someone is in such a depressed or foul mood as to preclude interaction, others may well see them as not being themselves. This sort of ready excuse acknowledges that a mood may so pervade a self as to undermine any situation that self enters even when there is no apparent connection between the mood and the situation. Such trans-situational occurrence of mood may incline friends and other intimates who feel a strong sense of communion with an individual, to express sympathy and, in fact, undertake with great empathy, to enter the individual's perspective more deeply in order to help. Normally, however, personal expressions of mood are thought to belong mainly in the private sphere and beyond the intrusion of public scrutiny except where collective ceremonies, such as funerals, require the public expression of ritual moods.

In addition to this initial mood assessment, people tend to make some sort of assessment about each other's worth relative to what they have achieved in the past and what they are likely to accomplish in the future. This assignment of value, referred to earlier, generally reflects some objective standard that has currency in a relevant social circle. It typically involves consensual goals about wealth, power, or prestige; achievement standards against which to measure the amount of progress one has made toward such goals; norms that govern the pursuit of the goals, and moral precepts that lay out preferred traits of character. In this fashion, identities are disclosed, elaborated, and refined. As individuals openly or tacitly appreciate each other's mood and appraise each other's value, they develop a more nuanced understanding of one another. Stone notes that, the distinction between value and mood is analytical, and in real time lived experience cannot be separated easily because individuals accomplish valued achievements that evoke good feelings and experience feelings that embody noble values. Stone also suspected that values are linked to identities while moods are linked to attitudes.

If appearance establishes the identity, value, and mood of a person, as stratified or located in social space, then, as Kenneth Burke (1936) has suggested, attitude indicates the activation of the individual and enables an assessment of one's trajectory: where has the individual come from, what is the individual doing, and where is the individual going? Attitudes represent anticipations; they are conveyed partly in appearance and summarize the past and present while signaling the future. They have an incipient, activating quality. More so than identity, value, or mood, attitudes are the process or tendency that both constitutes and pervades the trajectory of the actor–in-action. Attitudes do not refer to the conditions, contexts, or structures of action but to the ongoing embodied event as a tendency-in-process. Stone speculated that attitudes may well entail a different order of analysis from identity, value, and mood.

In any event, Stone has argued that the meaning of appearance, at least, as reflected in verbal responses to clothes, has four dimensions: (1) identities are placed, (2) values are appraised, (3) moods are expressed, and (4) attitudes anticipate. Following in the long tradition of William James, Charles H. Cooley, George H. Mead, Herbert Blumer, Harry S. Sullivan, Erik Erikson, Helen M. Lynd, Nelson Foote, Alfred Lindesmith, Anselm Strauss, and Erving Goffman, Stone is at pains to point out that this entire process has a self-reflexive character so that the individual who appears also reflects upon that appearance, responds to others who react to that appearance, who, in turn, incorporate in their reaction an assessment of the actor's own self-reflection.

This reciprocal process, of self-other awareness and reflection, to the degree it culminates in a coincidence of response, provides consensual validation to the appearance of the actor. And this turns out to be the self as Stone and Farberman (1970) put it: *"As the self is dressed, it is simultaneously addressed."* Selves are constructed and mobilized in appearance and thus intimately linked to clothing. Following Lindesmith and Strauss's (1952) general definition of self, Stone (1962) offers his own modified version: it is any validated program which exercises a regulatory function over other responses of the same organism, including the formulation of other programs. In sum, appearance gives rise to selves and constitutes an essential prerequisite for discourse.

The suggestion that the self emerges out of appearance has important implications that transcend the assessment and identification that city dwellers perform upon each other as they face off in anonymous situations; it applies with even greater force to the process of early childhood socialization because parents simply impose an appearance upon a child. A child dressed in blue is greeted by the world very differently from a child dressed in pink. Blue invests the child with masculinity, pink with femininity, and the world speaks to these children in different tones of voice using different words. Indeed, the world handles these children differently. The blue appearance invites roughhousing while the pink encourages gentility.

More generally, children develop a self-conception in response to the reflected attitudes of others and they learn these attitudes by acting out the roles of others, whether it is that of cowboy, policeman, or teacher. Either through what Stone calls *anticipatory socialization* in which the child plays a role that may be taken on in later life, or *fantastic socialization* where no realistic future possibility exists, in either case, the child will dress up for the part. Costume becomes an integral component of play because it enables the child to misrepresent itself during the role-playing episode and transform into someone it is not. Moreover, it allows the child to enter a collusion or conspiracy with the parents who share the secret concerning such playful deception, and may well strengthen the bond between them.

This process may be compared with the next stage of development in which the child begins to participate in games with peer group members and insists on wearing whatever is approved of as the group's uniform. The child adopts real (as opposed to) fantastic identities, and begins to learn the rules of the game. The uniform and rules of the peer group replace the costume and flights of fancy of individual play. The game of life has begun in earnest, but it does not end in childhood; it continues throughout the life span. Indeed, each pivotal point in life implies that a new game is about to begin, a new identity appropriated, and a new uniform put on. Life is a series of identities taken on and taken off, some with anguish, others with ease. Identities are aspects of selves that arise in the interplay of appearances; they are not established suddenly or all at once; each has a natural history that links its present commitments to its past involvements, and to its future expectations.

This summarizing, time binding, symbolic nature of identity suggests that any given identity transcends the situation that has mobilized it, or made it relevant to the encounter at hand. Stone speaks of *situated identity* or situationally appropriate identity, thereby emphasizing the criterial or axial importance of the situation for calling into action the one identity or meaning of the self that will be most efficacious in the situation. Moreover, Stone modified Robert K. Merton's (1949) ideas about role-sets and status-sets with the suggestion that identities may well be thought of as occurring in sets and sequences. That is, an *identity-set* is composed of those identities that imply and reciprocate each other such as husband-wife, while an *identity-sequence* suggests that certain sets logically lead into each other such that husband-wife leads to mother-father.

Stone and Farberman (1970) defined role as those *attitudes or incipient acts mobilized by an identity in a specified social situation.* Identity sits at the base of role and anchors it. And, any given identity typically has many roles flowing from it. For example, in the identity of professor one may be in a classroom situation that calls for performance of the role of teacher, or in a departmental meeting that calls for the role of colleague, or in a conference with a student that calls for the role of advisor. Stone was quite insistent that roles flow out of identity and not the other way round. For, unless people know who they are relative to others in each situation, they are unable to sustain role performance.

Similarly, if identity breaks down, or becomes inappropriate to a situation, it must be repaired for roles to be resumed. Indeed, Gross and Stone (1964) suggest that embarrassing developments are incipient in all situations and, as such, a constant threat to identity and role and that great care must be taken to forestall them. After analyzing over 800 reported incidents of embarrassment, Gross and Stone contend that they may be grouped into three basic descriptive categories: (1) inappropriate identity, (2) loss of poise, and (3) loss of confidence that the other will be able to remain in role.

Embarrassment in the form of discredited identity occurs when a professor loses his or her train of thought during a lecture and rambles off, or when a singer forgets the lines of the national anthem. Such displays of incompetent role performance disturb the occasion and cast doubt on the credibility of the perpetrator's identity. Embarrassment in the form of inappropriate identity occurs when a man mistakenly wanders into the ladies' room and finds himself in a situation in which he has no identity and can do nothing about it but flee. Or, when a woman's new husband moves into her apartment only to find a picture of her former husband (a symbol of a *relicit* or abandoned identity) still hanging on the wall. Or, when a judge's judicial robes part during a trial and reveal a tennis outfit underneath (a symbol of a *reserve* identity). Of course, each of these situations may (or may not) be retrievable, depending on how incongruent the embarrassing revelation is with the dominant role performance and the degree to which those present attends or disattend it. At minimum, there will be some disruption and some loss of credibility. Situations call forth and require appropriate identities and when they are not presented, or when they have been compromised, effective role performance suffers.

The ability, then, to control a situation is very much tied up with the prevention of embarrassment and the maintenance of personal poise and that means no impediments to the presentation of appropriate identities. What, then, must be done to forestall the emergence of embarrassment? Although Gross and Stone identified over forty elements of self and situation that should be managed for successful role performance to occur, they gave special attention to space, props, equipment, clothing, and the body.

Spaces, for example, have boundaries that range from obdurate to ethereal. A maximum-security prison, an apartment with thin walls, a large room with small groups of people in different corners, or an elevator full of strangers represent spaces whose boundaries exhibit different degrees of permeability. (This permeability of spatial boundaries represents a difficult, unsolved theoretical problem: How, in fact, shall boundaries be defined?) Normally, these spaces are part of some turf, under someone's control and arranged to facilitate some sort of dominant activity or role performance.

Sometimes these boundaries are patrolled and when those who enter do not belong, or when those who leave do so without permission, they risk considerable embarrassment or severe penalty. Sometimes those who do belong risk embarrassment especially when they arrive late, and need to catch up to get into the proper mood of the occasion, so that they do not ruin it for others.

Within any given space, there also are props that must be controlled. Wall paper or paint, wall-to-wall carpeting, heavy furniture, drapes, hanging mirrors, paintings, and appliances are arranged on a more or less long-term basis and only rarely re-arranged. When major re-arrangements do occur, it is usually during or after important transitions in life or lifestyle. Also, the decor of a setting tends to embody, in its very objects and esthetics, an identification with a certain social circle and status niche and thus intimates a degree of social exclusivity that may well make it impossible for people from different walks of life to sustain interaction.

Another element that requires manipulation is equipment. Unlike props, which are stationary during a transaction, equipment is meant to be handled and moved. Teachers use chalk, erasers, lecture notes, audio-visual aides, and computers; students use pens, note books, cellphones, tape recorders, and computers. Equipment are tools that facilitate dominant role performance. Clothing is another important element in that it both reveals and conceals the body and so projects an image of the person to the world. In fact, there are both (under) clothes and (outer) clothes and each must be kept under control to avoid embarrassment. Finally, the body itself must be nourished, rested, and kept in a general state of readiness. Loss of body control at any time because of incontinence, offensive emissions, kinesthetic imbalance, or insobriety may also produce profound embarrassment.

Perhaps the most crucial aspect of the self/situation domain that should remain undisturbed is the tacit and shared assumption that everyone can, and will, remain in role. That everyone will do the right thing and if anyone does get into trouble and falls out of role, others will help to overcome the embarrassment. This suggests that there are performance norms that work to offset major social debacles. Gross and Stone (1964: 126) speculate that one of them is: "standards of role performance almost always allow for flexibility and tolerance." In other words, lapses are permissible. Another one is that of: "giving the other . . . the benefit of the doubt." Together, these performance standards imply that people are considerate of each other a good deal of the time; otherwise, nothing would ever get done.

If, indeed, people tend to protect and preserve each others' dignity and role performance by smoothing over embarrassing developments, then that implies that during the socialization process, children learn to be tactful and to cope with their own and others' embarrassments. This learning process seems to proceed via deliberate attempts on the part of children to embarrass one another. Pushing, shoving, spinning, taunting, and name-calling seem designed to upend the target who then must struggle to regain some measure of poise and balance. Indeed, throughout the life span, each move from one reference group or social circle to another seems to contain a "rite de passage" in which some form of hazing, humiliation, practical joking, "frying," or "toasting" takes place.

There also may well be two other power related functions to the use of deliberate embarrassment. The first is to discredit someone who is performing a role that flows from an identity the person does not justly possess and thereby threatens the integrity of the collectivity, especially if it were brought to light by outsiders. The second is easing someone out of a role that they no longer are competent to perform by laying out a line of action for them to follow that contains a new identity (or social placement) to spare themselves and the group deep embarrassment. Thus, people can announce their resignation, or retirement, or acceptance of a promotion, up the line and out of the way, instead of being fired.

The gist of the foregoing discussion is that, while the occasional situated encounter may well survive an embarrassing moment or two, long-term enduring relationships, whether interpersonal or organizational, often contain ways to prevent potentially devastating embarrassments. Also, Stone insisted that role performance flows out of identity and not the other way around. This formulation brings into relief the ongoing debate that interactionists were carrying on, and continue to carry on, against the more traditional functionalist conceptions of status and role advanced by Linton (1938), Merton (1949), and Parsons (1951).

Although in full agreement with Gerth and Mills (1953) and Strauss (1959) that every specified social situation is set within a larger historical situation, so that there was no social psychology without history, Stone's view of history followed that of Mead (1934) and Teggart (1941); namely, that it is emergent, processual, and transformative, it passes through the minds, hearts, and hands of successive generations of concrete men and women each of whom leave an imprint. And while it was true, as Burke (1945) and Mills (1940) had argued, that each historical epoch has its own characteristic vocabulary of motives, people were as apt to deviate from the values embedded in those vocabularies as they were to conform to them. So, for Stone, as for his pragmatic forerunners, history did not occur in the grand terms of Hegel or Marx, that is, above the heads or behind the backs of people, but rather in the retail term of James, Mead, Dewey, Blumer, and Riesman, that is, in the narrow, concrete, passionate problematic situations of everyday life where actors confront the obdurate features of their epoch as they pursue what William James called "lived experience." For Stone, the enduring problems of life boil down to how individuals develop a sense of who they are, for themselves and others, in a fashion that connects them to some aspect of their communities so that the communities themselves achieve consensus and integration. Put another way, the fundamental question is: what are the social bases of personal life and the personal bases of social life?

Stone's focus on the importance of appearance as the pre-text and predicate to subsequent verbal discourse provided a corrective to the discursive, linguistic bias that he believed pervaded the otherwise seminal contributions of George H. Mead to a theory of the evolution and operation of the self. Stone rounded out Mead's approach by noting that participation in both a universe of appearance and a universe of discourse constituted a dialectical process that supported and sustained the self. The importance of appearance as a filter for beginning the process of developing a social identity for ourselves, and for each other, enabled Stone to operationalize key dimensions of Mead's theory of self. When individuals validate each other's appearances, they become objects that have a social identity, or in Mead's terms, they produce a *me*. They establish what, and where, they are in social terms, that is, what social circles they do (and don't) belong to and what positions they hold within them. As Perinbanayagam (2003) notes, Stone's work on identity thus vindicates and extends the great significance of Mead's contribution to a theory of self.

THE SOCIOLOGY OF SPORT

Stone's interest in the sociology of sport grew out of his long-standing involvement in the leading problems of urban sociology and social psychology. As we have seen, the problem for urban sociology was: how is modern, mass, anonymous, metropolitan life organized? For social psychology the problem was: how are personal and collective identity established in a society characterized by fleeting, instrumental, situated encounters, and, by implication, how are social organizations and personal and collective identity linked? Stone developed answers to these questions within the area of the sociology of sport. Along with Huizinga (1949), Riesman and Denny (1954) in Dunning (1971), Caillois (1961) in Dunning (1971), and Ellias (1939) in Dunning (1971), Stone (1955) laid the foundation for the study of sports as a serious scientific sub-discipline of sociology. Stone's particular contributions include: (1) successive historical epochs leading to communities of affinity engaged in leisure-time activities, (2) the development of the preconditions necessary for the emergence of professional sports, (3) the transformation of sports teams and star athletes into complex collective representations that can provide a basis for the development of collective identities within which individuals can anchor their personal identities, allowing them to maintain subjective identification with a virtual community even as they lose objective integration into a real community, (4) the eventual diffusion and weakening of collective representations, and (5) the emergence of sports as a platform for social change in the context of ongoing, societal power struggles.

Successive Historical Epochs Leading to Communities of Affinity

Stone was influenced by the views of Emile Durkheim ([1912] 1965) and David Riesman, Nathan Glazer, and Reuel Denny (1950), who saw the past 500 years of Western civilization as a succession of historical epochs. In line with Durkheim, Stone agreed that *landed estates* had given way to *economic classes* which, in turn, as Riesman and his collegues suggested, had given way to *mass society*. And, as Stone saw it, by the last half of the twentieth-century mass society had fractured into *communities of affinity* based on shared, leisure-time interests. Stone refined Durkheim and Riesman's general model of successive historical epochs by suggesting that, in fact, each historical epoch had its own: (1) dominant institution, (2) typology of social relationships, (3) typology of identities, (4) typical vocabulary of motives (or accounts), and (5) characteristic situations. Stone further suggested that the dominant institution of the epoch organized around landed estates was the *extended family*; the dominant institution of the epoch organized around economic classes was *work*; the dominant institution of mass society was *consumption*; and the dominant institution of the current epoch, organized around communities of affinity, was recreational activity.

Conditions for the Emergence of Professional Sports

Stone further argued that, in the contemporary era, five specific conditions were necessary for the emergence of *professional* sports as a significant, cultural activity: (1) an organized workforce, (2) a money economy, (3) a mass spectator audience, (4) the dramatization of performance on the playing field, and (5) a broader context where prevailing societal power arrangements were being challenged by rising social, political, economic, and racial groups (Stone n.d.a).

Sports Teams and Star Athletes as Complex Collective Representations

Viewing the emergence of professional sports against a background of social strife, Stone turned to Durkheim's concepts of collective representation, collective conscience, and collective symbols. For Stone, sports, like religion for Durkheim, can provide a basis for social solidarity. Stone (n.d.b), going beyond Durkheim, also warned that collective representations could turn out to be double-edged swords that exacerbate differences, not only binding people together but also driving them apart. Jackie Robinson and the Brooklyn Dodgers, the star athlete and the team, heightened and extended local, group solidarity and shared, collective identity as they were passionately embraced and defended by their fans, often quite aggressively, against outsider criticism, especially those coming from rival New York Yankee or New York Giants fans.

Stone also believed that sports teams, as collective representations, were equally important because they inspired participants and fans to tie their personal and collective identities to them. For example, Stone and Oldenburg (1967) suggest that spectator sports like professional wrestling allow fans to enter the social world of a dramaturgical spectacle that lifts them out of their humdrum everyday lives and enables them to identify with modern day gladiators who engage in a passion play of good and evil. Stone, with Viken and Krotee (1979), also offers research evidence that such participant sports as automobile drag racing often engulf enthusiasts to the point where it becomes a total way of life where normal occupational involvement becomes a mere interlude between racing events. Participants begin to live their lives within the time calendar and contact network of racing. Also, Anderson and Stone (1979), based on a fifteen-year analysis of socioeconomic strata differences in the meaning given to sports by metropolitan residents, argue that the introduction of a variety of professional sports teams into most large cities, combined with mass media television, has democratized *spectatorship* and reduced class distinctions among sports. They report, however, that some strata differences remain relative to actual participation in sports, particularly where expensive equipment and special locations are requisite to participation.

Stone regarded these developments as important and believed that they had general significance for traditional sociological thinking which held that the achievement of community identification, urban solidarity, and overall moral consensus in modern urban society was well-nigh impossible. As we have seen, Stone was inclined to believe that the massification of society was eroding traditional economic class distinctions and that new social forms based on new principles of organization involving *status, status symbols, and status aggregates* were emerging. It was important, for Stone, to acknowledge that wherever people engaged in regular and frequent communication, the possibility of them developing personalized or quasi-primary relationships existed, and which might in turn give them a sense of belonging to the larger community. Indeed, Blumer (1939) had suggested that a *mass* might be transformed into an *organized movement* around common objects and that a new social structure and culture might emerge. Stone actually hypothesized that, such a new *status-oriented* social structure and *leisure-oriented* culture were already emerging. Dunning (1971) suggests a similar view when he asks:

> In this sense, do sports act as a unifying agency which to some extent counteracts the divisive force of class, race, religion. . . . Do sports serve to give the

individual in the "lonely crowd "of our impersonal "mass society" a sense of belonging to some wider social grouping and help to bring order, meaning and a sense of continuity into . . . life? (xviii)

The Diffusion and Weakening of Collective Representations

Although Stone clearly was sympathetic to this view, he, also, cautioned against an overly simplistic emphasis of the positive role of sports. In a seminal article, titled "American Sports," published in 1955 in the *Chicago Review* he cautions that:

> The game, inherently ennobling of its players, seems to be giving way to the spectacle, inherently immoral and debasing . . . [where] spectators . . . encourage the spectacular [and] may be viewed as agent[s] of destruction as far as the dignity of sport is concerned. (Stone 1955)

Here, Stone was expressing his concern that professional sports may well contain the seeds of its own destruction, that the very spectators who he previously identified as a necessary pre-condition for the emergence of professional sports, especially in capitalistic societies like the United States, would likely become a major force in its relentless commercialization. What in earlier times had started out as locally oriented high school and college games were becoming professional entertainment, turning players into performers, and teams into purely business franchises intent on producing ever more fantastic, and profitable, consumer spectacles. Again, Dunning (1971), reflecting on the similar situation of soccer in England, echoes Stone's concern:

> [N]owadays . . . sport has come to form an important part of the "entertainment industry." . . . It regularly attracts countless thousands of paying spectators . . . [which] enables substantial numbers of people to be employed . . . [but] . . . What are the effects of the "sports industry" on the economics of production and consumption? . . . does its "product" help to refresh people who are tired . . . [or] does a profit orientation pose a threat to sports turning them into commercial spectacles which cease to be sports in any meaningful sense . . . ? (xx)

Both Stone and Dunning clearly see lurking in sports something darker than the utopian vision painted by Ashworth (1971) who saw in sports an ethos of

> equality . . . [based] on strict formal rules that make "extra-ability" factors equal for everyone . . . [where] the rich and the poor, the handsome and the ugly, the white and the black, are comparing themselves . . . in an egalitarian "communistic" utopia that subjects their respective beings to a test, a symbolic test, that is unhampered by . . . wealth or poverty, . . . looks or . . . color . . . [making] sport . . . a "symbolic dialogue." (45)

Ashworth's view reflects the spirit of the ancient Greek *contests* in which adversaries fought each other while naked in order to level social and economic differences and make the contest a matter of individual competence. But what, then, is the *meaning* of sport: an egalitarian utopia driven only by athletic excellence, or a fan-driven, profit-oriented, commercial spectacle? To be sure, professional sports, as collective representations, are complex, multidimensional social objects open to interpretation.

Michael Oriard (1993), who played professional football for the Kansas City Chiefs from 1970–1973 and went on to become a professor of English at Oregon State University, says that, at least one sport, football, cannot be understood on its own terms but rather as a *cultural text* or narrative that lends itself to multiple interpretations, depending on who is doing the reading. Players see football one way, coaches see it another, team owners another way, fans yet another way, etc. According to a quote from Oriard:

> when a quarterback releases a long and perfect, spiral pass and a down field receiver, galloping toward the end zone, looks back at the last moment to gauge the flight path of the ball, and makes a spectacular outstretched-arm, one-handed catch, only to be smashed in the ribs and dropped to the ground by the helmet of an opposing player. (83)

the meaning and value of this "*collision of artistry and violence*" is open to interpretation. Simone de Beauvoir (1961: 308, quoted in Stone 1972: 87) captures one meaning of this experience when she observed that violence (in sports) is "The authentic proof of each one's loyalty to himself . . . anger or revolt that does not get into the muscles remain a figment of the imagination." Another interpretation is offered by Robert S. Perinbanayagam (2006: 151), who argues that American football basically "has systematically restricted the opportunities for a [player] to act on his own initiative [but acts] under a tight discipline of plays and moves formulated ahead . . . by coaches, tacticians, and motivators." So, the very same action can be a demonstration of visceral, athletic excellence, remunerative, spectacular violence, scripted execution of a playbook, or, as Stone suggests, something more.

Societal Power Struggle: Sports as a Platform for Social Change

While Stone saw in sports both a playing field for authentic, individual excellence, and an arena in which fans might demand ever more dramatic spectacle that could undermine the integrity of the game itself, he also saw something else, perhaps of even greater importance; namely, that, in the history of sports, there always has been a "political" background or context surrounding the arena or playing field. For example, while the spirt of democracy infused and animated the ancient Greek *contests*, the Roman *spectacles* were quite different; there warriors (and others) from defeated and subjugated populations met in the arena as gladiators to determine their fate before a crowd of spectators. In other words, sports took place against a background of wider societal power relations and, in a way, a reflection of that struggle re-appears as a spectacle on the playing field. The arena might be a microcosm of democracy or a place where a defeated and enslaved population could be represented by a warrior-turned-gladiator fighting, despite the odds, for personal and collective redemption and destiny, at the same time entertainment of the masses.

Stone's conceptualization of sport teams and their star athletes as collective representations clearly reflects Durkheim's emphasis on the collective solidarity provided by religious groups who are bound together by a set of common beliefs and practices. But what happens when collective representations become more diffuse and multiple contradictory meanings and values that they contain emerge? There is perhaps no better example of this phenomenon than the contemporary controversy in the National Football League (NFL) in 2016 when players began to sit or kneel during the playing of the American national anthem as a protest against social inequality and recurring police brutality toward African American males.

Prior to 2016, players in the National Football League (NFL), following a tradition that began in 2009, when the US Pentagon paid the NFL millions of dollars to assist with the recruitment of US military personnel, began to stand at attention, with hand over heart, during the playing of the Star-Spangled Banner. All that changed when Colin Kaepernick, a San Francisco 49ers quarterback, remained seated during the playing of the national anthem prior to a 2016 pre-season game, in silent protest over incidents of police brutality involving African American men. Following a series of debates concerning Kaepernick's motives that involved a rarity of prominent sports personalities, public figures, and activist academics, the NFL owners and players agreed to a pledge that the NFL will establish a fund of $89 million dollars to be distributed among various organizations, including the United Negro College Fund (25 percent), Dreamers Corp. (25 percent), and the Players Coalition (50 percent). In addition, each NFL team owner, for each of the next seven years, will donate $250,000 to be matched with another $250,000 by each team's players, to be used for local initiatives. By 2024, these donations will total to close to $100 million dollars. However, David Zirin (2017) reports, a conflict has broken out among players concerning exactly how the money is to be distributed and managed. The NFL and some players (following Malcolm Jenkins of the Philadelphia Eagles, leader of the Players Coalition) want the money to stay within the designated organizations but others (following Colin Kaepernick and Eric Reid of the San Francisco 49ers) want it sent to local, grass roots, groups working outside established institutional structures.

How all of this will resolve itself remains to be seen. If Stone is correct, however, and collective representations (like the flag, the anthem, sport teams, and star athletes), are in the process of diffusing and weakening, then insurgent, contradictory, meanings and values will continue to emerge leading to more protests and counter-protests along cultural, social, political, economic, and racial lines.[1] The protests of professional athletes manifest real, not merely symbolic, power and what long-term effects these will have on owners, media outlets, fans, and political structures is an open question. Whether it culminates in profound institutional changes leading to a more open and inclusive society remains to be seen.

In sum, Stone's contributions to the sociology of sport locates it, in the current historical epoch, as an arena for social change, where sport teams and star athletes as collective representations function as iconic objects that people can build personal and collective *identities* on, which helps to hold together a mass society that has fractured into "communities of affinity" focused on recreational activity. Similarly, his contributions to Social Psychology emphasize the importance of "universes of appearance" (in contrast to universes of discourse), especially in mass societies where contacts are fleeting and anonymous. He also underlines the importance of establishing individual and collective identity both as the basis for situationally appropriate role performance and for social solidarity. Finally, Stone's contribution to Urban Sociology includes the concepts of "non-ranked status aggregates" and "personalization." In modern mass society, Stone believed that vertical social organizations were being replaced by non-hierarchical social forms organized around status aggregates and that, in this amorphous, impersonal environment, many individuals seek to personalize relationships in an effort to relate to others and to retain some connection to their larger communities.

NOTE

1. Stone's speculation that professional sport teams, as collective representations, may diffuse and weaken is supported by recent empirical evidence, that, at least, professional football has begun to lose its audience, especially among white men. Television sportscaster Bryant Gumbel, in a segment on Meet the Press (2/4/18) with Chuck Todd, suggests that the decline is due to several factors including: (1) antipathy to political protests on the playing field, (2) the increasing attractiveness of collegiate sports, (3) the escalating cost of tickets and parking at games, (4) the availability of multiple TV sports outlets, and (5) the mounting empirical evidence—and rising concern—about concussion and brain injury suffered by players.

WORKS CITED

Anderson, Dean F., and Gregory P. Stone. 1979. "A Fifteen Year Analysis of Socio-Economic Strata Differences in the Meaning Given to Sport by Metropoli tans." Pp. 167–84 in *The Dimensions of Sport Sociology*, edited by M. L. Krotee. West Point, NY: Leisure Press.

Ashworth, A. E. 1971. "Sport as Symbolic Dialogue." Pp. 40–46 in *The Sociology of Sport*, edited by Eric Dunning. London: Frank Cass & Co. Ltd.
Blumer, Herbert. 1939. "Elementary Collective Groupings." Pp. 241–44 in *An Outline of the Principles of Sociology*, edited by Robert E. Park. New York, NY: Barnes and Noble.
Burke, Kenneth. 1936. *Permanence and Change*. New York, NY: New Republic.
———. 1937. *Attitudes Toward History*. Boston: Beacon.
———. 1945. *A Grammar of Motives*. Berkeley, CA: University of California Press.
Caillois, Roger. 1961. *Man, Play, and Games*. Glencoe, IL: The Free Press.
———. 1971. "The Classification of Games." Pp. 17–39 in *The Sociology of Sport*, edited by Eric Dunning. London: Frank Cass & Co. Ltd.
Dunning, Eric, ed. 1971. *The Sociology of Sport*. Frank Cass & Co. Ltd.
Durkheim, Emile. [1912] 1965. *Elementary Forms of the Religious Life*. New York, NY: The Free Press.
Elias, Norbert. 1939. *The Civilizing Process*. Oxford: Blackwell.
Form, William H., Joel Smith, and Gregory P. Stone. 1954. "Local Intimacy in Middle-Sized City." *American Journal of Sociology* 60 (November): 276–84.
Form, William H. and Gregory P. Stone. 1957. "Urbanism, Anonymity, and Status Symbolism." *American Journal of Sociology* 62 (March): 504–14.
Gerth, Hans and C. Wright Mills. 1953. *Character and Social Structure*. New York, NY: Harcourt, Brace & World.
Goffman, Erving. 1951. "Symbols of Class Status." *British Journal of Sociology* 2 (December): 294–304.
Gross, Edward and Gregory P. Stone. 1964. "Embarrassment an Analysis of Role Requirements," *American Journal of Sociology* 70 (July): 1–15.
Hughes, Everett C. 1949. "Social Change and Status Protest: An Essay on the Marginal Man." *Phylon* 10 (First Quarter): 58–65.
Huizinga, Johann. 1949. *Homo Ludens: A Study of the Play Element in Culture*. London: Routledge and Kegan Paul.
Lindesmith, A. R., and A. L. Strauss. 1952. *Social Psychology*. New York: The Dryden Press.
Linton, Ralph. 1938. "Culture, Society, and the Individual." *Journal of Abnormal Psychology* 33: 425–436.
Mead, Gregory H. 1934. *Mind, Self, and Society*. Chicago, IL: University of Chicago Press.
———. 1936. *Movements of Thought in the Nineteenth Century*. Chicago, IL: University of Chicago Press.
Merton, Robert K. 1949. *Social Theory and Social Structure*. Glencoe, IL: Free Press.
Mills, C. Wright. 1940. "Situated Actions and Vocabularies of Motive." *American Sociological Review* 5 (October): 904–1013.
———. 1942. "Review of: Warner and Lunt, The Social Life of a Modern Community." *American Sociological Review* 7 (April): 263–71.
Oriard, Michael. 1993. *Reading Football: How the Popular Press Created an American Spectacle*. Chapel Hill and London: The University of North Carolina Press.
Parsons, Talcott. 1951. *The Social System*. London: Routledge and Keegan Paul Ltd.
Perinbanayagam, Robert. S. 2003. "Telic Reflections: Interactional Process, as Such." *Studies in Symbolic Interaction* 26 (1): 67–83.
———. 2006. *Games and Sport in Everyday Life: Dialogues and Narratives of the Self*. Boulder, CO: Paradigm Publishers.
Riesman, David, Nathan Glazer, and Reuel Denny. 1950. *The Lonely Crowd*. New Haven, CT: Yale University Press.
Riesman, David, and Reuel Denny. 1954. "Football in America: A Study of Culture Diffusion." *American Quarterly* 3 (4): 309–25.
Schmalenbach, Herman. 1961. "The Sociological Category of Communion." Pp. 331–47 in *Theories of Society I*, edited by Talcott Parsons et al. Glencoe: The Free Press.
Shibutani, Tamotsu. 1961. *Society and Personality: An Interactionist Approach to Social Psychology*. New York, NY: Prentice-Hall.
Shils, Edward. 1951. "The Study of the Primary Group." Pp. 44–69 in *The Policy Sciences*, edited by D. Lerner and H. D. Lasswell. Stanford, CA: Stanford University Press.

Smith, Adam. [1759] 2005. *The Theory of Moral Semtiments*, edited by Sálvio M. Soares. MetaLibri, v1.0p.
Speier, Hans. 1952. "Honor and the Social Structure." Pp. 36–52 in *Social Order and the Risks of War: Papers in Political Sociology*, edited by Hans Speier. New York, NY: Stewart.
Stone, Gregory P. 1952. *Sociological Aspects of Consumer Purchasing in a Northwest Side Chicago Community*. (Master's Thesis), University of Chicago.
———. 1954. "City Shoppers and Urban Identification," *American Journal of Sociology* 60 (November): 36–54.
———. 1955. "American Sports: Play and Display," *Chicago Review* 9 (3): 83–100.
———. 1956. "A Note on Gemeinschaft and Gesellschaft," *Alpha Kappa Delta* 27 (Autumn): 20–26.
———. 1959. *Clothing and Social Relationships: A Study of Appearance in the Context of Community Life*. Dissertation, University of Chicago.
———. 1962. "Drinking Styles and Status Arrangements." Pp. 121–40 in *Society, Culture, and Drinking Patterns*, edited by D. Pittman and C. R. Snyder. New York, NY: Wiley.
———. 1977. Review of: Donald W. Ball and John W. Loy (1975) *Sport and Social Order: Contributions to the Sociology of Sport*, *Contemporary Sociology: A Journal of Reviews* 6 (1): 110–12.
———. N.d.a. *Courage in the Intellectual Arena*. Unfinished, unpublished, hand written, autobiographical fragment.
———. N.d.b. *Role Performance*. Unfinished, unpublished fragment, hand written.
———. N.d.c. *Sport and Community*. Unpublished manuscript.
Stone, Gregory P. and Harvey A. Farberman, eds. 1970. *Social Psychology through Symbolic Interaction*. New York, NY: John Wiley & Sons, Inc.
Stone, Gregory, P. and Raymond Oldenburg. 1967. "Wrestling." Pp. 503–31 in *Motivations in Play, Games and Sports*, edited by R. Slovenko and J. Knight. Springfield, IL: Thomas.
Strauss, Anselm. 1959. *Mirrors and Masks: The Search for Identity*. Glencoe, IL: The Free Press.
Teggart, F. J. 1941. *The Theory and Process of History*. Berkeley, CA: University of California Press.
Tonnies, Ferdinand. [1887] 1957. *Community and Society*. East Lansing, MI: Michigan State University Press.
Veblen, Thorstein. 1899. The Theory of the Leisure Class. New York, NY: Macmillan.
Viken, James P., M. L. Krotee, and Gregory P. Stone. 1979. "Popular Culture and the Erosion of Class: Distinctions in the Mass Sport of Drag Racing." Pp. 127–40 in *The Dimensions of Sport Sociology*, edited by M. L. Krotee. West Point, NY: Leisure Press.
Warner, W. Lloyd, Marchia Meeker, and Kenneth Eells. 1949. *Social Class in America*. Chicago, IL: Science Research Associates.
Weber, Max. 1946. "Class, Status, Party." Pp. 180–95 in *From Max Weber: Essays in Sociology*, edited by Hans H. Gerth and C. Wright Mills. New York, NY: Oxford University Press.
Wirth, Louis. 1926. "The Sociology of Ferdinand Tonnies," *American Journal of Sociology* 32 (November): 419–20.
———. 1938. "Urbanism as a Way of Life," *American Journal of Sociology* 44 (July): 1–24.
Zirin, David. 2017. "Two Different Paths, Two Different Goals: Understanding the Rift in the NFL's 'Players Coalition.'" *The Nation.com* 4 (December).

Chapter Eight

Carl J. Couch

Michael Katovich and Shing-Ling S. Chen

One night at one of the American Sociological Association Meetings, Carl J. Couch (heretofore identified as just "Carl" in honor of his insistence to "just call me Carl") sat in his room, surrounded by his graduate students and "hangers on," telling often told stories and making what some might consider outrageous claims regarding his research. He never hesitated to say that what he and his students had accomplished constituted a "paradigm shift" about which Thomas Kuhn (1962) wrote. While none of us would dare interrupt Carl's flow once he began his raconteur-like style of talking, his old friend and competitor, Robert Stewart, sat in the room, making humorous and evocative comments. After a time, Carl and Robert began getting into "the dozens," each finding ways to one-up one another. Finally, Stewart said, "I get all the smart students—they are immediately attracted to me." Carl retorted, "I get all the dumb ones and make them smart."

Carl did indeed impart smartness and wisdom among many of his students. He lived an academic life that drew on a modernistic faith in scientific progress and the enlightenment ethos (Katovich and Reese 1993), but his narrative also had a mythological quality to it. After stints of service in World War II and Korea, interrupted by what he called "some odd jobs and wandering," Carl entered the Department of Sociology at the University of Iowa (then called The State University of Iowa) first as an undergraduate and then as a graduate student of Manford Kuhn, beginning, in all earnest, his career as a sociologist. By the late 1960s, after "bouncing around from place to place and getting fired from most of them," Carl returned home to the new-called University of Iowa. Eventually, after ten or so years at Iowa, Carl moved into Manford Kuhn's old office in McBride Hall, completing a mythological circle (Katovich 2017).

Carl combined seemingly contradictory but nonetheless authentic qualities associated with his performative self (Goffman 1959: 1963). This combination applies to the paradoxical remembrance of Carl, on which we elaborate later. He often showed a self-critical and effacing style, but did not shy away from announcing his or his students' accomplishments (or questioning those who did not accept his work as significant). Mostly, Carl impressed just about everyone with his passion. Everything he did comprised labors of love, whether pounding away at his electronic typewriter for years (until graduating to a computer), gathering data in the small groups laboratory at Iowa (known as CRIB—the Center for Research in Interpersonal Behavior—see Katovich 2017: xvii–xviii), delving into papers written by his students (and returning them with copious comments in a red pen, prompting one graduate student to call Carl's comments on any paper "The Red Sea"), teaching one of his many seminars on small group processes or methodology, drinking beer after such seminars, or just being with his family. Few others comprised the capacity for an honest, genuine, and straightforward interactional style with obvious displays of love, even if such love came along with it a gravelly, grumpy sounding voice, which often began and ended every sentence with "Goddamn it!" as in, "Goddamn it, get to work, goddamn it!"

In the following pages we wish to snatch Carl's body of work from the seemingly forgotten pile of thinkers to re-introduce such work into the qualitative sociological and symbolic interactionist circles. We will first provide a brief biographical sketch combined with his aforementioned return to the University of Iowa, including his focus on other areas of interest beyond Manford Kuhn's paper and pencil approach (Katovich, Couch, and Miller 1987; Couch, Katovich, and Buban 1994). This re-focus included a deep emotional investment in laboratory research, especially while employing audio-visual technology to engage in what he would often term "the research process" (Couch 1987: 25–28). Second, we explore Couch's particular scientific approach that correlated "the new Iowa School" (Buban 1986; Couch, Katovich, and Buban 1994) with a theory of methodology that emphasized generating generic concepts in the laboratory via the systematic examination of social processes (Katovich, Miller, and Stewart 2003). In this vein, we examine how Carl demonstrated allegiance to, but defiance of, scientific methodology (especially as established in American Sociology). Third, we examine how the new Iowa School's emphasis on laboratory research contributed to its outsider status within symbolic interactionism. Part of this status is linked to Carl's impressive presence that, again, became paradoxical, in that the presence overshadowed the work that he loved. In effect the work became a footnote to interactionist research. Finally, we look at applications of Carl's work that have kept not only his spirit but his core ideas alive in the twenty-first century.

BIOGRAPHICAL SKETCH

Carl J. Couch (1925–1994) was born in Blencoe, Iowa, growing up during a time and in an area deeply impacted by the Depression. Despite obvious hardships and what he called "the typical, dumb-dumb farm boy's childhood," Carl demonstrated a capacity for high achievement and distinct capacities for the "college-track" classes in the arts and sciences. However, the emergence of World War II interrupted his track to college, and Carl enlisted at seventeen in the U.S. Army, soon to be changed to the Army-Air Force. It did not take long for Carl to demonstrate his intelligence in the Army, earning the rank of Captain at age nineteen and flying on missions as the plane navigator. After World War II, as mentioned, Carl "drifted," until the emergence of the Korean War, in which he put his Captain's uniform back on, flew more missions, and ended up taking advantage of the GI Bill. Depending on the time of night one talked to Carl at his favorite Iowa City bar, Joes, Carl flew missions ranging from average to uncountable and dangerous. He did like to say, however, in regard to his missions that first, he "always got the plane back home" and second, despite his high scores in math, he "could never believe in statistics because statistically, I should be dead!"

Determined to "make up for lost time" Carl completed his BA, MA and PhD in four years (1951–1955), all from the University of Iowa. After receiving his PhD, Carl taught at Montana State University (1955–1957), Central Michigan University (1957–1962), and Michigan State University (1962–1965). After accepting a position at the Department of Psychiatry at University of Iowa (offered to him by a fellow graduate student with whom he matriculated, Harold Mumford), he began teaching and doing research in the university's Department of Sociology in 1966. He became a tenured associate professor at that time. In 1992, the department and university finally promoted him to professor and he remained in that position until his retirement in 1994.

During his time as a graduate student at Iowa, Carl became involved in Manford Kuhn's (1954, 1960) project, involving the now famous Twenty Statements Test (TST) that attempted to test G. H. Mead's (1925, 1930) general assumptions and conceptions of the self as social object. The project involved paper and pencil measurements of a more static and anchored self (Kuhn and McPartland 1954) and defined the foundation of the Iowa School of Symbolic Interaction (Meltzer and Petras 1970). After Carl left Iowa to pursue his craft as an independent scholar, he became disenchanted with Kuhn's static conception of the self and equally static methodological procedures. During this time, Carl had become drawn to Blumer's (1956, 1969) emphasis on the self as an intervening variable in the process of becoming. As we will discuss below, Carl went beyond Blumer as he became interested in Simmel's (1950) insistence that sociological forms of association must be an enduring focus when analyzing small social groups, especially interaction among dyads and triads. In effect, Couch adopted Simmel's belief that the central focus of research is social interaction, and not the dispositions or internal conversations of individuals. Carl's metamorphoses, from a researcher generating and analyzing static data to one concerned with studying social processes, stimulated an interest in studying various forms of coordinated activity from protest groups (Couch 1968) to basic dimensions of association generated within small social groups (Couch 1970).

Over time, Carl began to become more invested in the growth and sustainability of the symbolic interactionist perspective and the study of social processes. Recognizing a necessity to create an organization for this perspective, which had the reputation of a discipline without much in the way of systematic lodging with any institutional identity, Carl and Gregory Stone became co-founders of the Society for the Study of Symbolic Interaction (SSSI) in the mid-to-late 1970s. The organization elected officers such as president, vice president, and treasurer, created a flagship journal (*Symbolic Interaction*) and sponsored national meetings as well as regional symposiums. The origins of SSSI have become part of a legendary oral tradition, but the duration of the society has remained. The existence and duration of this society fulfilled, in part, Manford Kuhn's (1964a) call to move symbolic interaction into an "age of inquiry." Carl took his turn at fulfilling duties as an SSSI president (each president had one year terms) and always kept abreast of the business of SSSI.

As a Midwesterner by birth, temperament, and education, Couch also became seriously involved in the Midwest Sociological Society (MSS). He made sure that all of his graduate students became members of this society and encouraged them to present papers and get involved in committees. Couch also became president of the MSS and would send correspondence, with great pride, to anyone, using the masthead of this society. One of his more memorable correspondences to one of the authors used the MSS masthead and made reference to an article we published (Couch, Katovich, and Buban 1994). After sending the final draft to the editor with Couch's name listed as first author, Carl wrote (in his scrawl), "Mike, you're a jackass! I am not supposed to be the first author!"

While many saw Carl as "a white haired heretic" who scoffed at rules and procedures, an important aspect of his character involved his commitment to organizations such as SSSI and the MSS and his pride in holding positions that represented "hard time" service to these organizations. Couch had a healthy suspicion of authority, but believed strongly in the potential benevolence of an "interaction order" (Goffman 1983) and that SSSI and the MSS maintained the best aspects of this benevolent order. When asked how he resolved the apparent contradiction between his criticism of authoritarian policies and his devotion to organizations such as the SSSI and the MSS,

Carl would say, "I believe in the possibility of a controlled chaos." Carl's apparent contradiction between his anti-authoritarian style and his occasional status as an "organization man" also became evident in regard to his orientation to the scientific enterprise and the methodologies associated with such an enterprise.

FOR AND AGAINST THE SCIENTIFIC METHOD

Couch believed in hard science, based on hard data. He viewed such a belief as consistent with Mead's (1934, 1938) orientation to the scientific enterprise, placing him, at least to his way of thinking, squarely in the interactionist camp. But Couch also regarded Mead's conceptions as lacking in regard to explicit social dynamics. In particular, he believed in the possibility of developing a geometric theory of social life (Chen and Johns 2015: 347). Such geometry included the fundamental ideas inspired by Simmel (1950) that small social groups, specifically dyads and triads, created interdependent and interlocking "lines of action" (cf. Blumer 1969: 3) that encompassed the social *sui generis*. As described in more detail below, the drive for a hard science, for a geometric analysis of human interaction, informed various investigations in the laboratory. Such investigations would provide the basis for the aforementioned development of data generation within a new Iowa School.

Carl's belief in this hard science evolved. In the 1960s, Carl shared with other interactionists, less enamored with a hard science, data approach, a disdain for a sociological enterprise that had become heavily quantified and dogmatic in defining empirical in terms of sampling size and statistical summaries. Before he began emphasizing the hard science, data approach, Carl allied himself with those critical of a dominant and rigid methodological program of data generation. This method emphasized a fixed and stagnant paradigm that refused to regard any qualitative and interpretive approach to the worlds humans constructed as legitimate in the scientific sense of the term.

Later, as Carl began investigating the construction of dynamic conversations in the laboratory, he separated himself from other qualitative sociologists and began to view the scientific enterprise as requiring a theoretical view of the importance of observational placement. Specifically, he maintained a steady rejection of a purely quantitative approach, but viewed the accumulation of qualitative data as requiring a commitment to a scientific standpoint emphasizing stability of location (Couch 1982: 3–4). This stability explicated procedures for investigators to adopt a consistent and fixed standpoint while observing processual dynamics. In effect, Carl viewed the scientific enterprise in light of a Darwinian approach, involving systematic and qualitative searches for patterns while occupying a well-defined and enduring location for observing such patterns. In a way, his perspective resembled Feyerabend's (2010) critique of "methodological monism," or the over-dependence on one methodological strategy at the expense of other, valuable strategies.

Carl agreed with other qualitative sociologists that mainstream sociology had become overtaken by "the paper and pencil" methodology from which his original research emerged, but without the nuances and attempts to integrate such data with more qualitative approaches (Kuhn 1964b). Carl would frequently posit that sociologists adopted a positivistic and deterministic framework to not only quantify human experiences, but to render actual, ongoing experiences as irrelevant (Couch 1987, 2017a; Katovich, Couch, and Miller 1987). In effect, again similar to Feyerabend's critique, Carl became disenchanted with a "one size fits all" methodology that ignored ways in which social worlds could be constructed and examined as people embedded themselves in such worlds as minded and cooperative social agents.

Carl's dissatisfaction with the mainstream sociological framework emphasized how this framework eradicated the complex qualities of human action. It reduced human behavior to mere responses to ongoing stimuli. However, he also questioned the validity of most qualitative research that, in his view, seemed more content with providing interesting depictions or compelling stories than with generating abstract and generic concepts (Couch 1984a, 1984b). Instead, Carl set about to establish a sociology of complexity (Couch and Maines 1988). This sociology would involve the strict examination of sequences of social action. The strict examination would make use of existing technology so as to study humanity in a way that would fully encompass what it means to coordinate any type of social action, from the most taken-for-granted acts to those we deem problematic. In the attempt to articulate this endeavor, Carl began to search for a more adequate approach that allowed the examination of many important human qualities such as reflexivity, intentionality, and temporality (see Mead 1929, 1932).

In accord with his belief in examining the complexity and temporal qualities of life-worlds systematically, Carl advocated the use of emergent technology as tools that would alter methodological inquiry rather than using such inquiry to shape and define the function of the technological tools (Katovich and Chen 2017). However, Carl created his own version of a methodological framework, arguing for an across-time but point in space approach to examining social processes, which required commitment to studying social life in laboratory settings (Couch, Katovich, and Buban 1994). Carl's equation of a laboratory setting as the stable space necessary for a scientific analysis of social processes did not portray the laboratory as a staid or sterile environment that negated emergent behavior. Further, Carl's view of the laboratory differed from other experimental social psychologists of the time in that he did not view it as a place of deception. Rather, the laboratory could be a provocative stage (Katovich 1984) in which a scientist could cooperate with subjects in an open awareness context (Glaser and Strauss 1964) and eliminate extraneous variables. This stage created a theatrical environment in which subjects became "method actors" as their acts created emergent variables, contributing to the systematic study of ongoing social processes.

Even though Carl parted, at least methodologically, with fellow interactionists, he worked consistently within the symbolic interactionist tradition. In a twist of his interactionist allegiance, he advocated, strenuously, an alignment of Mead's and Simmel's works (Wieting 1994). He also regarded an ongoing qualitative approach in the laboratory as analogous to field observation in that his laboratory settings allowed for the examination of reflexivity, intentionality, and temporality. However, the limitations of field research techniques also prompted Couch to seek alternatives. For instance, the real-time naked eye observations made it difficult for field researchers to provide exact and patterned descriptions of the complexity social life in its entirety. Further, restricting examination to *in situ* performances invited errors in memory and symbolic reconstructions of the past that could distort, unintentionally, events as they transpired (Mead 1929). Researchers attempting to create more exact observations had to do what their name implied—they had to re-search, which made for the necessity of recording action to be replayed. Also, as implied above, even with observations over time, field researchers could not provide the precise articulation of social processes. Couch (1987) called for a methodology that could identify the precise sequence of how social acts were constructed (Couch 2017b). Therefore, without a complete record of social life, nor a precise sequence of social acts, Couch did not see field research as a viable approach to construct a hard science.

THE LABORATORY AND THE ACTION

As mentioned, Carl (1987) advocated the use of the laboratory so as to eliminate extraneous factors and bring the targeted research phenomena into focus. The laboratory served as a controlled setting that neutralized the interferences of unrelated factors that complicate the phenomena under examination. From Couch's perspective, "The removal of extraneous factors facilitates the systematic examination of those events deemed critical for acquiring greater understanding of phenomena under examination" (Couch 1987: 4). Further, the laboratory setting became a place "where the action is" (Goffman 1967: 149–50) that "magnifies selected features of social life" (Katovich 1984: 55) and highlights the phenomena under investigation. Rather than see the laboratory as a place that constrains human action, Carl maintained that,

"When properly used, the laboratory is a provocative stage that elicits vibrant social processes" (Couch 1987: 4).

Carl's conception of the laboratory began to take shape in the late 1960s, when videocassette recorders (VCR) decks and tapes became available. His commitment to interactionist principles notwithstanding, Carl's "long search for a hard science of sociology that addressed the intrinsic qualities of human behavior, and a research method that provided a complete and precise record of human actions, reached fruition" (Chen and Johns 2015: 349). The video recording capacity allowed Carl and his students to design scenarios in a laboratory to capture episodes of social interaction in their entire complexity. The playback system allowed them to articulate, with precision, the process of how individuals align themselves with one another to create social interaction. By applying this system to role-playing and theatrical endeavors in a controlled environment, "a hybrid" of conventional ways of obtaining and generating re-searchable data (within the laboratory) and using painstaking qualitative approaches to interpret such data became routinized (Chen and Johns 2015: 349).

Utilizing video recording technology, Couch and associates began a step-by-step and trial and error process involving the search for complex sequences of action (Miller 2011; Miller and Hintz 1995). Such complexity could be conceptualized and then expanded outside of the laboratory, providing what Couch considered a concerted and systematic quest for universal generic concepts and processes (cf. Turner 1953). With the creation of CRIB, Couch and his students constructed settings in which subjects, as mentioned, interacted as method actors as they would in daily life—rather than merely responding to artificial stimuli. The CRIB researchers then videotaped subjects' interactions for repeated viewing and analysis to identify important elements. In so doing, CRIB researchers allowed for complex interactions as well as elaborate sequences that involved fitting together interdependent lines of action.

An important principle that Couch advocated in his laboratory approach involved a regard for participants as intelligent agents who can anticipate and gain access to each other's intentions. This emphasis on intentionality and reflexive thinking further distinguished Carl's approach from traditional laboratory research. Based on such a conception of participants, Carl instructed laboratory researchers to establish a context, assign identities, and provide a social objective for participants to interact in the laboratory. The contexts established had an artificial quality in that CRIB researchers created them to elicit the specific social relationships under examination. CRIB researchers also constructed such contexts by using verbal instructions. Even so, the contexts created by the CRIB researchers allowed subjects to act as authentic agents, using their pasts to situate themselves and organize their actions (Mead 1929; Katovich and Couch 1992). Rather than put subjects in a disorienting position in which they could be overwhelmed by stimuli, CRIB researchers asked subjects "to suspend their disbelief and consider the researcher's environment on his terms" (Katovich 1984: 55).

In regard to approximating authenticity by encouraging subjects to use their pasts independent of the laboratory setting, CRIB researchers assigned subjects identities congruent to the established contexts. Carl maintained the desirability of assigning identities consistent or compatible with participants' everyday identities. For example, CRIB researchers asked individuals aligning themselves with management to play the managers, whereas those sympathetic to labor would play union leaders on a stage of workplace negotiation. The advantages of such alignment allowed participants to become more firmly situated in the context created, and also to have a better vocabulary for the enactment of identities assigned (Couch 1987). Further, a social objective in the laboratory setting, congruent to the context and identities assigned, became specified by the researchers and served as the goal for the participants as they coordinated their interaction.

Returning to Carl's fascination with technology and recording social action in the laboratory, one distinct advantage of using audio-visual recording allowed researchers to study social processes with precision. As Carl maintained, studying social processes requires researchers to describe, in precise detail, the sequence of social acts and "noting the sequential order of social events and specifying their formal qualities as well as their quantity" (Couch 1987: 137). While field research, unaided by audio-visual technologies, can produce descriptions of social relationships, field notes, although rich in details, may lack the comprehensiveness and the precision that are captured in the laboratory research reports (Leichty 1975). Carl stated that "field observations seldom are complete and accurate enough to allow for the precise specification of the sequential order of the construction of the elements of sociation that constitute various forms of social action and social relationships" (Couch 1987: 153). The recording and playback capacities of the video recording allow laboratory researchers to obtain a complete record of data, and examine the data over and over again to specify the sequences of social acts with precision.

The data generated in the laboratory called on CRIB researchers to provide analysis by first, transcribing the video recordings. Second, CRIB researchers needed to wade through "audio-visual recordings of social encounters (containing) so much data that it is usually impossible to complete an analysis of them by simply viewing and listening to the recordings" (Couch 1987: 73). In this light, Carl noted that it is necessary to make transcriptions from the recordings before an analysis can be performed, as "transcribing the tapes is time consuming, but allows for a more complete and thorough analysis of data" (Couch 1987: 73). To study social processes and relationships in a laboratory setting utilizing audio-visual recording is not only an approach that distinguishes the new Iowa School from other sociological perspectives, but also a setup that embodied all the sociological principles that Carl advocated—especially the aforementioned reflexivity, intentionality, and temporality (Buban 1986; Couch, Katovich, and Buban 1994).

The ingenuity and creativity of Carl and his students allowed for a multitude of role-playing and theatrical encounters, including planning sessions among constituents, bargaining and negotiation encounters, figurative assembly-line "factories," and interviews between employers and employees, to name a few. The combination of (1) a laboratory to generate research data for analysis and (2) the latest technologies in the 1960s, audio-video recording and playback systems for research in order to capture the processual aspects of human interaction (a newly available tool being tested in qualitative research), allowed for a vast library of recordings that could be re-searched and that could allow for comprehensive and verbatim conversation analysis that correlated with embodied coordination and non-verbal communication.

As mentioned, CRIB and the prolific research resulted from the use of the laboratory represented the establishment of the new Iowa School of sociology. The ethos of this school complied with and dissented from the conventional scientific methods established in sociology. On the one hand, Carl and his students believed in the systematic examination of social processes in controlled environments. They provided an elaborate defense of procedures that would constrain and "script" social action to the extent that such action would be confined to "artificial" environments, products of laboratory architecture. On the other hand, the new Iowa School was established to differentiate the work of Carl and his associates from sociologists who advocated similar pursuits of precision in sociological research, but employed the static methodology advanced by more quantitative researchers

Carl and his students provided a climax of the development of the new Iowa School in 1975, when Couch and Robert Hintz, Jr. edited and published *Constructing Social Life: Readings in Behavioral Sociology from the Iowa School* (Couch and Hintz 1975), a volume of research generated from the investigations of social interactions in CRIB. The volume contained analyses aimed at identifying social forms and creating theoretical concepts to articulate such forms. The anchor of this monograph contained the elaboration of Dan Miller's master's thesis, which, in general, examined the fundamental accomplishments of two individuals as they transformed their temporal and spatial being from independent agents to an interdependent dyad. Couch regarded this study, known as "Openings," as the breakthrough (2017b: 44–49) in regard to a scientific study of the elements of social action. The study became translated into a value added thesis (Miller, Hintz, and Couch 1975), identifying "a set of concepts that specified the elements and structure of social action" (Couch 1989a: 208). From this study, which identifies the key elements of social action that would be present in all complex action, even that which activated both micro and macro sociological processes simultaneously (Katovich 1986), all other laboratory studies could emerge. From Couch's perspective, the openings study represented the paradigm that would immortalize his research agenda.

The subsequent efforts of students following in the wake of the Couch and Hintz monograph became accessible through the publication of *Studies in Symbolic Interaction: The Iowa School* (Couch, Saxton, and Katovich 1986), and *Social Processes and Relationships* (Couch 1989a). The two volumes of *Studies in Symbolic Interaction: The Iowa School* not only contained many methodological considerations but also featured several exemplary research endeavors utilizing the new Iowa School approach. *Social Processes and Relationships* is a comprehensive treatment of all the concepts and theories put forth by the new Iowa School researchers to that date. Many insightful ideas and useful concepts constructed during the breakthrough stage received full attention and thorough development in these two publications.

Carl also began writing about what he considered to encompass more macro-sociological themes, based on the micro-sociological concepts generated in the laboratory. His views on charisma (Couch 1989b) keyed on "charismatic transactions" which, in part, resembled some of the interactions generated in various laboratory studies. He also attempted to construct theories of the state (Couch 1989c), markets (Couch 1986), and even civilizations (Couch 1984b), drawing upon the basic elements of interdependent action that emerged from Miller's study of openings (Miller 2011). In effect, Carl's use of the basic concepts generated in the laboratory displayed how such concepts serve as foundations for the emergence of broader forms of cooperation, coordination, negotiation, and even control. Carl's efforts did receive a good deal of positive attention; in 1992 he received the G. H. Mead Award from SSSI. Still, just before his death in 1994, Carl sensed an air of incompletion. Reflecting on his work one night he wondered if "all that I've done is just an exercise in catharsis."

A SURFEIT OF INTEREST IN THE NEW IOWA SCHOOL

The new Iowa School's mixed methods approach to research used a research setting, the laboratory, often equated with more positivistic approaches, as a provocative stage in which symbolic interaction occurred. During the 1970s until the late 1980s, Couch became acknowledged, even by critics, as the "father of qualitative laboratory research" (Katovich and Chen 2017). Indeed, some on the outside looking in regarded the new Iowa School a new paradigm in the sociological inquiry (Travisano 2015). This acknowledgment became embedded in evaluations of the prodigious accomplishments of those using the CRIB laboratory to generate data, publish works, and provide a historical audio-visual legacy that could be further re-searched by up and coming graduate students. However, the new paradigm that transcended a "singular methodology" would become, eventually, a marginalized approach to symbolic interaction, unacknowledged in sociology textbooks and sociological readings, and unread by many who devoted their lives to qualitative methodology. While the new Iowa School laboratory research yielded a fruitful outcome and established a significant scholarship well into the twenty-first century, neither the school nor its concepts became recognized in sociology, sociological textbooks, or readers emphasizing an interactionist orientation.

The lack of recognition is somewhat curious. Although few people advocated mixed methodologies in the 1960s and 1970s, current researchers employ them with great regularity. In retrospect, CRIB and the new Iowa School's mixed methodological approach emerged during a time when such an approach seemed unrecognizable. Carl and his students paid the price of being ahead of their time and being between research agendas (Katovich and Chen 2017). As mentioned, the 1960s and 1970s mainstream sociologists, quantitatively oriented, appreciated the laboratory setting. However, Couch's qualitative approach to generating laboratory research appeared inconceivable and lacked the alleged precision of quantitative results. On the other hand, field researchers, qualitatively minded, found the laboratory setting overly scripted even though they also valued the reflexivity, intentionality, and temporality that the new Iowa School emphasized. By the time mixed methodologies became acceptable to qualitative researchers (in the 1990s—Tashakkori and Teddlie 1998), Carl's works remained socially invisible by both quantitative researchers and qualitative researchers.

The new Iowa School's emphasis on utilizing audio-video recordings to analyze complex social action also appeared as ominous to interactionists, especially those who valued a more "naked eye" approach to analyzing social life. One of the sub-textual "points of pride" among interactionists had to do with relying on one's powers of observation as well as capacity for empathy to not only gain entrance into the social lives of inhabitants of particular life worlds, but also to understand the perspectives of these inhabitants (Lofland 1971). While schools of thought such as ethnomethodology (see for instance, Garfinkel 1967; Psathas 1995) had a great deal of success and garnered much admiration in regard to audio-taping conversations for purpose of analysis, the video aspect employed by the new Iowa School did not generate much enthusiasm among interactionists, some of whom felt that using video and equating laboratory interactions with interactions *in situ* went against the ethos of examining behavior in "unscripted environments." While students of Carl addressed such arguments (see Katovich 1984; Katovich, Saxton, and Powell 1986; Molseed 1994) and argued that videotaped interaction in the laboratory served as an extension of the sociological eye in emergent situations, few interactionists seem persuaded.

The new Iowa School has, at least in sociological and symbolic interactionist circles, seemed to take on an ephemeral past (cf. Mead 1929), but such a status does not mean the memory of Carl has become erased. Indeed, Carl's interactional style and dynamic presence created a paradox of remembrance. On the one hand, those who met Carl and got to know him could never forget him. He made lasting impressions on people who shared such impressions with others. One of the co-author's students, for instance, worked with a faculty advisor at the graduate program through which this student matriculated. The student made reference to how his faculty advisor could do a "spot on" imitation of Carl. Even though the student had never met Carl, he felt as if he knew something about him. This paradox of remembrance delves into the contrast between remembering Carl the person as opposed to remembering Carl as founder of the new Iowa School. Ironically, Carl's work became overshadowed by the "charismatic transactions" in which Carl participated with many others (Couch 1989a).

APPLICATIONS OF COUCH'S WORK IN INTERNET STUDIES

Despite the new Iowa School's apparent "fading away," memory of its accomplishments, spearheaded by Carl, has some institutional lodging. Former students do use his work in their classes and in the field of Communication Studies. Carl's students have continued to publish works in varieties of places, including *Symbolic Interaction, Studies in Symbolic Interaction*, or *The Sociological Quarterly* (the official journal of the MSS). Scholars identifying themselves with the new Iowa School in the field of Communication Studies have continued to seek broader applications of the theoretical concepts established while CRIB still operated as a going concern (Chen 2002).

Further, the recent publications of the second edition of *Constructing Social Life: Readings in Behavioral Sociology from the Iowa School* (Couch and Hintz 2015) and *Information Technologies and Social Orders* (Couch 2017c), edited by Mark D. Johns, indicates the continuous importance of Couch's work in sociology as well as in the study of communication technologies. In addition, Chen and Johns (2002) illustrated the application of the new Iowa School to study online interaction. In this work, the authors argued that the epistemological standpoints and methodological guidelines of the new Iowa School are useful in studying Web 1.0 interaction due to the various similarities found between the lab and the web. First, the magnified setting of the lab is similar to the filtered environment of online discussion. Second, the so-called artificial context in the lab is not much different from the virtual context of the web. Third, assigned identities are used in the lab, while in cyberspace, assumed identities are performed. Finally, both the lab and the web allow for the analysis of processes and sequences.

Katovich and Chen (2014) also demonstrated the utility of new Iowa School method in studying social media found in Web 2.0. The authors provided a comparison between the ethos, methodological mission, and theoretical standpoint of the new Iowa School and *Second Life*, a three dimensional virtual world that invites particular forms of sociation. Their analysis concludes that the methodological and conceptual emphases of the new Iowa School could provide a useful framework for research into the virtual worlds. Finally, one of Carl's unfinished manuscripts, originally titled *The Politics and Passion of Discovery*, has become a published memoir, *Carl J. Couch and the Iowa School: In His Own Words and in Reflection* (Katovich 2017). In this edited and, in part, "filled in" reflection, Couch recollects his journey from graduate student to founder of the new Iowa School. As was Carl's nature, he credits his students with most of the "founding," but does not, completely, cast himself as a "supporting actor."

Shortly before his death, Carl presented his presidential address at the Midwest Sociological Society (Couch 1995). Carl not only returned to the University of Iowa to occupy the office of his mentor, Manford Kuhn, but provided a "final word" at the Midwest Sociological Society, just as Kuhn had done years before. Interestingly, both Kuhn's and Carl's presidential addresses were published posthumously in *The Sociological Quarterly*. In his address and published article, Carl urged qualitative sociologists to find the fire in their belly and dare the art and science of seeking generic concepts that could have universal application. He also noted that such application would not represent science for the sake of science, but would be of use to many people seeking explanations and interpretations for occurrences in their own life worlds. While some interactionists have forgotten the new Iowa School and others may have never read the works that emerged from this school, the message advocated by Carl and his endeavors will always remain relevant (Chen 2017). At some point, in the near or far away future, Carl's quest will reappear.

WORKS CITED

Blumer, H. 1956. "Sociological Analysis and the Variable." *American Sociological Review* 21: 683–90.

———. 1969: *Symbolic Interaction*. Englewood Cliffs, NJ: Prentice-Hall.

Buban, S. 1986. "Studying Social Process: The Chicago and Iowa Schools Revisited." Pp. 25–38 in *Studies in Symbolic Interaction: The Iowa School*, edited by C. J. Couch, S. Saxton, and M. A. Katovich. Greenwich, CT: JAI Press.

Chen, S. L. 2002. "Renewing the new Iowa School of Symbolic Interaction in the New Millennium." *Studies in Symbolic Interaction* 25: 3–4.

———. 2017. Chapter 7, Ann, Pp. 159–60, in *Carl J. Couch and the Iowa School: In His Own Words and In Reflection*, edited by M. Katovich. Bingley, UK: Emerald Publishing.

Chen, S. L., and M. Johns. 2002. "Empiricism in Cyberspace: The new Iowa School Goes Online." *Studies in Symbolic Interaction* 25: 25–44.

———. 2015. "The Start of Something New: A Retrospective Look at the Iowa School." Pp. 347–59 in *Constructing Social Life: Readings in Behavioral Sociology from the Iowa School*, 2nd edition, edited by C. Couch and R. Hintz, Jr. Champaign, IL: Stipes Publishing.

Couch, C. J. 1968. "Collective Behavior: An Examination of Some Stereotypes." *Social Problems* 15: 310–22.

———. 1970. "Dimensions of Association in Collective Behavior Episodes." *Sociometry* 33: 453–71.

———. 1982. "Temporality and Paradigms of Thought." *Studies in Symbolic Interaction* 4: 1–34.

———. 1984a. "Symbolic Interaction and Generic Sociological Principles." *Symbolic Interaction* 1:1–13.

———. 1984b. *Constructing Civilizations*. Greenwich, CT: JAI Press.

———. 1986. "Markets, Temples, and Palaces." *Studies in Symbolic Interaction*. 7: 137–59.

———. 1987. *Researching Social Processes in the Laboratory*. Greenwich, CT: JAI Press.

———. 1989a. *Social Processes and Relationships*. Dix Hills, NY: General Hall Inc.

———. 1989b. "From Hell to Utopia and Back to Hell: Charismatic Relationships." *Symbolic Interaction* 12: 265–79.

———. 1989c. "Mass Communication and State Structures." *The Social Science Journal* 27: 111–28.

———. 1995. "Let Us Rekindle the Passion by Constructing a Robust Science of the Social." *The Sociological Quarterly* 36: 1–14.

———. 2017a. "Backdrop." Pp. 7–12 in *Carl J. Couch and the Iowa School: In His Own Words and in Reflection*, edited by Michael A. Katovich. Bingley, UK: Emerald Publishing.

———. 2017b. "The Breakthrough." Pp. 39–53 in *Carl J. Couch and the Iowa School: In His Own Words and in Reflection*, edited by Michael A. Katovich. Bingley, UK: Emerald Publishing.

———. 2017c. *Information Technologies and Social Orders*, edited by Mark D. Johns. New York: Routledge.

Couch, C. J., and R. A. Hintz, eds. 1975. "Time Intention, and Social Behavior." Pp. 35–58 in *Constructing Social Life*. Champaign, IL: Stipes.

———, eds. 2015. *Constructing Social Life: Readings in Behavioral Sociology from the Iowa School*, 2nd edition. Champaign, IL: Stipes.

Couch, C. J., M. A. Katovich and S. L. Buban. 1994. "Beyond Blumer and Kuhn: Researching and Studying Across Time Data Through the Use of Point-In-Space Laboratory procedures." Pp. 127–38 in *Symbolic Interaction: An Introduction to Social Psychology*, edited by Nancy J. Herman and Larry T. Reynolds. Dix Hills, NY: General Hall Inc.

Couch, C. J., and D. R. Maines, eds. 1988. *Communication and Social Structures*. Springfield, IL: Charles C. Thomas.

Couch, C. J., S. L. Saxton, and M. A. Katovich, eds. 1986. *Studies in Symbolic Interaction: The Iowa School.* Greenwich, CT: JAI Press.

Feyerabend, P. 2010. *Against Method*, 4th edition. New York: Verso Books.

Garfinkel, H. 1967. *Studies in Ethnomethodology.* New York: Prentice-Hall.

Glaser, B. and A. Strauss. 1964. "Awareness Contexts and Social Interaction." *American Sociological Review* 29: 669–79.

Goffman, E. 1959. *The Presentation of Self in Everyday Life*. New York: Anchor Books.

———. 1963. *Behavior in Public Places: Notes on the Social Organization of Gatherings*. New York: The Free Press.

———. 1967. "Where the Action is." Pp. 149–270 in *Interaction Ritual*. Garden City: Anchor Books.

———. 1983. "The Interaction Order." *American Sociological Review* 48: 1–17.

Katovich, M. A., ed. 1984. "Symbolic Interactionism and Experimentation: The Laboratory as a Provocative Stage." *Studies in Symbolic Interaction* 5: 49–67.

———. 1986. "Temporal Stages of Situated Activity and Identity Activation." Pp. 329–52 in *Studies in Symbolic Interaction: The Iowa School* (Volume 2), edited by Carl J. Couch, Stanley L. Saxton, and Michael A. Katovich. Greenwich, CT: JAI Press.

———, ed. 2017. *Carl J. Couch and the Iowa School: In His Own Words and in Reflection*. Bingley, UK: Emerald Publishing.

Katovich, M. A., and S. Chen. 2014. "new Iowa School Redux: *Second Life* as Laboratory." *Studies in Symbolic Interaction* 43: 63–84.

———. 2017. "From Galileo to Galilea to Carl Couch: Paradigm Shifts as Power Struggles." Pp. iii-vii in *Carl Couch and the Iowa School: In His Own Words and in Reflection*, edited by M. A. Katovich. Bingley, UK: Emerald Publishing.

Katovich, Michael A., Dan E. Miller, and R. S. Stewart. 2003. "The Iowa School." In *Handbook of Symbolic Interactionism*, edited by Larry T. Reynolds and Nancy Herman-Kinney. Lanham, MD: Alta Mira Press.

Katovich, Michael A., and William A. Reese. 1993. "Postmodern Thought in Symbolic Interaction: Reconstructing Social Inquiry in Light of Late-Modern Concerns." *The Sociological Quarterly* 34: 391–411.

Katovich, M. A., and C. J. Couch. 1992: "The Nature of Social Pasts and Their Use as Foundations for Situated Action." *Symbolic Interaction* 15: 25–47.

Katovich, M. A., C. J. Couch, and D. E. Miller. 1987. "The Sorrowful Tale of Small Groups Research." *Studies in Symbolic Interaction* 8: 159–80

Katovich, M. A., S. L. Saxton, and J. O. Powell. 1986. "Naturalism in the Laboratory." Pp. 79–88 in *Studies in Symbolic Interaction: The Iowa School* (Volume 1), edited by Carl J. Couch, Stanley L. Saxton, and Michael A. Katovich. Greenwich, CT: JAI Press.

Kuhn, M. H. 1954. "An Empirical Investigation of Self Attitudes." *American Sociological Review* 19: 68–76.

———. 1960. "Self-Attitudes by Age, Sex and Professional Training." *The Sociological Quarterly* 1: 39–56.

———. 1964a. "Major Trends in Symbolic Interactionist Theory Over the Past Twenty-Five Years." *The Sociological Quarterly* 5: 61–84.

———. 1964b. "The Reference Group Reconsidered." *The Sociological Quarterly* 5: 6–21.

Kuhn, M. H and T. S. McPartland. 1954. "An Empirical Investigation of Self-Attitudes. *American Sociological Review* 19: 68–76.

Kuhn, T. 1962. *The Structure of Scientific Revolutions*. Chicago: University of Chicago Press.

Leichty, M. 1975. "Sensory Modes, Social Action, and the Universe of Touch." Pp. 65–79 in *Constructing Social Life*, edited by C. J. Couch and R. A. Hintz. Champaign, IL: Stipes.

Lofland, J. 1971. *Analyzing Social Settings: A Guide to Qualitative Observation and Analysis*. New York, NY: Wadsworth.

Mead, George H. 1925. "The Genesis of the Self and Social Control." *International Journal of Ethics* 35: 251–77.

———. 1929. "The Nature of the Past." In *Essays in Honor of John Dewey*, edited by John Coss. New York, NY: Holt and Co.

———. 1930. "Cooley's Contribution to American Social Thought." *American Journal of Sociology* 35: 693–706.

———. 1932. *The Philosophy of the Present*. Chicago, IL: University of Chicago Press.

———. 1934. *Mind, Self, and Society*. Chicago, IL: University of Chicago Press.

———. 1938. *The Sociology of the Act*. Chicago: University of Chicago Press.

Meltzer, B., and J. Petras. 1970. "Symbolic Interactionism: Genesis, Varieties, and Criticism." Pp. 3–17 in *Human Nature and Collective Behavior*, edited by T. Shibutani. Englewood Cliffs, NJ: Prentice-Hall.

Miller, D. E. 2011. "Toward a Theory of Interaction." *Symbolic Interaction* 34: 340–49.

Miller, D. E., and R. A. Hintz. 1995. "Openings Revisited: The Foundation of Social Interaction." *Symbolic Interaction* 18: 355–69.

Miller, D. E., R. A. Hintz, and C. J. Couch. 1975. "The Elements and Structure of Openings." *The Sociological Quarterly* 16: 479–99.

Molseed, M. 1994. "Naturalistic Observation in the Laboratory." *Symbolic Interaction* 17: 239–51.

Psathas, George. 1995. "Talk and Social Structure." *Human Studies* 18: 139–55.
Simmel, Georg. 1950. *The Sociology of Georg Simmel*, compiled and translated by Kurt Wolff. Glencoe, IL: Free Press.
Turner, R. H. 1953. "The Quest for Universals in Sociological Research." *The American Sociological Review* 18: 604–11.
Tashakkori, A., and C. Teddlie. 1998. *Mixed Methodology: Combining Qualitative and Quantitative Approaches*. Thousand Oaks, CA: Sage.
Travisano, R. V. 2015. "Attitudes as Promises: A Symbolic Interactionist Approach to the Unconscious." Pp. 335–46 in *Constructing Social Life: Readings in Behavioral Sociology from the Iowa School*, 2nd edition, edited by C. Couch and R. Hintz, Jr. Champaign, IL: Stipes Publishing.
Wieting, S. 1994. "Obituary, Carl J. Couch." *Footnotes*, American Sociological Association, November. http://www.cccsir.com/whowas.htm.

Chapter Nine

Jack Douglas: The Reinvention of Society and Sociology

Creative Deviance, the Construction of Meaning, and Social Order

Thaddeus Müller

"All important creative acts are deviant acts..."

(Douglas 1976: 238)

Jack Douglas is the "creative deviant" sociologist par excellence. His deviance consists of criticising and rejecting dominant, classic ideas regarding, for instance, suicide, social order, and research methods. Reading his work over a period of twenty-five years my own reaction is still one of amazement and wonder. His work intrigues me deeply. I do not fully embrace his work and see his flaws, but I want to understand his resistance, his development, his work, and the person he is. The best way to do this is to submerge oneself in his work and relate it to the many layers of his biography and social worlds, in particular the persons who shaped and inspired him, and the sources he used to construct his texts. In order to do this I will first describe his deviance in being a sociologist and second I will offer an understanding of his sociological deviance by analysing his work, researching its developments, and relating them to his life history and to the social worlds he was part of.

It is impossible to consider all the works of Jack Douglas in the format of a book chapter. However, at the other extreme, focusing on one work cannot do justice to the complexity and development of his thought. Hence, I focus here on four books, which are closely related, as they all focus on transgression, creative deviance, the construction of meaning and social order: *The Social Meanings of Suicide* (1967), *American Social Order* (1971a), *Investigative Social Research* (1976) and *The Nude Beach* (1977). Douglas published these four ground-breaking books in just ten years.[1] They contributed to sociology in significant ways, in such divergent fields as qualitative research, suicide studies, cultural criminology and critical cultural studies.

METHOD

In order to get to the essence of Douglas's sociological approach I have submerged myself in his work. I have read, reread, and analysed not only the four books noted above, but all his work published between 1967 and 1977. This includes chapters in the books he edited in this period, such as *Deviance and Respectability: The Social Construction of Moral Meanings* (1970a), *Crime and Justice in American Society* (1971b) and *Existential Sociology* (with John Johnson 1977). I have especially paid attention to the references he uses in his work to create his new sociology. I have also used publications on Douglas's academic career and personal life (for example, Johnson 2015; Kotarba 2018; Melnikov and Kotarba 2015) and reviews of his work (for instance, Cavan 1977; Churchill 1972; and Manning 1971).

The method of analysis I used for Douglas's written work was constant comparison (Glaser and Strauss 1967). I engaged myself with his work, marked the most crucial passages and compared these with each other within each book and between books. I compared my findings with his other publications and publications on his works. I also compared the data from email interviews with my analysis of his work and vice versa.

In order to understand his work in relation to his biography I also interviewed Douglas himself via email. This helped me to better understand his work as, for example, he explained issues that were not clear to me and pointed out crucial elements of his biography often hidden in footnotes. I also used our emails to check my intuitive interpretations, especially on the relation between his publications and his biography. In recent years I have also talked informally about Douglas with some of his students (notably, Joe Kotarba, John Johnson and David Altheide).

The questions for the various interviews were developed while I was reading his work and as a reaction to the answers he gave in his emails to me. The email conversations we had were cordial, open, and honest. Douglas talked about his life, such as his traumatic childhood and how he experienced the different studies he did. I use some of his quotes in this chapter for the purposes of illustration, and to provide a deeper understanding of his work and himself. Before I do this, I will give a brief sketch of his biography and academic career.

SHORT BIO[2]

Jack Douglas was born on January 14, 1937 in Miami, Florida. Jack had a troubled and poor childhood. He had two younger brothers, born in 1938 and 1941. His mother was a barmaid and married five times. When Jack was five years old his mother left him and his brother, William. They were raised for several years in foster care. This was a traumatic experience for Jack. He states in an email to me that he loved his bright, young mum deeply and that his childhood was a world of love. He also describes the shock of being institutionalised:

> But 1942 overturned my world when I was barely five. World War II was not as destructive here as in Europe and Asia, but it did much to destroy my world of love. My mother went to work as an elevator girl in Miami Beach and apparently got caught up in the wild life of a beautiful young blond in a vast world of men training for war. My father went to war with the army and then the Pacific invasions. I have no idea how it happened, but I and my brother Bill woke up one day in a foster home prison surrounded by a high wrought iron fence and run by a monster tyrant we called "old lady Walton" behind her back. I was terrified and deeply depressed and anxious because it made no sense and no one would tell me how or why we were there.

Later his mother took both brothers and travelled with them across the US. This uprooted lifestyle in the underbelly of American society exposed Douglas to the seedy world of bars, where violence, alcohol, and desolation dominated. As a child, Jack was highly intelligent and sensitive. Because he was bookish, he was the target of bullies at school. One way of dealing with the world around him was escaping into the world of ancient times by reading the classic Greek and Roman philosophers, who would remain his role models and mentors for most of his career. At the same time, his intelligence became his greatest resource in getting ahead: Douglas received a full scholarship to Harvard and then to Princeton University. In these social surroundings he remained an observant outsider who refused to play the social game of status and becoming part of the in-group. He became critical of most scholars at both universities, whom he saw as careerist and not genuinely academic, searching for truths about human nature, which, for Douglas, was a lifelong quest. One crucial exception was Pitirim Sorokin, who became an academic role model for Douglas. Sorokin was a Russian refugee who partook in the revolution, but later came into conflict with the Bolsheviks. He became the founder and first head of Harvard sociology department and firmly disagreed with Talcott Parsons regarding the latter's structural functionalist sociology.

As Jack was on his way to becoming a "creative deviant" in academia, his brothers were participating in other forms of transgression. Jimmy, born in

1941, had spent many years in prison, and William, the brother Jack was closest with, passed away in 1958. William was a risk taker and, although his death resembled a suicide, it remained unclear whether this was the case.

Jack Douglas married in 1960 and in 1964 he took a teaching position at University of California, Los Angeles (UCLA), where he was in close contact with Harvey Sacks and Harold Garfinkel, whom he admired deeply and thought of as geniuses, especially Sacks. Their ethnomethodological approach shaped his reinvention of sociology, as we can see in his *The Social Meanings of Suicide*.

THE SOCIAL MEANINGS OF SUICIDE

The Social Meaning of Suicide (1967) is based on Douglas's dissertation and is probably his most well-known book. It is a full-frontal attack on Emile Durkheim. Douglas started his doctoral work with a hard-core positivistic statistical approach to suicide. Being as thorough as he is, he soon discovered crucial flaws in Durkheim's work and that of his followers. *The Social Meanings of Suicide* can be divided into two parts. The first part is a critique of the dominant positivistic structural functionalist sociology à la Durkheim. Douglas's work here is rigorous and fundamental. He starts with relating Durkheim to the cultural and academic ideas on suicide in his time. Douglas shows that Durkheim's theory of integration and suicide is actually a common sense approach, also used by others who studied suicide, such as the "moral statisticians." Douglas masterfully points out the logical contradictions of Durkheim's *Suicide* and the creation of a pseudo-scientific front:

> Theories of suicide have been pressed into the service of more general ideas and theories which the individual theorists assumed to be true before they came to the data on suicide. . . . But they have often gone one step further: they have tried to give the impression that they went from the data to the theory, that they had used an inductive method. This *positivistic rhetoric* has often given a scientific aura to these works when the actual methods used were anything but scientific. (Douglas 1967: 153)

Douglas criticizes Durkheim for using a simplified representation of society and its norms. Durkheim states that society is homogenous in the sense that everybody shares the same norms and values, and that behaviour and persons who diverge are abnormal:

> Durkheim did, of course, recognize that there are differences in normative evaluations of suicide, even in one nation, and tried, most unconvincingly, to banish such facts from consideration by developing his tortured theory of normality and pathology. (1967: 155)

Perhaps Douglas's main contribution is the next step in his dissection of Durkheim's study, a detailed and innovative account of how the social construction of (the meanings of) suicide biases the official statistics he employs. Douglas shows that the decision to define a death as suicide is not a clear and easy task for professionals. During the assessment process of the body, significant others of the deceased might try to influence the decision making process. One of Douglas's crucial findings is that the process of defining a death as suicide is closely related to integration:

> We would . . . expect that *the more socially integrated an individual is, the more he*[3] *and his significant others will try to avoid having his death categorized as a suicide, assuming that suicide is judged negatively*. (1967: 209)

Here, for example, we could point to significant others from a devout Catholic background who might try to change the definition of a death from suicide to an accidental death, because their theology suggests that suicide is a sin and will bring shame upon them and their loved ones. On the other hand, there are also people isolated from significant others and who, therefore, have no one who might want to influence the definition of a death by the coroner. Douglas shows that this mechanism biases the rate of suicides in relation to social status and urbanity:

> Regardless of any differences in moral judgement, one must expect that the greater average knowledge of an individual and his significant other in a smaller community will lead to a greater significance of the imputation of a negatively evaluated category such as suicide, so the effective *incentive* is greater to conceal any suicidal actions even where the moral judgement is less severe. Since there is usually a direct relation between social status and the degree of social integration, we would also expect that the official statistics would systematically underestimate the rates for the middle and upper classes. . . . Since the predominant social characteristics of the individuals residing in the "disorganized" core areas of the cities is that of a very low degree of social integration (and of social status), we would expect that the official statistics would systematically underestimate the rate of outer areas of the cities relative to their estimates for the core areas. (1967: 214–15)

Douglas shows in a rigorous and transparent way that Durkheim was wrong because he wasn't measuring what he thought he was. For Douglas, integration did indeed play a crucial role, not in the commission of suicide, but in the decision processes of defining the meaning of death and recording it.

The second part of the text, which follows the previously described critique of the nature and (mis)use of official statistics on suicide, can be seen as Douglas's first steps in his reinvention of sociology, which emphasizes the complexity of meaning-making in general and specifically in relation to such morally charged acts as suicide. Douglas states that we should focus our attention on the social construction of meaning:

> Moreover, I would argue that the only way one can go about scientifically studying the meanings of suicidal phenomena (or any other social phenomena) is by studying the specific meanings of real-world phenomena of this socially-defined type as the individuals involved construct them. (1967: 253)

Douglas describes the construction of the meaning of suicide as a process in everyday life influenced by a range of involved persons, such as the person who died, the coroner, family, and friends of the deceased and medical professionals such as general practitioners and psychiatrist. In order to describe and analyse the social construction of meaning, Douglas uses mostly secondary sources, such as the cases out of Cavan's (1928) study of suicide and reports in the media, to develop his alternative approach to understanding suicide. Based on the main text, one might conclude that Douglas is a bookish, armchair sociologist, but when one reads the footnotes, it becomes clear that many of the discussed cases are from data gathered by himself. Still, hiding observations in footnotes somewhat obscures his personal involvement with the topic and makes it difficult to understand fully how the research was conducted.

Based on the analysis of cases from secondary sources and his own observations Douglas identifies four meanings of suicide:

1. as a way of moving the soul from this world to the other world;
2. as a way of giving oneself a different meaning in the present world and the afterlife;
3. as an attempt to achieve sympathy and empathy;
4. as an attempt to get revenge.

Douglas states that to understand the meaning of suicidal action, one has to relate it to the suicidal process, which precedes the act itself. His conclusion is that the construction of social meaning is a complex process that cannot be reduced to the types suicide data used by Durkheim and others:

> [S]ocial meanings are fundamentally problematic both for the members of society and for the scientists attempting to observe, describe and explain their actions. (Douglas 1967: 339)

This part of the monograph reads like a hidden, formalistic form of symbolic interactionism, which is very similar to the work of Blumer, Goffman, Becker, and Kitsuse. Douglas does indeed make many references to these and other qualitative researchers in his footnotes, but he seems especially influenced by the ethnomethodologists, such as Garfinkel and Sacks, who deeply shaped his thinking on the construction of meaning.

Perhaps the biggest influence on his reflections on the ambivalence and complexity of the suicidal process is his own personal experience. Behind the façade of this rational and logical piece of work, we can sense the painful experiences in his personal life, notably the tragic death of his brother, to whom Jack felt very close. Jack explained in a long email to me:

> If you look at the frontispiece dedication of this book to my brother Bill, you will see that he died at 21, just before I started work on that book at Princeton Grad. College when I just had turned 22. He was walking with his back to the heavy traffic along the eastern edge of Miami Int. Airport in the winter darkness. A car went off the road, hit him from behind. He suffered a fatal head injury that killed him some days later after gruesome suffering. Bill was always taking big risks and I would beg him not to do so and he would laugh and do so? Why? Was he courting death that night? Gambling with life and death? Did he care? I do not know.

Douglas's first-hand experience with suicidal behaviour undoubtedly shaped his biography and perspective on this topic, but he did not show its explicitly here. Maybe it was too painful. Maybe he anticipated that it would have been rejected as being non-scientific. Later Douglas will integrate his own personal experiences into his work explicitly, but in his dissertation, the most personal act is his dedication to his brother William (1940–1961).

AMERICAN SOCIAL ORDER:
SOCIAL RULES IN A PLURALISTIC SOCIETY

American Social Order (1971a) is Douglas's second book. His main thesis here is that social rules are highly problematic in a pluralistic society, such as 1970s America. Douglas combines his focus on meanings and interactions with notions on power, inequalities, and oppression. We might today see this as a common approach, but back then qualitative research, especially in deviance studies, was criticized, particularly by critical sociologists. Coming mostly from the neo-Marxist tradition, their critique was that qualitative sociology focused too much on the social life of small groups or organisations, without paying attention to power-relations, politics, and social injustice. *American Social Order*, however, is probably the best example of how the two can be combined, but sadly, it is one of the least known of Douglas's books.

In the first part of the book, Douglas continues to reject Durkheim in a beautifully polemical and sometimes funny way, such as when he criticizes the assumption of "Moral Absolutism":

> To those sociologists who share the traditional structural-functional perspective on deviance, one of the great beauties of anomie theory is that it appears to explain the violations of the rules of society in terms of the absolute rules themselves; thus, it gives the appearance of explaining seeming rejections of the values of society in terms of an absolute acceptance of the values.... What might appear to be unsocial or anti-social, and what might be instances of freedom, "really prove" the absolutism of society. There is no way out of the closed system. (Douglas 1971a: 27)

Whereas in *The Social Meanings of Suicide* Douglas relies primarily on secondary data, in *American Social Order* his own research is of fundamental value to his thesis. Douglas uses his own interviews with coroners and medical examiners to show their biases in defining a death as a suicide. The process itself, he argues, depends on a range of circumstances that differ between individuals, depending on their income, legal, and medical knowledge and the local rules (or lack thereof) surrounding how a death is determined to be a suicide. Douglas makes use of different cases to demonstrate the extreme complexity in deciding whether someone committed suicide or not. The coroners have to look at (1) the consequences of the act; (2) the action itself; (3) the instruments used, such as a gun or knife; (4) the immediate situation of the act and that leading to the act; (5) expression of intention, such as a suicide note; (6) the long run situation; and (7) the type of person and any relevant previous acts. Finally, all these elements have to fit together in a narrative that makes sense.

For Douglas it is crucial that in order to solve the problems related to deviance, morality, social order and freedom, sociologists have to understand the social construction of meaning and the use of rules in everyday life. Therefore, just as in *The Social Meanings of Suicide*, Douglas focuses in *American Social Order* on the key principles of the construction of meaning, such as the influence of the situational and trans-situational context, freedom, and constraint (agency and structure), social interaction, negotiation and the public-private dimension.

A range of academics, such as Plato, Schutz, Garfinkel, and Burke, guide him in the development of his ideas. Douglas refers a few times to his own data to demonstrate on the construction of meaning. For instance, a transcribed interview about an attempted suicide is used to show its complexity. In the first five pages a woman explains the immediate context of her attempted and failed suicide. She describes her battle with depression: "Because I knew that if I felt better that night, that the same pain would come again another time. And I'd have to go through it all over again. And so primarily I just said I'm finished fighting this thing. I just want out" (1971a: 186).

In the following four pages the influence of interactions on the meaning of a suicidal action is described. The woman redefines her suicidal action based on what others communicate about her actions. As a result of what psychiatric professionals tell her, she redefines her first attempt as being not serious. In reaction to her second suicidal action, which became public through an article in a local newspaper, she reflects on the stories of her neighbours: "I kind of notice it but it doesn't bother me much. I know I have much more important things to conquer than what they think of me" (1971a: 210).

Douglas not only has criticized Durkheim and his followers, but also his fellow qualitative researchers who have published on rules and deviance, especially those who focus on labeling. He acknowledges that the labeling approach was the first to have discussed the problematic nature of social rules. Still, he does not embrace this approach because according to him they "still take the imputation process as non-problematic" (1971a: 142). Douglas shies away from anything that reeks of a structural approach and that does not problematize the meaning making process. Behind this rationale lies his firm belief in the freedom of individuals to shape their own life.

His perspective on freedom also shapes his critique on the labeling approach. He states that within their perspective, resistance, and autonomy are impossible. While not as robustly deterministic as the structural-functionalist approach, Douglas detects a milder version of determinism in the qualitative studies of the day. For instance, in his discussion of Becker's (1963) analysis of the stages of becoming a marihuana user Douglas states:

> In this sequence there is little consideration of the possibility that the individual who is having the use of marihuana defined for him by users would act as an independent agent in the construction of the meanings of use for himself. . . . There is little consideration of the ways in which individuals might fight such definitions of themselves, reject them, reinterpret them, convince society that they are wrong, and so on. (1971a: 205)

His critique of all forms of determinism and his focus on agency and freedom is also shaped by the cultural resistance and political revolt he saw all around him in the early 1970s:

> If anyone in America is fortunate enough to live in some state of moral bliss in which he is not in daily moral combat with others, and with himself, let him read newspapers, watch television or attend church services—or a revival, political rally or court hearing—or listen to a discussion between parents and children. . . . He will not find harmony over morals and social rules. (1971a: 150)

The America Douglas is describing here is one of great diversity in which the making of meaning is problematic in itself. Douglas does not mention a most important source of data here for his conclusion. But six years later he describes his experiences that shaped many of his ideas for *American Social Order* in the appendix of *Existential Sociology* (1977), where he reveals that he was active in university politics during the "Great Campus Turmoils" while he was working on *American Social Order* (1977: 295). In the footnotes to the appendix, he explains.

> Through this activity I learned about politics from the inside. I learned the difficulty of knowing what was going on, even of knowing what was happening with my closest associates. I learned how simple statements were distorted in the retelling. I learned how all sides, including our own, were involved in clandestine activities that they often did not understand. (1977: 307)

And

> throughout these practical activities I was intensely involved in trying to understand them and see their meaning for a better sociological theory. I believe they did reveal, in starker and more problematic forms, the kinds of struggles that go on all the time in the political arenas of our society in which social order must be constructed. . . . It was undoubtedly the most important field research I have yet done and . . . it has formed the background information for some of my most important work in recent years. (1977: 357)

In this period, many identified a massive transformation and rapid pluralization of morals leading to turmoil and polarisation, but Douglas provides a unique perspective on these changes in that he sees both order and disorder at the same time:

> The result has been that one has concentrated almost exclusively on explaining social order, the prime symbol of functionalism, while the other has concentrated on explaining social disorder or conflict, the prime symbol of the conflict theories. *Yet the obvious truth about society, especially our society, is that there is an abundance of both order and disorder, of both consensus and dissensus.* (1971a: 246)

So while, or maybe because, he takes this position, he does not close his eyes to the oppressive workings of organizations of control and how those in power stay in control:

> [They] use the legal definitions of crimes in an attempt to control the kinds of things lower-class individuals commit against them, in particular property crimes and certain acts of violence. The result is that *these acts as defined as "crimes" in our society will almost always be precisely the kinds of activities committed by lower-class individuals.* (1971a: 90)

Douglas's description of the criminal justice system accords well with critical sociological literature, inspired by Marx, Gramsci or Mills:

> The mandate of the police is to "maintain social order" and they have always understood that this is to be done even at the expenses of violating some of the most important and cherished laws in our society, especially concerning "civil rights." (1971a: 310)

On the final pages of *American Social Order* Douglas states that contemporary social disorder is shaped by the fact that some dominant groups of American society, supported by organizations of state control, are imposing their morals on a pluralistic American society:

> Those individuals and officials who have chosen in recent years to treat certain legal rules as absolute seem to have created the same massive circumvention and alienation from the law and from officials, and in some cases from America in general, as the enforcers of prohibition did a generation ago. For example, this seems clearly to have been the case in the attempts to enforce the laws against marihuana use. (1971a: 322)

In the final sentence of the book, Douglas suggests a way to get out the social situation of conflict, disorder and polarisation by recommending a libertarian approach of moral meaning in society. For him it is the cherishing and acceptance of a pluralistic society where there is freedom for individuals to create their own social life and construct their own morality:

> Only by deabsolutizing all social rules except those necessary for the construction of an "optimal" social order are we likely to avoid violent disorders as our society becomes more international, changeable, open, complex, and pluralistic. (1971a: 322)

Investigative Social Research. Individual and Team Field Research

Investigative Social Research (1976) builds upon *The Social Meanings of Suicide* and *American Social Order*. It rejects the quantitative approach of structural functionalism and is based on Douglas's conception of American society as being plural and conflicted, in which people will not tell the truth about things that are sensitive to them, such as social status, sexuality, and death. At the same time, this monograph conveys a non-moralistic stance toward doing research in which researchers have the sovereignty to get to the truth.

> The investigative paradigm is based on the assumption that profound conflicts of interest, values, feelings and actions pervade social life. . . . Instead of trusting people and experiencing trust in return, one suspects others and expects others to suspect him. Conflict is the reality of life; suspicion is the guiding principle. . . . It's war of all against all and no one gives any one anything for nothing, especially truth. (1976: 55)

Douglas's approach is inspired by the work of investigative journalists and detectives, and is demonstrated in concepts, such as "infiltrating groups," "penetrating misinformation" and "setting people up." Here he cites examples from a range of deviance studies conducted by his students and himself on topics, such as massage parlours, drug dealers, and the nude beach.

Douglas also discusses the social barriers to truth in a systematic and rigorous way. He starts with misinformation ("unintended falsehoods") which are commonly the result of the "complexities of things to the people being studied," such as organizational myths (1976: 57). He also focuses on evasions—intentional acts of hiding—which can have different forms, such as silence and avoiding (1976: 59) and lies and fronts, which can be understood as "socially shared and learned lies about the setting itself" (1976: 73). However, there are other barriers to the truth which are hard to reflect upon by those who are being studied, because they are not aware of them, such as taken-for-granted feelings and meanings. Another example of this kind of hidden barrier to the truth are problematic feelings and meanings. Because most persons, according to Douglas, prefer to present themselves as rational, they tend to shy away from articulating problematic feelings and thoughts.

Douglas discusses several strategies to get at the truth, such as testing and checking out, infiltrating the setting, and building friendly relationships and opening them up. Most of these belong to the standard research repertoire of any seasoned researcher of crime and deviance, but at times the polemic way he uses them and his examples make his view of investigative social research seem deceptive and, in some cases, unethical. For instance, this is how Douglas describes building and using friendly relations and checking them out:

> [T]he researcher exchanges intimacies with the subject. . . . Simply, he shows that he's into it too—that he is human, disreputable, etc. He thereby establishes commonalities, makes himself open to them, makes himself equal to them and, significantly shows he trusts them. (1976: 137)

It is clear that Douglas himself does not always feel good about his investigative strategies. He gives an example of Jon, whom he met on the nude beach. Jon said he did not want

> his life written down, even under a pseudonym, that he wanted to remain anonymous and not be written about. We liked Jon, regardless of the lack of trust, and always felt badly writing about him, even knowing the chance was slight that he or anyone he knew would read what we wrote . . . field research is inevitably a partly traitorous activity we had accepted as necessary. He, of course, was right not to trust us. His mistake was in liking us. (1976: 139)

Also, in Douglas's third major monograph, his relation to other qualitative researchers is problematic. Probably the most remarkable element here is his rejection of ethnomethodology. Douglas criticizes the fact that ethnomethodologists do not examine real life experiences, but only study recorded highly scripted interactions, such as doctor/patient conversations, that, according to Douglas only show the front stage of social life and provide little insight into the true nature of human beings. Though he seems here to be more favourably disposed to the Chicago School fieldwork tradition inspired by symbolic interactionism, he also criticizes their research methods, on three grounds: their denunciation of full emergence because of their fear of losing "objectivity," their focus on only one perspective in the research field, and their lack of team field research.

Douglas rejects the criticism of full emergence, an active full member of the community one studies. He insists that researchers should "use subjective experience, gained from interaction with other people and from introspection, to understand them and oneself" (1976: 25). In the context of those days, this stance is highly innovative and daring. He gained this insight through his own research experience and that of others, especially John Johnson (1975), who wrote *Doing Fieldwork* in which he describes how in his research feelings and thoughts were fused. Douglas similarly states that the researcher should take:

> his own experiences as a vital source of insights, as a means of grasping and understanding partial truths of the setting. (1976: 127)

The researcher also should focus on testing:

> out the relevance and the limitations of his inner, unspoken experience by getting the members to talk, at least, indirectly, about the experiences. (1976: 127)

Douglas's second critique of the Chicago School fieldwork tradition is its focus on the description of the worldview of one group. This "uni-perspectival" (1976: 48) approach only shows one side of a social world and ignores the "multi-perspectival picture of society" (1976: 48). Finally, the uni-perspectival approach is related to what Douglas calls the "Lone Ranger researcher," where fieldworkers work alone. To create a "multi-perspectival" perspective on society, Douglas developed the idea of team field research:

> Team field research involves a number of people working together in a flexibly planned and coordinated manner to get at the multiperspectival realities of a group, . . . utilizing the specialized abilities and opportunities of the various team members, providing both support and crosschecks on the work of each member by the other members, and all members ideally providing creative inputs to the research, the grasping, the understanding and the final report. (1976: 194)

Investigative Field Research became his third ground-breaking book in ten years. It is vastly dissimilar from other textbooks on research in those days, which Douglas dismisses as "research cookbooks" (1976: 3). Douglas frames his narrative in a sort of warfare jargon that sounds ruthless and exploitative, and was seen by some as unethical (Cavan 1977). This way of describing urban social life in the 1970s was not uncommon, however. For instance, Lyn Lofland, in an earlier (non-published draft) version of *A World of Strangers*, employed concepts such as "psychological warfare" and "battle tactics" (1985: xii). But, more importantly, *Investigative Social Research* was shaped by the fact that Douglas and his students studied controversial topics such as transgressive, deviant behaviour, about which most people are not usually straightforward to others they do not know personally.

Still, my experience is that there are also many occasions in which one can trust others and rely on what they say, which Douglas acknowledges, almost fleetingly, in one of less polemic moments:

> While the emphasis is put on the differences between the cooperative and investigative methods, thus making them look extremely different, in actual practice as investigative researchers we necessarily rely upon some degree of trust and cooperation at some stage of our work. (1976: 56)

THE NUDE BEACH

In the early 1970s while Jack Douglas was jogging on the beach near his house, he noticed that increasing numbers of people were bathing nude. He became professionally interested because he saw this sort of behaviour as a potentially revolutionary act that could change society and also function as a gateway to understand human nature. He began participating in this social world and researched it for several years, during which he cooperated with Paul Rasmussen and Carol Ann Flanagan in an example of team field research.

There is a close relation between *The Nude Beach* and *Investigative Social Research*. In addition, many themes that dominate *The Social Meanings of Suicide* (for example, the complex process of giving meaning to morally charged activities) and *American Social Order* (for instance, the plural and conflictual character of American society) also play a crucial role in *The Nude Beach*. Its central theme concerns the process of giving meaning to public nudity and how this is infused with experiences of both pleasure and shame. For instance, chapter 2, "Joining the nude beach" is all about the fear, anxiety, and shame in exposing one's naked body in front of strangers. Because the exposure of the naked body in public is such a highly emotionally and morally charged act, it also leads to fierce reactions from others who are repulsed by it and try to prevent it. Douglas, Rassmussen, and Flanagan describe all these aspects of how people give meaning to the nude beach, including Douglas's own:

> I was able over many years (nine thus far, but only five of which have been nude years) to observe individuals repeatedly dealing with shame and so came to recognize the patterns (I should point out that my own feelings of shame, especially of aggressive moralism and certain forms of self-deception, long "hid" much of this from me. But I have become conscious of them and am now even watching them. I must admit it was more fun when I was deceived and could more "sincerely" vent my aggressive moralism on those "voyeurs creeps" who made me feel shame subconsciously or even momentarily consciously before I could vent it and pull the warm layers of self-deception over myself). (Douglas et al. 1977: 86)

In the introduction and conclusion of the book Douglas indicates that he favours the nude beach, describing it as a pleasant physical experience of nature and freedom. He also sees public nudity as a revolutionary action coming from within society to experience freedom and to reject absolute moral norms:

> We think there is little doubt that nude beaches . . . are truly revolutionary. If they become an accepted part of our social world, fundamental parts of ourselves, our very body feeling, images, and sexual expression will change in important ways. (1977: 228)

One of the more innovative qualities of *The Nude Beach* is the description of a wide range of perspectives on nudity, such as the regular casual nude beachers, voyeurs and exhibitionists, the gay scene, the swinging scene, the media, the police, the courts and those who are against the nude beach, such as property owners. Where conventional ethnography tends to focus on one group, Douglas and his co-authors focus on this wide range of voices. So, for instance, they describe the stance of the police, which in general is relaxed. They tend to stick to warnings and oversee minor violations on beaches that are isolated. But they do not tolerate "lewd" behaviour on any beach and nudity on beaches that are easy to enter. Only in situations of political pressure do they become more proactive, showing up more frequently and giving out warnings. One of their main strategies is to:

> "keep them uncertain." While it is true that the police aren't themselves clear on this, it is certainly true that they know they do not intend at this time to arrest people for nudity on the well-established beaches unless there is some lewd behaviour associated with it. But they never make this known publicly. (1977: 211)

A detailed description of the politics around the nude beach is a great example of uncovering "fronts" via a multi-perspectival ethnography. The property owners who are against the nude beach were trying to convince the city to build an access road. But their real reason for proposing the road was to make the beach accessible to the general public, so that public nudity would no longer be allowed. The nude beachers knew this and formed the committee "Save Eden Beach:"

> The Committee got totally idealistic and moralistic right away. They contended the access road would bring so many people it would ruin the natural ecology of the beach. . . . Hence the word save in the committee name. But, of course, the word was meant to have a double, secret meaning for the nude beachers—Save Nudity on Eden Beach. (1977: 219)

There were two dominant perspectives on the nude beach: (1) the nude beachers' view that it was all friendly, natural and pleasant, and that there was no sex going on and (2) their opponents who argued that its users were a bunch of perverts involved in an orgy of sex. Though it is clear that Douglas himself enjoys being naked on the nude beach, he does not simply confirm the nude beachers' perspective. Rather, his conclusion is that both parties are constructing a set of meanings to protect their interests, neither of which is in line with his team's observation of the nude beach.

For example, Douglas and his co-researchers provide many descriptions of sexual behaviour that might discredit the nude beach. They confirm that sex acts do take place on the beach, but that there is "always some degree of concealment, so they are not simply "open to plain view" . . . (1977: 106). They also describe the beach as a "pick up-scene" where "sexual hunting" takes place (1977: 165). In their description of the different strategies employed, Douglas does not shy away from identifying discrediting behaviours such as the harassment of women by men, as in the behaviour of "yawanna-fuckchick types" who approach women with the line: "Hey, yawannafuck?" (1977: 170). Douglas shows that the nude beach is not a paradise where people enjoy nature and their bodies in freedom by describing examples of sexual harassment by exhibitionists and voyeurs:

> One day we saw Ben, a heavy organ-displayer, follow a young girl into the water and get erect as he stood there talking to her. She then came out of the water and started to jog down the beach. Ben jogged along beside her, swinging back and forth violently. She then abruptly turned, with no warning, and ran the opposite direction, leaving him to the other way. (1977: 144)

And . . .

> One of the heaviest bits of voyeurism we ever saw on the beach was perpetrated by a couple of straight camera-voyeurs. . . . The straights followed them, zeroing in for their close-up beaver shots as the girls whirled to confront their tormenters. One of the girls, apparently maddened beyond control, shouted out, "All right, buddy, fuck off!" The straights beat a hasty retreat, but kept their camera rolling. We later observed them sitting down the beach, shooting any female nude who moved (1977: 119).

Douglas reports these examples of harassment of women because he wants to be truthful in his depiction of order and disorder on the nude beach.

Confirming his earlier ideas, most people experience the beach as a cool scene where both conflict and cooperation are experienced:

> I was beginning to see it's a really beautiful and mellow scene. It's really sexy, no matter what people tell you, and I don't think anyone would bother to come down here if they didn't really enjoy seeing others' bodies and showing their own body. I've met some guys here that I really liked and sometimes we get it on together after we left. . . . Sure, there are bound to be some creeps running around, but that doesn't bother me, generally . . . that's their thing. But it is also really beautiful. The nude beach is a cool scene (1977: 20, 22).

The Nude Beach marks the end of a decade long journey for Jack Douglas. While in *The Social Meaning of Suicide* Douglas relies primarily on secondary data. *The Nude Beach* features a rich ethnographic description, based on his own full emergence in the social world of nude beachers. It is almost as if Douglas has freed himself, left his iron cage of rationality and objectivity, and fully participated in society. In his next publication, an edited volume *Existential Sociology*, Douglas rejects, in his habitual polemical style, sociological studies (including his own, especially *The Social Meaning of Suicide*) that emphasise symbols, morality and meaning in their analysis of society. Instead he states that social life is all about feelings and that emotions rule our behaviour.

This personal and academic transformation coincides with the vast societal and cultural changes in America, and especially in California, which emphasized individual freedom and emotions over societal constraints. The nude beach was a profound example of this shift. Jack Douglas was shaped by these societal changes, making him a child of his times, while remaining a creative deviant and discovering (his own) emotions as a tool to understand society and human nature.

CONCLUSION

In only a decade Douglas published four ground-breaking monographs, each of which had a major impact in such sociological subfields fields as suicide studies, qualitative research, and (cultural) criminology. In order to understand the construction of these four studies we have to look at Douglas's biography and especially how he interacted in the social worlds in which he participated.

First, one has to understand that Douglas was not trained in any qualitative tradition, such as Hughes, Becker, and Goffman, who were schooled in the Chicago School tradition. These scholars accepted the premises of qualitative research, fieldwork, and symbolic interactionism. Instead Douglas was formed by a range of disciplines, including philosophy, psychology, natural science, and sociology. In essence, this made him a social scientist in a positivistic sense. For him, every study was about getting access to the truth of humankind. As a young scholar, he even at one time embraced a mathematical approach to social life. *The Social Meanings of Suicide* should be seen through the eyes of someone slowly discovering the merits of qualitative research, especially ethnomethodology, and trying to develop an alternative approach to the then dominant structural functionalist approach to suicide. His representation of himself in his first book is still that of an armchair sociologist, though in the footnotes there are, albeit sparse, references to his own research.

In his perception of suicide, Douglas was also shaped by the death of his brother Bill and encounters with other persons who were considering suicide. The primary characteristics of the death of his brother are its ambivalence and complexity, which the Durkheimian approach fails to address. In a way, Douglas is trying to create a new approach to makes sense of his brother's death. At the same time, he is also changing the meaning of suicide provided by Durkheim and his followers. Douglas makes it clear that suicidal action is not pathological and abnormal in itself, but that suicidal actions contain different meanings constructed by different actors in everyday situations.

American Social Order grows out of *The Social Meanings of Suicide* and is, therefore, shaped by the same social and intellectual context. Still there is a definitive and distinctive transformation in his perspectives on society and sociology visible in this second book. In it he adds two crucial elements, the pluralisation and the polarisation of American society, that make the construction of meaning even more complicated and problematic.

American Social Order is shaped by Douglas's daily experience of conflict in the media and the political situation he was involved in during the "Great Campus Turmoils," but he only mentioned this years later in the appendix to *Existential Sociology* (Douglas and Johnson 1977). Also, he extensively uses his own research material in *American Social Order*, but he does not include any methodological discussion, making only a minor reference to the sources of his data. This also indicates that Douglas at this time does not see himself as a qualitative researcher in a traditional sense. He is more a philosophical student of social life who feels free to use his own observations, media coverage, and secondary literature.

His sociological stance is remarkable for its time, as he rejects the then dominant structural functionalist and neo-Marxist approaches, mainly because both are divorced from human lived experiences. At the same time, he has a love-hate relation with qualitative studies. He acknowledges their contribution to studies of deviance, but criticizes them also for focusing too much on how society shapes or in his words "determines" people, and not paying enough attention to agency, freedom, and autonomy.

Investigative Social Research has a radically different feel. Where Douglas was a hesitant researcher in his first study, here he fully embraces the direct experience of fieldwork. What is interesting is that he was already aware of the problematic nature of deviance studies in 1970, as he published a reader and an anthology on this topic that could have defined him. But what profoundly shaped him in the first half of the 1970s was mentoring a group of talented young graduate students, such as John Johnson, Joe Kotarba, David Altheide, Andrea Fontana, Paul Rasmussen, and Patti and Peter Adler. Working with them turned him into a qualitative researcher, albeit with a hard core positivistic and scientific aim to describe the truth about humanity that remained with him from his teenage reading of classic philosophers and his education at Harvard and Princeton.

If Douglas had been trained in any qualitative tradition he probably would have taken the lies and deceits for granted and found his way around them, like any experienced qualitative researcher. But because he was a relative outsider he did not and focused instead on the investigative aspect of fieldwork. His weakness became his strength.

One significant example of Douglas's unique methodological position is that when he became a participant researcher, he argued that going native, in the sense of experiencing the feelings of the people you study, can help you better understand their world. At the same time, he was supported and shaped by a group of outstanding young researchers noted above. For instance, *Doing Fieldwork* by John Johnson (1975), on the fusion of feeling and thinking, is probably the most cited book by Douglas in which he did not himself participate. At the same time, his deep involvement with ethnographic fieldwork had a fundamental impact on his relation with ethnomethodology. He rejected it for being sterile and superficial, because, according to him, ethnomethodologists were only interested in the "frontstage" of accounts and did not investigate any deeper meaning.

The Nude Beach is written in the same period in which Douglas wrote *Investigative Social Research* and they overlap in many ways. *The Nude Beach* is in method, form, and substance the ultimate investigative social research-ethnography. Still, Douglas has not completely severed himself from his past. He is still interested in the construction of meaning in a pluralistic and polarized society. But he seems to be less interested in sociology. Douglas ends this monograph with reflection on humanity and our existential being in the world. He, sadly, hardly reflects on the relevance of his work for sociology. This is a shame because the book is now narrowly seen primarily as an insightful study of a nude beach, while it more accurately is a monograph on the construction of social problems, labeling and moral panics, arguably doing a better job covering the topics than Becker (1963) and Cohen (1972). *The Nude Beach* is a thick ethnographic description of the nude beach in which all perspectives are covered. It is about real people who in everyday life construct meaning. Also, Douglas does not shy away from controversial topics concerning discrediting information of the nude beach. His concept of the creative deviant and his description of the pleasure of transgression make this text the forerunner of cultural criminology, more so perhaps than Jack Katz's *Seduction of Crime* (1988). Unfortunately, however, *The Nude Beach* is not recognized as such.

One reason for this perhaps is that Douglas did not publish any further research on deviance or transgression. In fact, he stopped publishing for six years. His experience of the nude beach changed his perspective on society as is clear in *Existential Sociology* (Douglas and Johnson 1977), where he rejects all forms of sociology because they do not recognize emotion as the guiding force in human life. He also distances himself from the classical philosophers, who had influenced him during his teenage years, because they were too rational and also ignored the significance of emotions in understanding humanity. With this stance, he returned to his position of being an outsider in sociology, as he had begun his academic career a decade earlier. The difference was that in the late 1970s he entered a world of feelings that confronted him with emotional issues shaped by his traumatic youth. Again, he dealt with this, trying to understand the emotional disorder in his personal life in *Creative Interviewing* (1985), which focusses on trust, emotions, understanding and cooperation, and *Love, Intimacy and Sex* (Douglas, Atwell and Hillebrand 1988).

NOTES

1. In the period 1967–1977 he published in total 16 books, which consist of monographs, anthologies and readers. In almost all the anthologies and readers he published one or more original chapters.
2. This is mostly based on the publication by John Johnson (2015).
3. As many others in those days, Douglas used the male pronoun in a generic sense.

WORKS CITED

Becker, H. S. 1963. *Outsiders: Studies in the Sociology of Deviance.* New York: The Free Press.

Cavan, R. S. 1928. *Suicide*. Chicago: The University of Chicago Press.
Cavan, S. 1977. Review of "Investigative Social Research: Individual and Team Field Research." *American Journal of Sociology*, *83*(3), 809–11. Retrieved from http://www.jstor.org/stable/2778178.
Cohen, Stanley. 1972. *Moral Panics and Folk Devils: The Creation of the Mods and the Rockers*. London: MacGibbon & Kee.
Churchill, L. 1972. Review of *Jack D. Douglas: American Social Order*. *Social Forces*, *51*(2), 237.
Douglas, J. D. 1967. *The Social Meanings of Suicide*. Princeton, NJ: Princeton University Press.
———, ed. 1970a. *Deviance and Respectability: The Social Construction of Moral Meanings*. New York: Basic Books.
———, ed. 1970b. *Observations of Deviance*. New York: Random House.
———, ed. 1970c. *Understanding Everyday Life: Toward the Reconstruction of Sociological Knowledge*. Chicago: Aldine.
———. 1971. *American Social Order: Social Rules in a Pluralistic Society*. New York: Free Press.
———, ed. 1971. *Crime and Justice in American Society*. Indianapolis, IN: Bobbs-Merrill.
———. 1976. *Investigative Social Research*. Beverly Hills, CA: Sage.
———. 1985. *Creative Interviewing*. Beverly Hills, CA: Sage.
Douglas, J. D., F. C. Atwell, and J. Hillebrand. 1988. *Love, Intimacy, and Sex*, 20. Sage Publications, Inc. Newbury Park, CA: Sage.
Douglas, J. D., P. K. Rasmussen, and C. A. Flanagan. 1977. *The Nude Beach*. Beverly Hills, CA: Sage.
Douglas, J. D., and J. M. Johnson, eds. 1977. *Existential Sociology*. Cambridge, UK: Cambridge University Press.
Glaser, B. G., and A. L. Strauss. 1967. *The Discovery of Grounded Theory: Strategies for Qualitative Research*. Chicago, IL: Aldine.
Johnson, J. 1975. *Doing Fieldwork*. New York: The Free Press.
Johnson, J. M. 2015. "Freedom Works! The Vision and Broken Heart of Jack D. Douglas." *Symbolic Interaction*, *38*(2), 285–97.
Katz, Jack. 1988. *Seductions of Crime: Moral and Sensual Attractions in Doing Evil*. New York, NY: Basic Books.
Kotarba, J. 2018. The La Jolla Salon and the Search for Human Nature. *Studies in Symbolic Interaction*, 45.
Lofland, Lyn. [1977] 1985. *A World of Strangers. Order and Action in Urban Public Space*. Prospect Heights, IL: Waveland Press
Manning, P. K. 1971. Review of *Deviance and Respectability: The Social Construction of Moral Meanings*. *Sociological Quarterly*, *12*(4), 548.
Melnikov, A., and J. Kotarba. 2015. "Existential Sociology." In *The Blackwell Encyclopedia of Sociology Online*, edited by G. Ritzer. Boston: Blackwell. doi:10.1111/b.9781405124331.2007.x.

Chapter Ten

Ben Agger

Social Theory as Public Sociology

Lukas Szrot

SOCIAL THEORY AS PUBLIC SOCIOLOGY:
BEN AGGER (1952–2015)

> Imagine a circle inscribed inside a rectangle. The circle represents all that can be known with positivist methodology in the social sciences. The rectangle represents empiricism. That's my question: can you be an empiricist without being a positivist? I think you can. There's nothing wrong with being a card-carrying positivist, but there are other ways of knowing, of doing sociology. (Agger 2013)

While such a statement would be at home in the "positivist-constructivist" debate that animated the methodological schisms of twentieth century sociology, Agger went further, and took a rather different approach. Borrowing from theoretical ideas in the humanities innovations loosely referred to as poststructuralism, deconstructionism, and postmodernism,[1] Agger sought to fuse these elements of each with critical theory, resulting in an alternative vision of sociology that appears at once democratic, radical, and markedly different. His critique of social *science* methodology turned on challenging the artificial disjuncture between science and non-science as methods of inquiry in the context of sociology—his "re-reading" promises a sociological approach at once open-ended, theory-driven, publicly engaged, and participatory (Agger 1989a).

Agger would have argued that to separate the life of a theorist from the theory s/he articulated would be to risk Sartrean (1987) "bad faith."[2] Thus, before contextualizing the contemporary relevance of Agger's critique of disciplinary sociology, I offer a brief biographical sketch. Then, I focus on his *avant-garde* efforts to infuse critical theory with postmodern ideas evoking a public vision of sociology rooted in practical reason. Finally, I consider how Agger's critical insights enable us to re-imagine the role of social theory via public discourse and alternative future visions that address present injustices.

BEN AGGER: BIOGRAPHY AND SOCIOLOGY

Agger relocated to Canada after completing high school, earning a degree in political science in 1973, followed by an MA in sociology one year later. He received his PhD in political economy from the University of Toronto in 1976, and then taught first at Bishop's University then moving to SUNY-Buffalo, as professor of sociology until 1994, with an affiliation with the department of comparative literature in 1990. Agger then moved to the University of Texas at Arlington as Dean of Liberal Arts in 1994, before assuming a professorship in sociology there in 1998, where he served until his untimely passing on July 14, 2015.

A native of Eugene, Oregon, Agger came of age against the backdrop of the Vietnam War and the social turmoil of the 1960s. His involvement in the countercultural youth movements there was inspired and supported by his father, University of Oregon political scientist Robert G. Agger. Agger remembered his father as "a very influential person in terms of supporting and encouraging African American students in particular, and all students in general, encouraging us to continue to struggle for change in this society" (2009: 216). Agger is in turn remembered fondly by colleagues: "If perhaps not in demeanor, Ben was in spirit and thought an unreconstructed North American '68er" (Antonio 2015: 827). A pivotal year for the antiwar movement, feminism, and Civil Rights in the United States was 1968. Agger was an antiwar activist, and, with his father, actively dialogued with Eugene's Black Panther Party and other movements that emerged in his home town to combat racism (Agger 2009). These early experiences left their mark on Agger, as his extensive body of work always maintained a critical edge echoing Marx's famous eleventh thesis on Feuerbach: "heretofore the philosophers have tried to understand the world. The point, however, is to change it."[3] Agger notes elsewhere the influence of these formative years: "Sometimes, only half-joking, I tell my own sociology students that 1969 was the last best year!" (2002: 31).

There are several related reasons why Agger's extensive body of work has been relatively neglected in professional sociological circles. For one, Agger spent much of his career at the University of Texas at Arlington, an institution catering primarily to non-traditional, commuter students and which does not have a doctoral program in sociology. However, the primary reason why Agger's work is not more widely discussed in contemporary sociological circles is perhaps his role as an interdisciplinary "gadfly" who prodded sociologists who came across his work to think, and re-think, what sociology is, how it is done at present, and how it might be done differently. An extended example from *Postponing the Postmodern* is illustrative:

> This book demonstrates, and argues for, a de-professionalized sociology, a sociology that is merely a version, a way of being human a literary activity that can be pursued without advanced degrees or appeal to the higher power of almighty Method . . . too few sociologists are intellectuals in the sense of asking big questions about society and composing their work in an accessible language. Instead, they plow narrow fields and write for other experts, destining their work for obscurity . . . necessity of expertise has become a cult, with knowledgeable insiders talking only to other insiders as the discipline entrenches a master narrative of math and method. (Agger 2002: 22–23)

To blur boundaries between the academic and public spheres and challenge the foundations upon which one's discipline has been erected is to jeopardize both one's position within the academy and one's standing among one's peers. This may be particularly true in this difficult era for universities, in which funding for disciplines like sociology has become a political football. Agger's pointed critique of the kind of sociology being done by many of his colleagues and peers may suggest why his work has not been more widely recognized in sociological circles.

In his extensive body of work, Agger wrote on a variety of substantive topics: the sociology of food, the body, the 1960s, families, education, culture, and the Internet. However, his work bears a common thread in its connection to both the cultural project of the Frankfurt School of critical theory as well as postmodern thought as means by which to reimagine both sociology and society. While Agger generated a substantial oeuvre, I wish to focus on his critique of disciplinary sociology that took shape in works such as *Reading Science* (1989a), *Socio(onto)logy* (1989b), *Public Sociology* (2000), and *Postponing the Postmodern* (2002).

AGGER'S CONTRIBUTIONS TO SOCIOLOGY: CRITICAL THEORY, POSTMODERNISM, AND PUBLIC SOCIOLOGY

Drawing on and synthesizing elements of postmodernism and critical theory, Agger theorized a public sociology with a transformative aim. In all four of the aforementioned works, Agger extensively cites the work of postmodernists alongside that of the critical theorists. Regarding these two broad categories of thought, the injudicious reader might be tempted to conclude (1) that "postmodernism and critical theory" can be lumped together as collaboratively posing a danger to the broadly empirical project to which disciplinary sociology is ostensibly devoted, if not a threat to the broader university and society itself; and (2) in advocating some version of *deconstructionism* for sociology, Agger was yet another academic who came of age in the late 1960s and was caught up in what some regarded as a pernicious intellectual fad.

Postmodernism has been perennially lampooned by critics as pseudo-profound gibberish that willfully misunderstands concepts from mathematics and the natural sciences (Gross and Levitt 1999), a pseudointellectual radical political project (Kimball 1990), a product of (perhaps deliberate) philosophical confusion (Sokal 2008), and even a means by which relativizing reality and absolutizing difference gives license to far-right religious and nationalistic identity movements (Antonio 2000; Nanda 2003). In short, by jettisoning epistemic objectivity and undercutting the possibility of the separation of fact and value, an academy committed to the pursuit of truth is irreparably fragmented by the question: "Whose truth?"

One of the most recognizable contributions of what is broadly called *postmodernism* (itself comprised of thinkers and schools of thought whose ideas often radically diverge from one another) is a re-characterization of both self and society predicated on the rejection of "grand narratives," which can be criticized as foreclosing of transformative possibilities vis-à-vis self and society (Lyotard 1984). Postmodernism may be considered in terms of a *subjective turn* away from the old Kantian Enlightenment clarion call: *what can I know? What should I do? And for what can I hope?* (Lash 2010). Descriptively, postmodernism describes a new era in which the line between subjective-objective, self-world, human-nature dichotomies that shaped Western Enlightenment philosophy are blurred. Normatively, certain possibilities that arose out of *modern* constellations of thought, including essentialist categories of what is true, good, beautiful, even possible, may become irrelevant or even obsolete. Selves are assembled out of bits of ephemera; societies are fragmentary, lacking shared hopes, norms, and ideas. The conception of the present as *postmodern* challenges the very foundations of knowledge, belief, and morality.

With the compression of space and speeding up of production time (Agger 2004),[4] reality is reduced to an illusion created by words, symbols, images; reality at the same time becomes a *desert* replaced by "the generation by models of a real without origin or reality: a hyperreal. The territory no longer precedes the map, nor survives it. Henceforth, it is the map that precedes the territory" (Baudrillard 1983: 2). The hyperreal is the model onto which this unreal reality is then mapped. For Baudrillard, the map comes to precede the world: this latest "historical" phase is controlled by a *code*, a cybernetic mimesis that links human to machine in which "All the transcendent finalities [are] reduced to a dashboard full of instruments" (1983: 109) and a loss of a sense of history forecloses on revolution by erasing critical distance. "Every image, every media message, but also any functional environmental object, is a test. . . . Both objects and information result already from a selection, a montage, from a point-of-view" (1983: 120).

A postmodern world as depicted in this way has no ontological or teleological moorings; philosophically it is anti-foundationalist, anti-universalist, and anti-essentialist, as well as ahistorical. If postmodernity has an essence at all, it is in the self-perpetuating dissolution of any shared future vision or goal. Agger saw something ominous lurking in this: "People are taught to be what we might loosely call postmodern—self-absorbed and yet globally knowledgeable about practical matters—precisely to protect this economic and political arrangement (termed capitalism by Marx)" (2002: 5). The future is no longer futuristic, so to speak—it does not include alternative visions of social organization or different transformative possibilities. The social organization of the present, severed from the past, is projected, indefinitely, into the future. Postmodernity convinces us that we have reached what Hegel termed *the end of history.*[5] The results, according to Agger, are stark:

> The loss of meaning is occasioned by a peculiarly ahistorical view of the world, which is flattened into an eternal present. The world we experience appears to exhaust all possible worlds. We don't know who we are, or what formed us. . . . Conservatives and progressives alike notice that people lack certain basic values, a solid inner core of identity that transcends the ephemera of various particulars such as fashion, news, entertainment, work. (2002: 3–4).

Critical theory, on the other hand, denotes a *liberatory* critique of what Marcuse (1964) called the administered *"welfare-warfare state."* Critical theory in this vein is a systematic attempt to understand why, if crisis and contradiction are inherent in capitalism, as Marx argued, moments of widespread political-economic crisis led to Nazism and totalitarianism rather than liberation. In Agger's words: "Critical theory as developed by the original Frankfurt School attempted to explain why the socialist revolution prophesied by Marx in the mid-nineteenth century did not occur as expected" (1998).

In critical theory, then, there are many elements that stand in opposition to a postmodern reading of the present. *Critical* theory presupposes the possibility of critique, and critique in turn presupposes some position *from which* to criticize, as well as standards by which to criticize, specifically in terms of those contained in the position being criticized, which critical theorists refer to as immanent critique (Antonio 1981). In this sense, the conflation of postmodernism and critical theory is problematic. A tension emerges between a normative vision predicated on human liberation, as with the Frankfurt critical theory, and the fragmentation of the self and the social as characterized as postmodernism. In the *Postponing the Postmodern*, Agger foregrounds the disjuncture between the two schools of thought in their incompatible understandings of the self:

> Derrida and Foucault abandon the notion of the subject or self as an archaic residual from Western philosophical logocentrism, arguing that the subject is positioned by language and thus loses a great deal of transformational efficacy. Although Marcuse, like Adorno, recognizes that subjectivity has become politicized in an era of total administration, he holds out hope that the subject can liberate itself from what he calls "false needs." The notion of false needs earns the wrath of postmodernists, who insist on the relativity of needs as well as of language. (2002: 182–83)

Per critical theory, theorizing *false* needs requires some criterion to which one can appeal in order to establish what *needs* are in the first place, as well as how to separate *true* from *false* needs. Agger would insist that the possibility of *false* needs is irrelevant if not pernicious in postmodernism. This is in part why the fragmentary tendencies of postmodernism, read through the lens of critical theory, represent the means by which consumer capitalism becomes legitimated rather than a denoting qualitative break with modernity. To illustrate, Agger discusses the Marcusean notion of "false needs" which emerge in the context of rapid economic growth, particularly after World War II, to "fill the gap threatened by a structural disproportion between production and consumption. . . . These needs trigger endless consumption from the acquisition of basic necessities, an activity that scarcely needs to be theorized, into the appropriation of sign values—sources of meaning in fast capitalism" (2002: 182–83).

Wondering aloud why the Marxist revolution never took shape (or so frequently resulted in human rights catastrophes where it ostensibly did) presumes the veracity of both the Marxian critique of capitalism as well as normative and political categories of understanding from which such criticism can emerge. Such efforts stand in tension with an era described as "postmodern," hence the title of Agger's work: *Postponing the Postmodern* (2002). Postmodernism was to be "postponed" because it was tantamount to post-politics—its fragmentation risked a dissolution of the possibility of meaningful social change.

Agger's work challenges established modes of social science, seemingly going further than either postmodernism or many in critical theory. He emphasized that "critical theorists of the Frankfurt School largely accepted Marx's economic analysis of capitalism, but they tried to develop a critique of civilization even more far-reaching than Marx's," in which "they argue that the Enlightenment in particular is to blame for fascism and totalitarianism, inasmuch as Enlightenment (mathematical method)" (2002: 9) "behaves toward things as a dictator toward men" (1989a: 8), "rejecting nonquantitative knowledge as illegitimate" (1989b: 33).[6] What Agger opposed was not the efforts of science, or of scientists, but the potential for the technocratic deployment of maps and models in the social sciences to become undemocratic reifications of present circumstances and social relations.

Agger's project was avant-garde in its attempt to wed these theoretical projects, and to distill from them a transformative, publicly oriented sociology: "The best antidote to Adorno's depressive negative dialectics and to postmodern theory's abandonment of the political is, as I have indicated, a differentiated concept of everyday life, from which all sorts of cultural and political projects spring" (2002: 187). Agger's vision of the postmodern critique of objectivity and the turn to the subject stands out in that it is explicitly political, and intended to re-energize critical theory, and its emancipatory potential, rather than bury it (1989a; 2002). The possibility of such a liberatory project, energized by postmodernism and critical theory, renders sociology public—sociology becomes something that everyone can, in principle, do. While Agger's own political vision, including the possibility of utopia, was heavily informed by the writings of Karl Marx, one does not have to share his political viewpoint to participate in the broader sociological vision he offered:

> Although I contend that we can create a classless society, I cannot demonstrate this conclusively to people who would tell a different, perhaps Platonist or Weberian, story. My story, however well told, involves a certain circularity—my definition of social class, my theory of inequality, my conception of the good—that begs questions that cannot be answered without inviting further circularity. (2000: 256–57)

Several years after the publication of Agger's 2000 book, the idea of *public sociology* was enthusiastically embraced by the American Sociological Association (ASA) in an anthology featuring several of the discipline's prominent figures (Clawson et al. 2007). Despite Agger's book-length contribution to the topic, his name appears neither in the bibliography nor the index of the ASA volume. In subsequent years the focus on public sociology has become part of the American sociological mainstream, but Agger's contribution remains conspicuous in its absence (but see Agger 2008 and Szrot 2017).

AGGER'S VISION: SOCIAL THEORY AND PUBLIC SOCIOLOGY CONFRONTING INJUSTICE

In discussing the rise of Pythagorean and Platonic philosophy in ancient Greece, Carl Sagan warned of the danger to both science and democracy posed by an elite class of specialist keepers of knowledge (Sagan 2013). For similar reasons, Agger relentlessly criticized the tendency for sociology to become insular and disconnected, from both the human beings under study and their conflicting visions of what can be known and what should be done.

Aligning with those critics who took to task what they viewed as obscurantism and wooly logic of some postmodern writers (Gross and Levitt 1999; Sokal 2008), Agger called for a more readable, more engaging, less *obscurantist* (but ultimately not anti-mathematical) sociology, as part of a broader effort toward public outreach and engagement beyond the confines of the academy. Agger undertook such a project even though he realized that this might entail his being marginalized vis-à-vis what he called disciplinary sociology.

Many of the internal debates in American sociology, concerning qualitative and quantitative methodologies, macro- and micro-sociology, positivist and non-positivist approaches, today seem to have been settled by truce. However, a methodologically pluralistic discipline may conceal a "sacred project" with specific social, moral, and political agendas that go unquestioned in a discipline that has de-emphasized theory (Smith 2014). Social theory's insights, including Agger's, offer new possibilities for constructive engagement with the societies toward which (and Agger would insist, *from within which*) we sociologists direct our respective gazes. For Agger, theoretical issues are sidelined by positivist sociology, limiting the potential of the discipline. It follows that important, high-stakes questions risk becoming distorted by unspoken assumptions, silently foregrounding increasingly technical analyses, many of which deploy methods and models inaccessible to those without a graduate-level education in statistics.

For example, the median income for a Black family in the United States is far lower than that for a white family (Perlberg 2013). Women, people of color, and political liberals care more about the environment on average (McCright and Dunlap 2011). An increasingly large proportion of the world's total wealth is concentrated in increasingly fewer hands (Slater 2016). "Social facts" such as these are important as they guide research and public policy. However, the mere statement of statistical relationships elides larger questions, often dismissed as speculative and thus outside the conventional sociological purview. To wit: when the ASA declares its mission to end inequality, are there different sorts of (in)equality? Is it possible to eliminate all of them at the same time? Regarding the above social facts, are existing institutions amenable to reform of racial disparity, environmental risk, and the consolidation of global wealth into ever fewer hands, or must these be dismantled (perhaps violently, some might argue) and replaced in order to build new ones that more adequately address the vital issues of our time?

As noted above, Agger shared the broader goal of the ASA, and a commitment to a more just and equitable society, but argued that the methodology of mainstream sociology is incompatible with these stated goals, and that the stated goals of the discipline may be more adequately addressed by other possible narratives. Agger's goal, then, was to open up the sociological project, to make public what is overly specialized, to permit a true plurivocality in the study (and future) of society. "An epistemological pluralist, I am intolerant only of intolerance! That is, the positivist program as I understand it necessarily excludes non-positivist ways of knowing and writing" (2000: 231). Sociology is not physics, and need not be restricted to sophisticated mathematical modeling; interviews and fieldwork can capture depth and nuance that are often lost in survey research and large data sets. But perhaps more importantly for Agger, *theory* allows us to challenge and revisit one another's—and our own—assumptions about the kinds of social worlds we perceive as actualities or potentialities, as well as our relationships (as both scholars and citizens) to them. Such conversations do not necessarily need to take place at an ethereal plane of abstraction.[7] They can be rooted in *practical reason*—"scripting a life understood by theory—self-questioning about what forms us, and how we can undo our formation and thus change the forms themselves" (2002: 24).

Declaring what kinds of worlds do and do not really exist, and the constellations of possibilities that inhere within them, has historically been the purview of philosophy, not sociology (though one might reasonably argue that certain philosophical assumptions underpin all human intellectual endeavors). The assumption that social reality can be more or less accurately *mapped* (particularly numerically) is a base assumption of much of the work conducted by contemporary American sociologists. Such mapping is, Agger (2000) argues, ideological where it pretends not to be; it is a simplified vision of the social world that risks reification of the present. He applies a similar criticism to the (mis)representation of theory—Agger (1989a) argues, for example, that Marx has been domesticated by sociologists via conflict theory, associated with a vision of social conflict between competing groups and interests as inevitable, ongoing, and de-contextualized rather than as oriented toward a qualitative transformation of society rooted in history. One could argue (though Agger focused on primarily on the transformative potential of Marxian thought in this sense) that there is also a *sociologized* Durkheim in theories such as *structural-functionalism* and *consensus theory*, and a *sociologized* Weber who is depicted as absolutely separating fact and value, claiming that capitalism arose in Europe because of the Protestant Reformation, and prophesizing a bureaucratized world stripped of meaning. In these *sociologized* versions, other important aspects of these respective theories are occluded.

Yet, as Agger insightfully notes, even if we get the Grand Theorists right, theory too often remains within the conventional boundaries of sociology rather than offering a constructive means by which to clarify or carve out new areas of study. Alternatively, in our approach to sociology that does not sanctify (but does use) mathematics, and embeds itself in a living and dynamic social world, theory becomes emphasized anew: "Non-positivists argue that sociology will never arrive at laws because people, who are defined by their 'historicity' as well as free will, are not like pieces of matter in the physical world in that people can organize together in order to change their social and economic circumstances, as they have throughout human history" (2000: 100). People are not particles. Models are not reality, and what they might tell us about social reality does not exhaust all possible social worlds. The map, then, must not be allowed to precede, and therefore dictate, the real (see Baudrillard 1983 and Harvey 1990). Method is a form of argument based on certain assumptions that can be challenged, re-visited, and re-imagined in different spatial, temporal, and personal contexts. And perhaps most significantly, the present constellation of social organizations cannot be taken for granted—it must be argued for, *defended* or *critiqued*, in whole or part. Theory lives, breathes, animates sociology; when we are most inclined to dismiss it, assumptions go unexamined, and sociology risks becoming insular, unreflective, and irrelevant.

Such a sociological perspective is expected to fluctuate over the course of a lifetime, to delve into new areas of inquiry, open to re-examination, reflexivity, and interdisciplinary forays. Additionally, this also involves considering alternative possible social worlds and relations. To this end, Agger's own vision changed over the course of his lifetime, regarding theory and methods in sociology, as well as envisioning alternatives. Near the end of his life, cut short by unexpected illness, Agger developed an interest in the body as a site of both alienation and liberation. In *Body Problems* he proffered a pithy articulation of a *slowmodern* vision: "I have written about a good society that blends the pre-modern and modern, borrowing the best from each. From modernity we would take literacy, science, medicine, global consciousness, human rights, participatory democracy. From pre-modern cultures we take reverence of nature, rural life, small communities bonded by face-to-face relations" (2011: 53). Agger bequeathed to twenty-first century sociology an inspired vision of the possibilities of a critical vision of the modern social, rooted in the possibilities of the postmodern self.

NOTES

1. Jacques Derrida, "Structure, Sign, and Play in the Discourse of the Human Sciences," *The Critical Tradition: Classic Texts and Contemporary Trends* (New York, St. Martin's Press, 1989), 959–71. Catherine Belsey, *Poststructuralism* (New York, Oxford University Press, 2002). These two relatively brief and accessible works helped me to understand some of the implications of these schools of thought relative to social theory and Ben Agger. It would, however, be difficult to summarize each of these schools of thought, let alone to discuss how and why they differ from one another. In the context of

this chapter, I have used the term "postmodernism" to loosely describe multiple schools of thought emerging out a specific set of historical circumstances and deploying a broad family resemblance of critical tools and methods. I admit that this is a conflation on my part for the sake of simplicity.

2. Jean-Paul Sartre, *Existentialism and Human Emotions* (New York, Citadel Press, 1987). Ben Agger, "Postmodern Gibberish: Derrida Dumbfounds the Positivists," *New York Journal of Sociology* 1, no. 1 (2008): 187–206. Lukas Szrot, "(Auto)biography and Social Theory: A Perspective on the Life and Work of Ben Agger (1952–2015)," *Fast Capitalism* 14, no 1 (2017), www.uta.edu/huma/agger/fastcapitalism/14_1/home.html. "Bad faith" may be understood as a form of phenomenological inauthenticity, a refusal to acknowledge the choices demanded by one's existence—a work on Agger as theorist would be an act of "bad faith" insofar as it attempted to sunder authorial perspective from a text. And so that I do not end up acting in bad faith myself for the purposes of authorial expediency, I have been rather selective in authoring this text—the image of Agger that spills forth from this text is connected to, and contextualized in, the specifics of certain aspects of his social theory. For a broader-ranging, more personal tribute to Ben Agger's life, work, and influence see issue 14 of *Fast Capitalism*.

3. Marx's eleven "Theses on Feuerbach" have been published as an addendum to Marx's work *The German Ideology*. The significance of the eleventh thesis as it relates to Marx, as well as how Agger utilized them in his critique of disciplinary sociology, will become evident below.

4. While David Harvey, in *The Condition of Postmodernity: An Enquiry into the Origins of Cultural Change*, conceived of "space-time compression" as a phenomenon related to postmodernity, but one which had roots in both the Enlightenment and the globalization of capitalism, Agger conceived of the era, particularly beginning with the late 1970s, as "fast capitalism," which shares some of the nuance of Harvey's analysis. The idea of a "speeding up" is foundational to Agger's understanding of the present.

5. Also see Francis Fukuyama, *The End of History and the Last Man* (New York, Avon Books, 1992). Fukuyama's is a thoughtful but widely criticized Hegelian (but not "postmodern") examination of the historical time period following the collapse of the Soviet Union and the fall of the Berlin Wall. A vision of an "end of history" that projects implicitly or explicitly projects some form of liberalism or capitalism into the indefinite future as Fukuyama did must be resisted insofar as the development of a critical project focused on social transformation is deemed possible. Indeed this contention in many ways marks where liberal and leftist social theorists part ways. Agger frequently questioned whether capitalism was "the end of history," both implicitly in his work as well as explicitly in dialogue with scholars and students he mentored.

6. This is a rather stark claim but Agger's view became more nuanced between the late 1980s and the early 2000s.

7. Agger frequently stressed in his courses, especially to graduate students, the difference between being "obscure"—that is, dealing with ideas that are abstract, complicated, counter-intuitive, or difficult to wrap one's head around—and being "obscurantist"—writing in such a way that ideas appear more complicated or abstract than they need to be. Being obscure, he used to say, was at times necessary, because some things are complicated. Being obscurantist should be avoided judiciously, however.

WORKS CITED

Agger, Ben. 1989a. *Reading Science: A Literary, Political, and Sociological Analysis*. Dix Hills, NY: General Hall, Inc.

———. 1989b. *Socio(onto)logy: A Disciplinary Reading*. Urbana: University of Illinois Press.

———. 1998. "Critical Theory, Poststructuralism, Postmodernism: Their Sociological Relevance." *Illuminations*. www.uta.edu/huma/illuminations/agger2.htm

———. 2000. *Public Sociology: From Social Facts to Literary Acts*. Lanham, MD: Rowman & Littlefield Publishers, Inc.

———. 2002. *Postponing the Postmodern: Sociological Selves, Practices, and Theories.* Lanham, MD: Rowman & Littlefield Publishers, Inc.
———. 2004. *Speeding up Fast Capitalism.* New York: Taylor & Francis.
———. 2008. "Postmodern Gibberish: Derrida Dumbfounds the Positivists." *New York Journal of Sociology* 1: 187–206.
———. 2009. *The Sixties at 40: Leaders and Activists Remember & Look Forward.* Boulder, CO: Paradigm Publishers.
———. 2011. *Body Problems: Running and Living Long in a Fast-Food Society.* New York: Routledge.
———. 2013. "Social Theory" Lecture, Social Theory, September 3, 2013, University of Texas at Arlington.
Antonio, Robert J. 1981. "Immanent Critique as the Core of Critical Theory: Its Origins and Developments in Hegel, Marx and Contemporary Thought." *The British Journal of Sociology* 32(3): 330–45.
———. 2000. "After Postmodernism: Reactionary Tribalism," *American Journal of Sociology* 106 (2): 40–87.
———. 2015. "Remembering Ben Agger," *Critical Sociology* 41(6): 825–27.
Baudrillard, Jean. 1983. *Simulations.* Translated by Paul Foss, Paul Patton, and Philip Beitchman, Cambridge, MA: Semiotext(e).
Belsey, Catherine. 2002. *Poststructuralism.* New York: Oxford University Press.
Clawson, Dan, Robert Zussman, Joya Misra, Naomi Gerstel, Randall Stokes, Douglas L. Anderton, and Michael Burawoy, eds. 2007. *Public Sociology: Fifteen Eminent Sociologists Debate Politics and the Profession in the Twenty-First Century.* Berkeley, CA: University of California Press.
Derrida, Jacques. 1989. "Structure, Sign, and Play in the Discourse of the Human Sciences," *The Critical Tradition: Classic Texts and Contemporary Trends.* New York: St. Martin's Press.
Fukuyama, Francis. 1992. *The End of History and the Last Man.* New York: Avon Books.
Gross, Paul R. and Norman Levitt. 1999. *Higher Superstition: The Academic Left and Its Quarrels with Science.* Baltimore, MD: Johns Hopkins University Press.
Harvey, David. 1990. *The Condition of Postmodernity: An Enquiry into the Origins of Cultural Change.* Cambridge, MA: Blackwell.
Kimball, Roger. 1990. *Tenured Radicals: How Politics has Corrupted Our Higher Education.* New York: Harper & Row Publishers.
Lash, Scott. 2010. *Intensive Culture: Social Theory, Religion and Contemporary Capitalism.* Los Angeles, CA: Sage.
Lyotard, Jean Francois. 1984. *The Postmodern Condition: A Report on Knowledge.* Minneapolis: University of Minnesota Press.
Marcuse, Herbert. 1955. *Eros and Civilization: A Philosophical Inquiry into Freud.* Boston, MA: Beacon Press.
———. 1964. *One Dimensional Man.* Boston, MA: Beacon Press.
Marx, Karl. [1867] 1992. *Capital, Vol. 1: A Critical Analysis of Capitalist Production.* Edited by Friedrich Engels. New York: International Publishers.
McCright, Aaron and Riley E. Dunlap. 2011. "Cool Dudes: the Denial of Climate Change among Conservative White Males in the Unites States," *Global Environmental Change* 21: 1163–72.
Nanda, Meera. 2003. *Prophets Facing Backward: Postmodern Critiques of Science and Hindu Nationalism in India.* New Brunswick, NJ: Rutgers University Press.
Perlberg, Steven. 2013. American Median Incomes by Race since 1967. *Business Insider.* http://www.businessinsider.com/heres-median-income-in-the-us-by-race-2013-9.
Sagan, Carl. 2013. *Cosmos.* New York: Ballantine Trade Books Paperbacks.
Sartre, Jean-Paul. 1987. *Existentialism and Human Emotions.* New York: Citadel Press.
Slater, Jon. 2016. 62 People Own the Same as Half the World, Reveals Oxfam Davos Report. *Oxfam International.* https://www.oxfam.org/en/pressroom/pressreleases/2016-01-18/62-people-own-same-half-world-reveals-oxfam-davos-report.

Smith, Christian. 2014. *The Sacred Project of American Sociology.* New York: Oxford University Press.
Sokal, Alan. 2008. *Beyond the Hoax: Science, Philosophy and Culture.* New York: Oxford University Press.
Szrot, Lukas. 2017. "(Auto)biography and Social Theory: A Perspective on the Life and Work of Ben Agger (1952–2015)." *Fast Capitalism (University of Texas at Arlington)* 14. www.uta.edu/huma/agger/fastcapitalism/14_1/home.html.

Index

activism: Agger and, 7, 214, 223n3; Douglas and, 199–200; Weber, Marianne, for, 4–5
Addams, Jane, 3, 28, 30, 35, 98, 125, 136n24
Agger, Ben: as activist, 7, 214, 223n3; on assumption influences, 220, 221; biography, 214; on "end of history," 217, 223n5; on fast capitalism, 217, 223n4; as interdisciplinary gadfly, 214–215; Marx and, 214, 217, 219, 221, 223n3; on models and present, 218–219, 223n6; on modern with premodern, 222; on obscure and obscurantist, 220, 223n7; on positivist versus empiricist, 213; for publicly oriented sociology, 219; public sociology not including, 219; on readable sociology, 219–220, 220–221; on research and simplification, 221–222; social justice supported by, 220; on theory misrepresentation, 221–222
agricultural societies, 24
AJS. *See The American Journal of Sociology*
altruism: Sorokin and, 5, 119, 125, 128; study of, 127–128, 129
American Institutionalism, 102
The American Journal of Sociology (AJS), 27, 30, 32, 33

American Sociological Association (ASA), 3, 68, 86, 219, 220
American Social Order (Douglas), 191–192, 197, 208–209
amitology, 125
animism, 20
"The Applications of Psychology to Social Problems" (Bernard, L.), 77–78
ASA. *See* American Sociological Association
Ashworth, A. E., 166–167
assumption influence, 220, 221
attitudes: appearance with, 158; identity roles and, 159; moods as, 157; trajectory from, 157
"Authority and Autonomy in Marriage" (Weber, Marianne), 54–55
autonomy, 54–55, 63
axial age, 12; cost of, 23; dangers from, 23; for human history, 17; moral revolution in, 11, 14; Stuart-Glennie on, 4; transcendent God in, 21

BDF. *See* Federated Women's Association
Becker, Howard, 2
behavior: Bernard, L., on environment and, 81; CRIB and, 174, 180–181, 183–184, 185; Douglas on emotions ruling, 207; prosocial, 128–129
Bellah, Robert, 12, 21, 23
Belsey, Catherine, 222n1

Index

Bernard, Jessie, 5, 73; Bernard, L., husband to, 68, 71–72; independent work by, 88–89; on Jews, 88–89; *Origins* with Bernard, L., 90; on sociological feminism, 68

Bernard, Luther Lee, 77, 78; on American ignorance, 81–82; autobiography, 70–71; CSS student, 67, 73; doctoral dissertation of, 74–75; early life of, 68–69; on early sociology, 67–68; on environment directing behavior, 81; on ethics, 78; on eugenics, 81, 84; experiencing, 72; on "feeling" and "act," 75; female relationships and, 90–91; footnotes by, 76; on hedonism and self-realization, 77; *Instinct* by, 79, 83; on instincts, social science, 5, 79, 80; instincts data, 80; on Jews, 88–89; on Latin America, 81–83; on marriage to Bernard, J., 68, 71–72; on Mead, 74–75; on naturalistic life, 90; Onion Skins of, 67, 84–85; *Origins* with Bernard, J., 90; private life of, 77; on pursuits, 70; as scholar, 91; social betterment and, 78; social control and, 5, 74, 76, 81, 89; on society shaping people, 78; sociological innovation by, 76; sociology pedagogy by, 73; on sociology research, 69, 85–87, 87–88; standards of, 68; vocabulary by, 75, 76; war as institution and, 90; as writing machine, 84, 85

Body Problems (Agger), 222

Branford, Victor, 14

Canada, 31, 34

capitalism, 28, 32; fast, 217, 223n2, 223n4; postmodernism and consumer, 218; spirit of, 47, 52, 54–55

Carver, Thomas Nixon, 119, 135n12

Center for Research in Interpersonal Behavior (CRIB): actors and authenticity in, 181; behavior and, 174, 180–181, 183–184, 185; data, publishings, audio-visual legacy of, 183–184; ongoing, 185; settings and actors in, 180–181

Chapin, Stuart F., 118, 135n10

Chicago, 28, 36, 38

Chicago school of sociology (CSS), 29, 144; Bernard, L., student of, 67, 73; democracy informed by, 29; Douglas criticism of, 203; MacLean in, 4, 27, 30; men and women roles at, 29; qualitative and quantitative methods at, 29; social betterment and, 78; social class and labor relations by, 37–38

children, 53; Christianity raising, 23; costumes and roles for, 158–159; embarrassment and, 161; home and morals for, 59; human nature and raising, 22–23; March For Our Lives for, 60; men responsibility to, 56; *panzoonism* and, 24; parenting and, 22–23; peer group uniforms for, 159; problems studied, 37–38; school culture for, 62; school walkouts by, 63–64; as working and shaping, 63–64

Christianity, 13; child raising in, 23; moral revolution and, 15–16; as religion of the book, 15, 17, 20, 24

class, 102; CSS and HHSS studying, 37–38; sports and democratization of, 165; Stone on status versus, 148; working, 28, 32

climate change, 109

clothing, 146–147, 155

collective representations, 164–165, 166–167

community, 6, 149; anonymous and urban, 149; anti-urban bias on, 150; communion in, 150; scientific, 1; sports and affinity, 164; transformations in, 150

complexity sociology: CRIB and actors for, 180–181; with laboratory theater, 178–179, 179–180; sequences of social action, 178

conflict: in media, 208; nudity with cooperation and, 207; status, sexuality, death and, 201

conservative bias, 2

construction of meaning, 195–196; Garfinkel and Sacks on, 196–197; marihuana user and, 199; situations, constraint, negotiations on, 198; *The Social Meanings of Suicide* and, 191–192, 194, 208; suicide and, 196;

U.S. on diversity and, 199
consumerism, 148–149, 149, 153, 166, 167, 218
Contemporary Sociological Theories (Sorokin), 122, 136n19
cooperative movement, 103–104, 111
costumes, 158–159
Couch, Carl J.: as ahead of time, 184; charisma of, 185; group activity studied by, 176; on laboratory and extraneous factors, 178–179, 179–180; on observation and scientific methods, 174, 177–178; on paradigm shift, 173; qualitative laboratory research and, 183; on recording action, 179, 180, 181, 182; on selves becoming, 175; SSSI co-founded by, 145, 176; style of, 174; TST and, 175; World War II service of, 173, 175. *See also* Center for Research in Interpersonal Behavior; Iowa School of symbolic interaction
CRIB. *See* Center for Research in Interpersonal Behavior
The Crisis of Our Age (Sorokin), 123
critical race, 1–2
critical theory, 2, 213, 214; on crises and liberation, 217; Frankfurt School, 215, 217, 218; postmodernism versus, 217–218; social theorists, 4; transformative public sociology, 215; true, false needs in, 218
CSS. *See* Chicago school of sociology
cultural sociology, 124–125

data: census, 56; CRIB, 183–184; hard, 177; on instinct, 80; sources, 208
death, 131, 201. *See also* suicide
democracy, 29, 165
Derrida, Jacques, 222n1
determinism, 199
deviance, 210; Becker studying, 2; creative, 6, 191, 191–192; Douglas on creative, 6; negative and positive, 120; qualitative research on, 197–198, 209
disability sociology, 37
disciplinary sociology, 215, 220
discourse: apparent, 155; appearance for, 155, 158; on clothing, 155; self validation in, 156; selves from, 163

diversity: history mined for, 3; indigenous, 5, 110; U.S. on, 199
Dostoyevsky, Fyodor, 118, 134n7
Douglas, Jack, 2, 197; biography of, 193; books by, 192, 210n1; on civil rights and police, 200–201; on construction of meaning, 195–196; creative deviance and, 6, 191, 191–192; on criminals defined, 200; CSS criticized by, 203; on data sources, 208; Durkheim attacked by, 194, 195, 197–198; email interviews with, 192; emotions and, 207, 210; as experiencer, 203; for humankind truth, 208; male pronoun use by, 195, 210n3; on micro and macro levels, 6; on morals and libertarian pluralism, 201; on nudity, nature, freedom, 205; on order and disorder, 200; on pleasure, pain, shame, 204–205; on pluralism and state control, 201; on pluralistic society, 208; on polarization, 208; research by, 198, 203, 209; on resistance and revolt, 199; social interactions by, 207; sociology outsider, 210; Sorokin and, 193; suicide and, 193–194, 196, 197, 208; trust and, 202, 204; on truth, 202, 209; university political activity by, 199–200
Drever, James, 79
Du Bois, W. E. B., 3, 36, 107
Dunning, Eric, 163, 165, 166
Durkheim, Emile, 208; Douglas attacking, 194, 195, 197–198; on scientific rules, 33–34; suicide theories by, 194
dyads and triads, 177, 182

early Chicago school of sociology (ECSS), 28, 29
East/West dichotomy, 105
economics: Indian, 99, 102; Neolithic, 24; politics and, 145
ECSS. *See* early Chicago school of sociology
Eli Lilly Foundation, 119, 136n16
embarrassment: avoidance or deliberate, 162; children and, 161; identity with, 160; props controlled and, 161; roles and, 161; space controlled and, 160

emotions: behavior ruled by, 207; emphasis, 210; practical value judgements and, 51, 51–52
"end of history," 217, 223n5
environment degradation, 109, 111
ethics, 47, 52, 54–55; Bernard, L., on, 78; Jaspers on religion and, 11–12; women, men and marriage, 55–56
ethnography, 2, 36, 209
ethnomethodology, 202–203
eugenics, 81, 84

factory system, 35
family finances, 57
Fast Capitalism, 223n2
FCSS. *See* female Chicago school of sociology
Federal Children's Bureau, 37–38
Federated Women's Association (BDF), 47
female Chicago school of sociology (FCSS), 28
feminism: Bernard, J., on sociological, 68; Integral model segregation on, 133; lived experience and, 52; patriarchy and, 52–53; pragmatism, 28; theory scholars, 1–2; Weber, Marianne, contributing to, 4, 45, 47, 50
The Foundations of Indian Economics (Mukerjee), 99, 102
Frankfurt School, 215, 217, 218–219
Freudian model, 71, 125, 155
From the Axial Age to the Moral Revolution (Halton), 12
Fukuyama, Francis, 217, 223n5

Galpin, Charles, 110
Gandhi, Mahatma, 102, 136n24
Garfinkel, Harold, 194, 196–197
Geddes, Patrick, 14, 99
gender roles, 57–58
Germany, 48, 49
Gilman, Charlotte Perkins, 3, 56, 107
God, 21, 132
Golden Rule, 129
Gouldner, Alvin, 87
Great Depression, 135n13
Guha, Ramachandra, 108
Gumbel, Bryant, 169n1

Hayes, E. C., 118, 135n9–135n10
Hell religions, 13
HHSS. *See* Hull-House social settlement
historical comparative method, 101
historical shifts, 1
Hull-House Maps and Papers, 34
Hull-House social settlement (HHSS): Addams leader of, 28; democracy informed by, 29; ECSS men and, 28, 29; liberation sociology founding by, 37; MacLean active in, 27, 30; qualitative and quantitative methods at, 29; social class and labor relations studied by, 37–38
human ecology. *See* social ecology
human nature, 22–23
Hunger as a Factor in Human Affairs (Sorokin), 121
hunter-gatherer societies, 18, 22, 24

ideational cultures: sensate cultures and, 117, 122–123; Sorokin on, 122, 124, 129
identity, 155; achievement assessment in, 157; anonymous, 156; appearance and, 158, 159; attitude and role as, 159; children and, 63–64, 159; in city and rural environments, 153–154; embarrassment on, 160; as husband-wife, 159; interpersonal, 156; relations and elaborated, 157; for roles, 162; self as social, 156; sequence of, 159; situated, 159; in social psychology, 153; sports and, 163; structural, 156; universal, 156; values and, 157
immanent causation, 123
India, 5, 95, 96–97, 102
Indian Institutionalism, 102
The Indian Sociological Review (Mukerjee), 5, 97
The Indian Working Class (Mukerjee), 102
indigenous peoples, 15; disagreement by, 17; diversity and, 5; hunter-gatherer societies, 18, 22, 24; regional social ecology and, 95–96, 104, 110
inequalities, 47, 48, 197
infectious rheumatism, 28, 30
infighting, 2

instinct: Bernard, L., on, 5, 79, 80; Bernard, L., textbook on, 79, 83; data on, 80; eugenics and, 81, 84
Instinct (Bernard, L.), 79, 83
Instinct in Man (Drever), 79
Integral model: feminism and segregation in, 133; for fragmentation, polarization, 5; on knowledge and members, 132–133; science and unification in, 133–134; spirituality and, 132
interactionists: on hard science-hard data approach, 177; on recordings, 184. *See also* symbolic interactionism
internal disciplinary politics, 1
An Introduction to Sociology: A Naturalistic Account (Bernard, L.), 90
intuition, 18, 21, 130
Investigative Social Research (Douglas), 191–192; conflict on sexuality, death, 201; fieldwork in, 209; research cookbooks dismissed in, 204
Iowa School of symbolic interaction, 182–183, 184; interactionist approach and, 177; mixed methods research of, 183; for online interactions, 185–186; for social media and virtual worlds, 186; SSSI and, 6, 145, 176; students continuing, 185; symbolic interactionists and, 174, 179. *See also* symbolic interactionism
Islam, 15–16, 17, 20, 24

Jaspers, Karl, 12; axial age and, 11, 17, 21; folk cultures undervalued by, 15; on religion and ethics, 11–12; on science and technology, 21; Stuart-Glennie and, 12, 16, 19; on transcendence, 16
Johnson, John, 210n2
Judaism, 15–16, 17, 20, 24

Kelley, Florence, 35–36
Komi, 117, 134n1
Kovalevsky, Maxim M., 118, 134n5
Kuhn, Thomas, 1

labelling: freedom and, 199; moral panics and, 209–210
labor relations, 37–38
Latin America, 81–83

liberation sociology, 37
Liedloff, Jean, 22–23
lived experience: Bernard, L., and, 72; Douglas and, 203; "feeling" and "act," 75; feminist movement and, 52; NDE and, 131; women valuing, 52, 53
living wages: coal fields and women, 38–39; factory system and, 35; Kelley on, 35–36; MacLean comparing, 32, 33, 35, 39; Weber, Marianne, on, 56; women and, 32–33, 56
love, 5, 119, 125–126
Lucknow School, 96–97, 98, 101–102, 105
Luther's Onion Skins, 67, 84–85

MacLean, Annie Marion: AJS publishing, 27, 30, 32, 33; Canadian sociologists with, 31; Chicago, feminist pragmatism for, 28; in CSS, 4, 27, 30; disability sociology by, 37; at ECSS, 28; in HHSS, 27, 30; infectious rheumatism for, 28, 30; intellectual achievement of, 32; liberation sociology by, 37; living wage comparison by, 32, 33, 35, 39; "new women" generation with, 28; pioneering subjects of, 30–31; qualitative ethnography by, 36; quantitative methodology and, 34–35; on social justice, 39; women, working class, race, age by, 28, 32; with women, 28, 29, 30; women historical foundation by, 39; on women's issues, 31
male pronoun, 195, 210n3
March For Our Lives movement, 5; for autonomy and survival, 63; genesis of, 60–61, 61; for schoolchildren, 60; silencing efforts on, 61, 63; social media and, 61
marginalized theorists, 1
marriage, 54–55, 159; Bernard, L., on, 68, 71–72; family finances manipulation in, 57; men in, 55–56, 56; Weber, Marianne, on, 55; women, ethics and, 55–56
Marx, Karl, 13, 46, 98, 106, 129, 134n5, 200; Agger and, 214, 217, 219, 221, 223n3; economics over politics and, 145
mass shootings, 60–61, 62

Mead, George H., 74–75, 155, 163, 175
media, 208; online interactions, 185–186; social, 61, 186
men: Bernard, L., on society and, 78; CSS and, 29; family finances manipulation of, 57; gender roles for, 57–58; marriage and, 55–56, 56; objective, subjective culture and, 58, 59; as patriarchy, 52–53, 54–55; professors, 28, 30, 52, 53; sociological research and, 53
Merton, Robert K., 127, 134, 135n13, 136n19, 136n21, 159
methodology bias, 2
middle-mass society, 148–149
Midwest Sociological Society (MSS), 176, 186
Mill, John Stuart, 13
moods, 157, 158
moral revolution: axial age as, 11, 14; conscience, prophets, self-reflection for, 14, 15, 19; cost of, 23; 500-600 BCE changes, 11, 14; Judaism, Christianity, Islam in, 15–16; from mythologic polytheism, 16; Stuart-Glennie on, 14–15, 15; timing of, 15; as transitional phase, 17–18, 18
morals: children, home and, 59; Douglas on, 201; nude beach and, 209–210; pluralistic society and, 200, 201; shopping and, 151
MSS. *See* Midwest Sociological Society
Mukerjee, Radhakamal: on American human ecology, 108–109, 109–110; on art sociology, 106, 106–107; cooperative movement and, 103–104, 111; on East/West dichotomy, 105; historical comparative method used by, 101; on Indian Institutionalism, 102; on indigenous diversity, 5, 110; on industrialization and villages, 100; international speaking by, 97–98, 98; multidisciplinary proponent, 98, 101–102; published, 99–100; on regional social ecology, 95–96, 104, 110; on regional sociology, 95, 96, 100–101; on rural communalism, 101; on rural Western bias, 110; for rurbanization, 5, 110–111; social ecology and, 107–109, 111; on social work, 97; on urban/rural planning, 102–103; on Western influence, 96–97, 98–99, 101, 105; on working class, 102
Mumford, Lewis, 12

naturianism, 11
near-death experiences (NDE), 131
Neolithic civilization: diet, 17, 22; economic problem of, 24
"new women" generation, 28
non-ranked status aggregates, 147–148, 153; clothing study in, 146; as local community organization, 149; monopoly and, 147; Stone for, 146; symbols and, 165; in urban sociology, 145; "Y" and vertical order in, 146–147, 149
The Nude Beach (Douglas), 191–192; ethnography of, 209; on labelling and moral panics, 209–210; on pleasure, pain, shame, 204–205
nudity, 204–205; conflict and cooperation on, 207; morals and, 209–210; nature and freedom of, 205; police on beach, 205; property owners on, 206; sexuality, harassment and beach, 206–207

objective culture, 74, 175; children and walkouts as, 63–64; mass shootings disrupting, 60–61, 62; men and, 58, 59; polytheism and, 18; women shaping, 59–60, 61
obscurantist, 220, 223n7
"On the Valuation of Housework" (Weber, Marianne), 56
oppression research, 197
oral tradition, 2
Oriard, Michael, 167
The Origin and Goal of History (Jaspers), 11
Origins of American Sociology (Bernard, L., and Bernard. J.), 73, 90

panzoonism, 11; *animism* and, 20; as first stage, 17–18, 20; holism from, 24; for parenting, 24; Stuart-Glennie on, 15; sustainable wisdom in, 22

parenting: Christianity on, 23; human nature and, 22–23; *panzoonism* for, 24; sustainable wisdom on, 23
Park, Robert E., 101, 108
Parkland, Florida, 60–61, 62, 63, 63–64
patriarchy, 54–55
personalization, 145, 151, 152–153
Petrazhitsky, Leon, 118, 134n6
Petrovna Baratynskaya, Elena, 118–119, 121, 134n8, 135n11
pluralistic society: Douglas on, 208; moral meaning and libertarian, 201; morals transforming in, 200; social rules in, 197; state control and, 201
polarization: Douglas on, 208; Integral model for, 5; positive and negative, 132; status and vertical, 147
politics: Douglas and university, 199–200; economics and, 145; infighting and, 2; internal disciplinary, 1; power and sports, 167–168; Sorokin and subversive, 117–118
polytheism, 16, 18
positivist approach: empiricist versus, 213; sociology and, 2, 120, 128–129
postmodernism, 215; consumer capitalism and, 218; critical theory versus, 217–218; critics of, 216; future vision dissolution in, 217; self, society recharacterized in, 216; social change postponed in, 218; space-time compression and, 216, 223n4; use of, 213, 222n1
Postponing the Postmodern (Agger), 215, 218
power, 119, 125; anthem kneeling and, 168; hiding, 2; protests diffusing, 169, 169n1; qualitative research on, 197; socio-cultural dynamics of, 1; sports and political, 167–168
practical value judgements, 51, 51–52, 156
pragmatism, 4, 28
proletariat literature, 107
The Protestant Ethic and the Spirit of Capitalism (Weber, Max), 47, 52, 54–55
Protestant Reformation, 55
protests: power diffused by, 169, 169n1; status and, 2, 148, 168

public sociology: Agger for, 219; Agger not included in, 219; critical theory and, 215
Public Sociology (Agger), 215

qualitative methodology, 34, 39; Bernard, L., using, 73; Couch and, 183; deviance and, 197–198, 209; HHSS and CSS using, 29; MacLean and ethnography as, 36; on oppression, power, inequalities, 197
quantitative methodology, 34, 39; clarity versus complexity of, 33–34; HHSS and CSS using, 29; for living wage, 35; MacLean using, 34–35; on women paid labor, 33
queer theory scholars, 1–2

Reading Science (Agger), 215
Reconstruction of Humanity (Sorokin), 125
recordings: of behavior, 174, 180–181, 183–184, 185; Couch and action, 179, 180, 181, 182; CRIB for, 174, 180–181, 183–184, 185; interactionists on, 184; role playing in, 180–181, 182; transcription of, 181–182
regional sociology, 95–96, 100–101
Regional Sociology (Mukerjee), 100
religions: of the book, 15, 17, 20, 24; custom to conscience in, 14, 15, 19; God and, 21, 132; growth and tolerance of, 132; with Hell, 13; Jaspers on ethics and, 11–12; Sorokin on, 129; spirituality and, 129, 131; Stuart-Glennie on, 18, 21
research methodology: Bernard, L., on, 69, 85–87, 87–88; collaborative, 88; cookbooks, 204; Couch and qualitative, 183; CRIB and, 174, 180–181, 183–184, 185; Douglas, 198, 203, 209; infighting over, 2; numerical mapping as simplification, 221–222; with personal experience, 203; social facts guiding, 220; sociological, 2, 53, 87; on suicide, 194, 196; team field, 203
review misrepresentations, 2
Roberty, Evgeni Valentinovich De, 118, 134n5
Rockefeller Foundation, 122, 136n20

roles: actors in, 180–181, 182; attitudes and identity in, 159; children and, 158–159; costumes for, 158–159; embarrassment and, 161; gender, 57–58; identity for, 162; women and, 58
Ross, Edward A., 118, 121, 135n9–135n10, 135n12
rural identity, 153–154
rural impoverishment, 109
rurbanization, 5, 110–111
Russia, 117–118, 120, 121, 124, 134n3, 136n23
Russia and the United States (Sorokin), 124
Russian Revolution, 117–118, 134n3

Sacks, Harvey, 194, 196–197
Sagan, Carl, 219
Sartre, Jean-Paul, 213, 223n2
Schmalenbach, Herman, 150, 156
schools: children walkouts from, 63–64; cultural transmission in, 62; safety, 62
science and technology dominance, 21
scientific methodology, 174, 177, 177–178
selves: appearance and, 155, 158, 163; Bernard, L., and realization of, 77; discourse and, 156, 163; everyday life for, 162; identity and, 156, 159; moral revolution and, 15; postmodernism and, 216; Sorokin on multiplicity of, 120–121; variable in becoming, 175
sensate: change and, 123, 126, 131; ideational cultures and, 117, 122–123; sensuous versus, 136n21
Sermon on the Mount, 136n25
sexuality, 201, 206–207
Shaw, George Bernard, 12–13
shopping: aspiration, marginality, success on, 152; four types of, 151, 152; personalization and, 151, 152–153; social and moral sentiment in, 151
Simmel, Georg, 57–58, 59, 156
Small, Albion, 73, 74, 135n9
Social and Cultural Dynamics (Sorokin), 119, 122–123, 136n20
social betterment, 78
social change, 167–169, 218
social control, 5, 74, 76, 81, 89, 91

social ecology, 95; environment degradation and, 109, 111; Mukerjee on, 107–109, 111
Social Ecology (Mukerjee), 108
social groups, 120–121
social integration, 195–197
socialist movements, 121
social justice, 128; Agger and ASA on, 220; liberation sociology for, 37; MacLean for, 39; urban/rural planning and, 102–103
social life geometric theory, 177
The Social Meanings of Suicide (Douglas), 191–192, 194, 208
social media, 61, 186
Social Mobility (Sorokin), 121
social order, 191–192, 197, 200, 208–209
social psychology, 153, 162, 163
social relations, 156–157
Social Revolutionary Party, 117–118, 134n4
social rules, 199
social theorists, 3–4
social welfare, 38
social work, 97
Society, Culture and Personality (Sorokin), 124–125
Society for the Study of Symbolic Interaction (SSSI), 6, 145, 176
socio-cultural power dynamics, 1
sociological research, 2, 53
sociology, 89; art, 106, 106–107; Bernard, L., on early, 67–68; of calamity, 121; complexity, 178–179, 179–180, 180–181; cultural, 124–125; disability, 37; disciplinary, 215, 220; Douglas as outsider, 210; gaps and interpretations in, 2–3; of knowledge versus ideology, 133; liberation, 37; MacLean in American, 4, 27, 30; 1902 pedagogy of, 73; pathology and, 128; positive, 120, 128–129; public, 215, 219; readable, 219–220, 220–221; regional, 95–96, 100–101; Sorokin criticizing, 119, 135n14; Stuart-Glennie before, 11; theories, 122, 136n19; theorists marginalized in, 1; theory misrepresentation, 221–222; Western bias in, 1. *See also* urban sociology

The Sociology of Revolution (Sorokin), 121
Socio(onto)logy (Agger), 215
Sorokin, Pitirim: on altruism, 5, 119, 125, 128; biography of, 117–118, 134n2; on criminal governments, 126; on crisis and spiritual worldview, 119, 123, 132; on culture, 122, 124; on deviance, 120; Douglas and, 193; Harvard reorganization and, 119, 136n15; human personality and, 124–125; on ideational cultures, 117, 122–123, 129; on immanent causation, 123; Integral model and unification from, 133–134; on love, 5, 125–126; politics and, 117–118; on religious doctrines, 129; on revolution and famine, 121; on rural-urban sociology, 122; Russians rediscovering, 120; on self multiplicity, 120–121; on sensate and change, 123, 126, 131; on social mobility, 121; on sociology, 119, 122, 135n14, 136n19; statue of, 120, 136n18; on superconscious intuition, 130; U.S. and, 118, 118–119, 124; on valid knowledge, 133; on values-based approach, 119–120, 136n17; working habits of, 135n11
space-time compression, 216, 223n4
Spengler, Oswald, 122, 136n22
spirituality: atheism and, 132; consciousness and, 19, 130; custom and conscience in, 14, 15, 19; death, thanatology and, 131; Integral model and, 132; in medicine, education, business, 129–130; mindfulness and, 130; miracles, angels in, 130; positive and negative polarization, 132; religions and, 129, 131–132; secular, 129; Sorokin on, 5, 119, 123, 132
sports: affinity community and, 164; collective representation by, 164–167; commercialization of, 166, 167; identity and, 163; political power and, 167–168; professional emergence of, 164; protests and changes in, 169, 169n1; for social change, 169; social change by, 167–169; Stone on, 6, 163–169; violence and, 167
Srole, Leo, 143, 149

SSSI. *See* Society for the Study of Symbolic Interaction
status: consumption for, 148, 153; horizontal competition of, 147; instability modes of, 147–148, 149; platforms, 148; protest, 2, 148, 168; sentiment, 147; symbols, 154; transformers, 148; vertical polarization of, 147. *See also* non-ranked status aggregates
Stone, Gregory P., 6, 143; clothing study used by, 146–147; on community, 6; on consumerism and middle-mass, 148–149; on identity, 153; on non-ranked status aggregates, 149; on production to consumption, 148, 153; on situated identity, 159; on sports, 6, 163–169; SSSI co-founded by, 145, 176; on status aggregate versus status group, 147; on status group and hierarchy, 146, 153; on status platforms, transformers, 148; on status symbols, 154; on status versus class, 148; on universe of appearance, 153; World War II with, 143–144; "Y" and instability found by, 146–147, 149
structural-functionalism, 2
The Structure of Scientific Revolutions (Kuhn), 1
Stuart-Glennie, John: on *animism*, 20; on axial age, 4; on custom to conscience, 14, 15, 19; in footnote, 12; ideas ignored, 14; Jaspers and, 12, 16, 19; on moral revolution, 14–15, 15; Mumford and discovering, 12; on nature and consciousness, 19; *panzoonism* of, 15, 24; on religion, 18, 21; on scientific racism, 13, 21; social contacts of, 12–14; before sociology, 11; on third age of humanity, 18, 21; on transitional phase, 17–18, 18
subjective culture, 58, 59, 60–61, 62
suicide: construction of meaning and, 196; death, 131, 201; Douglas and, 193–194, 196, 197, 208; Durkheim theories on, 194; four meanings of, 196; research on, 196; social integration on, 195–197; statistical approach to, 194; transcribed interview on, 198–199

sustainable wisdom, 22, 23
Symbolic Interaction, 6
symbolic interactionism, 2, 177, 184, 196; Couch on, 6, 174, 176, 179; CRIB marginalized in, 183–184; social theorists, 4

thanatology, 131
theoretical value relationships, 51, 51–52
theory scholars, 1–2
third age of humanity, 18, 21
timeless values, 59
Tolstoy, Lev, 124, 125, 129, 136n24
transcendence, 16, 21, 23
transformation, 148, 150, 200, 215
The Transition to an Objective Standard of Social Control (Bernard, L.), 74
translations lack, 2
trust, 202, 204
truth: Douglas for human, 208; getting at, 202; misinformation and evasion of, 202, 209; trust and, 202, 204
Twenty Statements Test (TST), 175

United States (U.S.): Bernard, L., on ignorance in, 81–82; Canadians migrating to, 34; diversity and meaning in, 199; human ecology in, 108–109, 109–110; producer to consumer of, 148, 153; social order of, 191–192, 197, 208–209; Sorokin and, 118–119, 119, 124, 136n15; Weber, Max, influenced by, 51
universe of appearance: discourse influenced by, 155, 158; gestures, posture, dress, language, settings in, 155; identity, values, moods, attitudes in, 158; identity and selves in, 159; judgments in, 156; permanent acceptance in, 155; self and, 156, 163; in social psychology, 153; status symbols in, 154
urban sociology: anonymous roles in, 149; anti-urban bias and, 150; identity from symbols, 153–154; Mukerjee and, 102–103; non-ranked status aggregates in, 145; personalization in, 145; Sorokin on, 122
U.S. *See* United States

value-neutral perspective, 4, 52, 53
values: appearance with, 158; identity and, 157; systems, 104
values-based approach, 119–120, 136n17

Wage-Earning Women (MacLean), 32, 33, 35, 39
war, 90, 124, 143–144, 173, 175
Warner, Lloyd, 145–146, 149
The Ways and Power of Love (Sorokin), 119, 125
Weber, Marianne Schnitger: activism of, 4–5; BDF president as, 47; cousins and housekeepers of, 45–46; on culture and timeless values, 59; erasure of, 53; on family budgets, 57; feminism and, 4, 45, 47, 50; on gender inequality and family law, 47, 48; Germany efforts by, 48; Hitler exiling women and, 48–49; on marriage, 55; on men and progeny, 56; on Nazi guilt, 49; patriarchy and, 52–53; persistence of, 49; scholarly work of, 54; university entrance for, 46–47; on value-neutral perspectives, 4, 52; Weber, Max, support by, 45, 47, 48, 50; on women, 56, 58; on working, 59, 63; writing versus procreation and, 53
Weber, Max, 4, 47, 52, 145; biography of, 50, 54; illness of, 47, 47–48; supporting Weber, Marianne, 47, 48, 50; on theoretical and practical values, 51, 51–52; U.S. influence on, 51; Weber, Marianne, for, 45, 47, 48, 50
Western bias: influence of, 96–97, 98–99, 101, 105; rural ecology neglect as, 110; scholarship with, 98–99; sociology with, 1
women, 37; Bernard, L., and, 78, 90–91; coal and wages for, 38–39; CSS and, 29; experience valued by, 52, 53; factory system for, 35; FCSS and, 28; gender roles, 57–58; Hitler exiling, 48–49; Integral model segregation on, 133; issues for working, 32–33; living wages and, 56; MacLean as new, 28, 29, 30, 31; MacLean history for, 28, 32, 39; in marketplace, 28, 32; marriage ethics and, 55–56; objective culture and, 58, 59, 59–60, 61; paid labor, 33;

social welfare supporting, 38; sociological research and, 53; suffrage for, 38. *See also* feminism

"Women's Special Cultural Tasks" (Weber, Marianne), 57

Young Women's Christian Association (YWCA), 35

Zimmerman, Carle C., 119, 122
Zolberg, Vera, 106

About the Authors/Editors

Nicholas M. Baxter is acting assistant professor of sociology at Indiana University Kokomo in the Department of Sociology. His teaching and research areas include urban and community sociology, environmental sociology, social theory, leisure studies. His research focuses on the intersection of community and the physical environment, specifically among river town communities along the Mississippi River.

Christine Bucior, MA, is a doctoral candidate in sociology at Pennsylvania State University.

Shing-Ling S. Chen is professor of mass communication in the Department of Communication Studies at University of Northern Iowa. Trained as a symbolic interactionist, she researches information technologies and social orders. She is the co-editor of *Symbolic Interaction and New Social Media*, and *Constructing Narratives in Response to Trump's Election*. She is also the founder and program manager of Carl Couch Center for Social and Internet Research (www.cccsir.com).

Christopher T. Conner is visiting assistant professor of sociology, in the Department of Anthropology and Sociology, at Knox College. His teaching and research interests include social theory, crime and deviance, subcultures, inequalities and intersectionality, and LGBT studies.

Mary Jo Deegan is the founding director of the Jane Addams Research Center and emeritus professor of sociology at the University of Nebraska-Lincoln. She has published over 200 articles, essays, and reviews, and written or edited 22 books including *Jane Addams and the Men of the Chicago*

School, 1892–1918 and *Race, Hull-House, and the University of Chicago.* Her most recent book is *Annie Marion MacLean and the Chicago Schools of Sociology, 1894–1934.* She is an international lecturer on nonviolence, feminism, pragmatism, education, and democracy.

David R. Dickens is professor of sociology at the University of Nevada, Las Vegas. His primary areas of research and teaching specialization include classical and contemporary sociological theory, critical theories of culture, and qualitative methods.

Harvey A. Farberman is professor emeritus of social welfare policy and research at Stony Brook University where he served on faculty from 1966–2015. He was a founder of the Stony Brook University School of Social Welfare and founding director of the New York State Center for Aging and Policy Research at the Stony Brook University Health Sciences Center. He was a visiting scholar and NIMH Fellow in sociology at the University of California, Berkeley, and a visiting professor at the University of Bath. Farberman was co-chair of the steering committee that led to the creation of the Society for the Study of Symbolic Interaction (SSSI) and served as president of the society and as editor of the journal *Symbolic Interaction.* He was elected to Sigma Xi, received the SSSI Distinguished Service Award, named a SSSI Annual Distinguished Lecturer, and received the Albert Nelson Marquis Lifetime Achievement Award. He also served for many years as a member of the board of directors of the New York State Federation of Organizations, Inc., and as a consultant to the New York State Office of Aging, the Suffolk County, New York, Office of Aging, and the New York Academy of Medicine.

Eugene Halton is professor of sociology at the University of Notre Dame. He has written extensively on consumption and materialism, pragmatism, and the problematic nature of modern civilization and the civilizational mindset more generally. His most recent book is *From the Axial Age to the Moral Revolution: John Stuart-Glennie, Karl Jaspers, and a New Understanding of the Idea* (Palgrave Macmillan, 2014). His previous book, *The Great Brain Suck* (University of Chicago Press, 2008), explores the problematic role of techno-consumer culture in America. Earlier books include *Bereft of Reason: On the Decline of Social Thought and Prospects for its Renewal* (University of Chicago Press, 1995) and *Meaning and Modernity: Social Theory in the Pragmatic Attitude* (University of Chicago Press, 1986). He is co-author, with Mihaly Csikszentmihalyi, of *The Meaning of Things: Domestic Symbols and the Self* (Cambridge University Press, 1981) regarded as a keystone in material culture studies and translated into four languages.

Michael A. Katovich is a professor of sociology and chair of the Department of Sociology and Anthropology at Texas Christian University (TCU). He received his PhD from the University of Iowa, where he studied symbolic interaction and social processes under the tutelage of Carl J. Couch. His research and teaching emphasizes symbolic interactionist approach advocated by Couch. He has published in various professional venues including readers, journals such as *The Sociological Quarterly, Qualitative Sociology, the American Sociological Review, Symbolic Interaction*, and *Studies in Symbolic Interaction*. He has also edited or co-edited three books, including *Carl Couch and the Iowa School: In His Own Words and in Reflection*. He has taught a variety of courses at TCU, including required courses for a major in sociology. He has also taught and published in areas that key on media images, interaction processes, and death and dying.

Thaddeus Muller is a Senior Lecturer in Criminology at Lancaster University. His research focuses on transgression and resistance among a variety of subgroups including cannabis users, rock/pop musicians, and defaulting homeowners "fighting Wall Street." He is an active member in both the European Society for the Study of Symbolic Interaction, as a board member, and the American Society for the Study of Symbolic Interaction. In addition to his publications in a wide variety of international journals, he has also guest edited several different journals including *Studies in Symbolic Interaction*.

Lawrence T. Nichols is professor of sociology and former chair of the Department of Sociology and Anthropology at West Virginia University, where he teaches courses on criminology, mass media and social problems, sociological theory, and the sociology of business. He is co-author of books on alternate dispute resolution and corporate social responsibility, and editor of a volume on public sociology. Dr. Nichols has published extensively on the history and sociology of social science, with a particular focus on Harvard University and the careers of Pitirim A. Sorokin, Talcott Parsons and Robert K. Merton. Since 1998 he has edited a national quarterly journal, *The American Sociologist*, and in 2012 he served as president of the North Central Sociological Association. In spare moments Dr. Nichols enjoys choral singing and the never-ending quest to become a competent golfer.

Diane M. Rodgers, associate professor of sociology at Northern Illinois University, is author of *Debugging the Link between Social Theory and Social Insects* (LSU Press). The book analyzes natural and social scientific co-constructed theories of social organization, including the race, class, and gender hierarchies within entomological discourse. Some of the author's other publications are in the following journals: *The Sociological Quarterly, Sociological Spectrum, Symbolic Interaction, Humanity and Society, Organization: The*

Critical Journal of Organization, Theory and Society, History of the Human Sciences, and *Minerva: A Review of Science, Learning and Policy*.

Alan Sica is professor of sociology and founding director of the Social Thought Program at Pennsylvania State University. He was editor and publisher of the international journal *History of Sociology* and editor in chief of two ASA journals, *Sociological Theory* and *Contemporary Sociology*. Over the last 40 years he as written or edited a dozen books concerning social theory, with particular attention to Max Weber.

Stacy L. Smith is a visiting professor of sociology at the University of Alabama Birmingham. Her research focuses on meaning-making, identity-creation, and social cohesion in marginalized groups, with a particular interest in identifying the mechanisms that are responsible for social cohesion. Her dissertation, titled *Dead and Still Grateful: Deriving Mechanisms of Social Cohesion from Deadhead Culture*, explores seven different mechanisms that help group members maintain a sense of cohesion. She is currently conducting qualitative research on the cosplay subculture. In this study she seeks to understand the complex interaction between sublimated and realized identity among cosplayers. Stacy's research interests include social theory, group behavior, sociology of culture, social psychology, emotion, religion, and ritual. She has taught a wide array of courses, including sociological theory, social interaction, social problems, social movements, religion, and popular culture. Her work has also been featured in in *Teaching Sociology*.

Lukas Szrot is currently a PhD candidate in sociology at the University of Kansas. He studied sociology under the guidance of Ben Agger at the University of Texas at Arlington from 2013–2015. His primary substantive areas of interest are sociology of religion, environmental sociology, and historical sociology, and his work examines historical shifts in the relationship between religious affiliation and environmental concern in the United States. Szrot has a background in social theory as well as quantitative research methods, and has written and conducted research on epistemology in the social sciences, public understanding of science, dynamics of social organizations, and the role of religious traditions and movements in shaping culture and politics.

Lightning Source UK Ltd.
Milton Keynes UK
UKHW011321130722
405800UK00010B/187